The American Sporting Collector's Handbook

THE

AMERICAN

SPORTING

COLLECTOR'S

HANDBOOK

Revised Edition

Edited by Allan J. Liu

Winchester Press
Tulsa, Oklahoma

Library of Congress Cataloging in Publication Data
Main entry under title:

The American sporting collector's handbook.

    Includes index.
    1. Hunting—Implements and appliances—Collectors
and collecting. 2. Fishing—Implements and appliances—
Collectors and collecting. I. Liu, Allan J.
SK275.A45 1982   799'.075   81-23168
ISBN 0-87691-325-7   AACR2

Published by Winchester Press
1421 South Sheridan Road
Post Office Box 1260
Tulsa, Oklahoma 74101

Printed in the United States of America

1 2 3 4   85 84 83 82

Contents

Foreword

Since *The American Sporting Collector's Handbook* was first published in 1976, there has been a demand for an update. With this update, the prices have been made current and the book has been expanded to 31 chapters. Of particular interest is Chapter 31, Decorating. Not only have collectors been requesting this kind of information, but makers of custom furniture and cabinets are listing these types of decorating items in their catalogs.

Sporting collecting is still growing by leaps and bounds. More and more dealers complain about the scarcity of fine items. Auction houses are anxious to include sporting items in their catalogs. Yet there is still time to get in on the ground floor. Collectible sporting items are all over the countryside. Much can be gotten by doing your homework and by intense looking.

If there's any advice I can give the novice collector it is to collect what you like and buy the best you can afford. Be wary of bad condition and forgeries. Price ranges listed are for items in excellent condition. On consignment items, reputable dealers charge 33⅓ percent commission. If you wish to sell an item directly, most dealers will pay about 50 percent for an item in demand and less as the demand decreases. Many times they will have poor items in their inventory for years. Don't begrudge the dealers their cut—they can save you a lot of shoe leather. For man-to-man sales (dealer omitted), 75 percent of the price listed is usually fair unless the item is a really "hot" one.

The sky's the limit on sporting collecting. Some prices lately have been $75,000 for a shotgun, $5,000 for a fly rod, $20,000 for a decoy. As the finer points of items become known and demand becomes greater, prices will naturally rise. Sporting collecting is a good hedge against inflation. The beauty of this collecting is that an item can be bought, utilized, and then sold for at least what you paid for it. If you've been discriminating in your buying, you'll probably walk away with a nice profit.

Happy collecting!
Allan J. Liu
December 1981

Chapter 1 ❧ *Original Art*

DREW HOLL

From the very beginning, a connection has existed between art and sport. Long before a written language was established, primitive man felt the desire to record his contests with the animals around him in crude cave drawings. Thousands of years later appeared medieval scenes of boar, stag, and, of course, unicorn hunts. The hunt with its ever-growing fraternity spread into England from France. Stag hunting was probably the most popular, with its elaborate ceremony and pageantry. Certain rituals that developed during this time have been retained to this day.

In time, the wealthy of both Europe and England developed highly sophisticated forms of sport. Fox hunting became immensely popular, as did horse racing, shooting, and angling. Other sports gained in popularity—hawking, cockfighting, coursing, and, to a lesser degree, bearbaiting, otter spearing, and owling. All these activities generated various forms of art.

For the English country gentleman, racing and hunting remained the popular and fashionable pastimes through the eighteenth and nineteenth centuries. Sporting paintings of this time were in great demand and many fine artists developed a reputation that has lasted to the present. While some artists earned their reputations and then livelihoods from commissions to record famous horses and hunts, it is interesting to note that many shooting and angling paintings of this period were not the result of commissions, but were rather a pleasant record of personal experiences.

It is important for the collector to have some knowledge and background of some of the major English artists and the contributions they made to the sporting scene, although this chapter will deal primarily with American artists. Sporting art in America was slow in developing. It wasn't until the early 1800s that scenes depicting the hunter and his quarry began to appear, and these differed greatly from the sporting art that was so popular in England during the same period. Early American sporting scenes were not graced with manicured gentlemen—rather by frontiersmen in the act of pursuing game for food.

American sporting art in most instances is a sound investment. In the late 1950s and early 1960s, paintings by Ogden Pleissner were offered for between $400 and $800. These same paintings today command prices of $6,000 to $15,000. Rungius paintings that sold for $2,000 to $3,000 in the late '50s have appreciated to $12,000 and $20,000. Remington and Russell paintings that were virtually given away at the turn of the century are today worth incredible sums.

Historically, paintings were almost always purchased because they pleased the buyer, who gave little, if any, thought to future values. Today, with the loss of faith in standard investment procedures, more and more people are turning to art as a hedge against inflation. But the owner still has the pleasure of enjoying his paintings over the years as they are appreciating in value.

Most of the artists discussed in this chapter saw their art appreciate in value during their lifetimes. Unfortunately, the greatest appreciation usually occurs after an artist's death. Collectors scramble to acquire what paintings are still available, and after they are gone, prices climb. It seems almost unfair that artists cannot participate in this renewed interest in their efforts.

HOW TO COLLECT

Art is a personal thing. No two people see the same thing in a painting. A man who owns a setter and primarily hunts woodcock and grouse can't really relate to a painting of a bull moose in a meadow; and, conversely, the big-game hunter would respond little to a portrait of a flushed woodcock. But sporting art fortunately offers a limitless range of subjects, styles, and price ranges; every collector can pursue his own interests.

Once the collector has decided what direction he's going, one way to start a collection is to visit as many galleries as possible to see what's available. (A list of galleries appears later in this chapter.) Probably the best time to visit galleries is in June or July when they are putting their fall catalogs together. This is when you have first pick, as all the art to be reproduced in the catalogs has to be either physically present or represented in photographs. Of course almost every gallery keeps a "want list" and would be most happy to add your name and advise you when a particular artist's work becomes available.

Another way to start or add to a collection is through estate sales and auctions. Many a fine piece of art has been acquired this way and often below present market value. Of course, it is important to know what the present value is so you don't overbid.

With the current interest in garage sales, tag sales, and so forth, it is often possible to pick up interesting and even valuable pieces of art, and, occasionally, antique shops are sometimes the source of some fine old art. A word of caution, though: some unscrupulous "dealers" have been known to offer what seems to be a real find at a ridiculously low price. This could only mean two things — stolen art or possibly a copy. If the art is stolen, you run the risk of losing it at some future date. Most good art is insured, and insurance companies are very persistent in trying to recover stolen art of any value. If it's a copy, you will have purchased just that — a copy.

Any reliable source will guarantee the authenticity of any painting sold and will gladly refund your money if it is later proven not authentic. If you doubt your source, ask for a written description on the bill of sale for the item in question with the written understanding that it may be returned within a reasonable time. The description should include the dimension, medium (oil, watercolor), and signature. Signature, for example, should read "signed by Frank Benson." The wording "signed Frank Benson" could mean just that — someone signed the name Frank Benson.

Forgeries and copies, unfortunately, exist in the realm of sporting art. There is a fine line of distinction between a forgery and a copy. A forgery is a deliberate attempt to duplicate the work of another with the intention of representing it as an original. A copy, on the other hand, is usually an innocent attempt to reproduce the subject and style of another with no thought of representing it as an original. Through the ages, it was common and accepted for artists to copy paintings they admired, and it's not surprising that this practice has been carried over to present times; occasionally a copy of a Frost or Remington appears.

CARE AND PROTECTION OF PAINTINGS

Just as important as having your acquisitions authenticated by reputable sources is protecting them once you own them. Paintings must be insured against possible damage or theft. An appraisal is in order, and photographs of each item should be submitted to your insurance company. The purpose of the photographs is twofold: to substantiate possession of the art, and to have a visual record in the event of a theft. Make two sets of photos, one for your insurance company and one for yourself. Appraisals are available through some galleries, and some experts who specialize in appraisals advertise in the yellow pages of the telephone directory.

Oil paintings and watercolors are subject to deterioration and should be given proper care. Oil paintings in particular should receive special attention. Because of its very nature, canvas shrinks and stretches with atmospheric conditions; therefore, it is important never to subject canvases to rapid changes in temperature. Many a fine oil has been damaged sitting over a fireplace in a cold room; once a fire is lighted, the temperature rapidly climbs and the canvas stretches too quickly. If this is repeated often enough the painted surface can crack.

Watercolors, while not as sensitive as oils to rapid changes in temperature, are also affected adversely. Watercolors are usually behind glass, and a rapid change in temperature can cause the glass to sweat. This moisture on the surface will often mildew, leaving small, unsightly brown stains on the painting. Watercolors are also subject to fading, so avoid placing them in direct sunlight. While extreme temperature fluctuations rarely exist in today's modern homes, they do often exist in vacation homes and, in particular, ones near water.

Oils should be periodically cleaned and revarnished. This is best left to a professional if they are particularly dirty, but in some cases an effective job can be done with mild soap and water applied with cotton. However, if there is a break in the canvas or if the surface is cracked, under no circumstances should you attempt to clean the painting yourself. Moisture under the surface of the painting can make it lift, causing it to discolor, or worse, fall off.

Restoration of paintings is an art in itself. A competent restorer can take a painting dark with age and rent with holes and bring it back to its former beauty. This type of quality work is often expensive, but certainly worth it. Good restoration work does not detract from the value of a painting, and it is safe to say that many fine old works of art have had some work done on them. Most galleries can recommend good restorers.

SPORTING ARTISTS

Sporting artists, by definition, have one common denominator — their love for nature and the outdoors. Most of them hunt and fish, and these activities inspire them. More often than not, a great painting is the result of a special day outdoors.

Most of the remainder of this chapter is an introduction to a few of the great names in sporting art. No such brief listing can pretend to be comprehensive, and I apologize if a favorite artist of yours is not included.

Please note that for each artist I have given a price range in which his or her paintings are currently being offered. There is a very wide range in some instances, because value is affected by size, condition, and quality of the work. Also, many artists worked in various mediums – pencil sketches, pen and ink, watercolor, oil. A small pencil sketch by Charles Schrevogel might bring only $4,000 to $6,000, while his most famous oil, "The Silenced War Whoop," is valued at $275,000.

The artists are listed in alphabetical order.

Bob Abbett has become one of America's most popular animal artists. Specializing in sporting dogs in action, his scenes literally breathe the intense excitement of the point or the flush. He gives the sure touch to his work that only familiarity with the scene brings. Range $6,000 to $15,000.

Harry Adamson, paying strict attention to authenticity and precise detail, displays a fine talent for expressing his strong and colorful approach to naturalism in all his oils. Range $3,000 to $10,000.

Henry Alken, Sr. *(1785–1851)* was an artist with a delicate touch. He handled his subjects with meticulous care; every feature of each fox hunter and mount was always carefully recorded. His thorough knowledge of horses and the hunt enabled him to portray events that were often ignored by other artists of his time. His paintings are crisply detailed and fully animated, frequently including scenes of fallen riders and runaway horses. Range $8,000 to $50,000.

Les Anderson's fine interpretation of sporting dogs places his paintings in a class by themselves. His attention to detail is virtually without equal, and he displays a fine talent for expressing the life in the animal he portrays. Range $2,500 to $4,000.

John Atherton *(1900–1952)* was a fishing artist. He was an expert fly-tier, the author of the book *The Fly & the Fish*, and a member of the Anglers Club of New York. His art factually and honestly depicts the American fishing scene. Range $1,000 to $5,000.

John James Audubon *(1785–1851)* emigrated to Philadelphia from Paris in 1803. He devoted his entire energies to the outdoors – fishing, hunting, and collecting specimens. Some of his subjects seem stiff and awkward, for he relied heavily on mounted specimens; but he developed a sureness of technique and skillfully depicted wildlife in natural settings. His Birds of America series earned him an unrivaled reputation. Audubon paintings are extremely rare; no range can be given, but $50,000 is a fairly typical price.

Al Barker, a prolific artist, is best known for his small watercolors and oils. His subjects cover a wide range of activities – fishing, hunting, and wildlife studies. His works are carefully composed, yet simple in design. Range $150 to $1,000.

Frank Benson *(1862–1951)* drew his inspiration from his own shooting experiences. A prolific artist, he shared his many moments afield in drawings, watercolors, and oils. Benson's style is not that of stark realism, rather subtle portrayals, relying on the importance of composition and the interesting use of color. Range $2,000 to $15,000.

Ed Bierly was the award winner of the first Federal Duck Stamp design to be reproduced in color. In addition to wildfowl paintings, his treatments of big-game animals are equally important. Range $1,500 to $6,000.

Albert Bierstadt *(1830–1902)*, German-born, developed an insatiable appetite for American wilderness and big game. He spent most of his life in the Rockies and Yosemite, and his canvases portray these areas in all their grandeur. Bierstadt paintings are characterized by a special use of color, imparting a moody feeling and giving the feeling of infinite depth. Yet his works have an unquestionable authenticity of detail and are awesome and powerful. Range $25,000 to $100,000.

Richard Bishop *(1887–1975)* was one of America's most prolific artists, undoubtedly best known for his waterfowl paintings. An avid hunter and keen observer, he was extremely versatile and was at home with every medium — pencil sketches, pen-and-ink drawings, watercolors, and oils. His transformations of Edgar Queeny's photographs from the book *Prairie Wings* into line drawings have been the bible for many artists. He was one of the first winners of the Federal Duck Stamp design award. His work ranges from $400 to $15,000.

Herb Booth, like many artists, is basically self-taught. His nationwide travels observing wildlife and background material have given his work both variety in composition and accuracy in portrayal of game birds in their habitat. Range $800 to $3,000.

George Brown painted with a softness that gives his subjects animation and movement. His oils were almost always game-bird portrayal — great flocks of geese or the twittering flush of a woodcock — which exhibit a special realism. Brown's work is difficult to obtain. His career was terminated by an unfortunate accident before he reached his full potential. Range $4,000 to $15,000.

Paul Brown *(1893–1958)* fell in love with horses at an early age, and they remained his favorite subject throughout his life. His specialty was horses in action — polo matches, hurdle races, flat races; almost anything to do with horses. He worked in various media — pen and ink, pencil sketches, pastels, watercolor, and oils — and was equally proficient in all. Range $200 to $4,000.

Charles L. Bull *(1874–1932)* is considered by many to be one of the greatest of animal artists. He was an accomplished taxidermist, working for many years for the Smithsonian Institution in Washington, D.C. He was an undisputed expert on anatomy, and his work reflects his thorough understanding of his subjects. Range $2,000 to $10,000.

Greg Caron showed a major interest in painting throughout his school years. He spent a year in Chicago at the American Academy of Art. Later apprenticing at an industrial art company, he began his career as a full-time wildlife artist in 1970. Range $500 to $2,000.

George Catlin *(1796–1872)* was a lawyer turned portrait painter. Great interest in the West, and especially its Indians, led him to be known as the dean of Indian painters. Living with more than 40 tribes, he accurately recorded their culture with sketch pad and brush, creating an invaluable pictorial history of a complex society before the influence of the white man. His Indian portraits are especially appealing. Range $25,000 to $50,000.

Diana Charles specializes in animal portraits, and a great deal of her effort is concentrated on sporting dogs. She has the special facility of capturing the spirit of the animal in her watercolors, resulting in very pleasing and accurate studies. Range $500 to $1,500.

Roland Clark *(1874–1957)* was a sportsman-artist and writer with few equals. Although mostly known for his etchings and dry points, his watercolors and oils are well executed and skillfully composed. His favorite theme was ducks, and in the foreword to his book *Pot Luck* he writes, "Doubtless youth sees with a glamorous eye, magnifying certain pictures and treasured memories of them for all the years to come. I believe I had that sort of eye. A hundred ducks were a thousand; the geese filled all the sky. There were forty quail in an average covey — once upon a time. To picture them on canvas and copperplate, to give them true resemblance of life has been my earnest endeavor for many, many years." He indeed accomplished what he intended. Range $1,000 to $18,000.

Guy Coheleach is well known as a painter of African wildlife, but his work runs the gamut of sports. Range to $25,000.

Art Cook's primary interests in school were the outdoors and sketching wildlife. His career began as an illustrator, and he ultimately became industrial-art director for a large corporation. After winning the coveted Federal Duck

Oil painting of geese by Roland Clark. Clark worked in both oils and water-colors; his paintings have a certain softness and feeling that men who know the coldness of the blind appreciate.

Stamp design award in 1972, he left the business world to devote his full time to wildlife painting. Range $500 to $5,000.

"Whiskey Jack and Blue Belle." A. B. Frost.

Peter Corbin is an artist of great promise. His paintings are brilliantly executed and always carefully researched. His salmon and trout scenes are particularly appealing. Range $1,200 to $3,000.

John Cowan follows more in the earlier traditions of wildlife artists. His paintings come alive with sportsmen and dogs in action. His creations are original, dramatic, and intensely colorful portrayals with true life-like character that can't be faulted. Range $1,500 to $4,000.

Montague Dawson painted oils of seas and ships that give the feeling of wind on your cheek. Range $6,000 to $70,000.

Nick Eggenhofer came to America from Bavaria as a young man, was strongly influenced by Remington and Russell, and devoted his full talents to Western art. His subject matter is spirited, and scenes of Western Americana predominate in his efforts. Range $3,000 to $10,000.

Bill Elliott draws constantly on his experiences in the field. He is a dedicated fisherman and a great deal of his effort lies in that direction. He is particularly noted for his finely rendered pencil drawings. Range $300 to $1,500.

Churchill Ettinger is an artist of great accomplishment, and his subjects cover the range of the whole outdoors — trout fishing, woodcock shooting, big-game fishing, harness racing. Equally proficient in both watercolor and oils, he is also known as a fine etcher. Range $750 to $2,500.

John Fernely, Sr. *(1782–1860)* epitomized the spirit of fox hunting. His canvases are full of activity, with hounds and huntsmen going full tilt. He was very much a master of detail and reproduced all the blemishes and features of his subjects. He was extremely popular in his day and rather prolific. Range $2,000 to $40,000.

A. B. Frost *(1851–1928)* was the artist of rural America, and his paintings reflect all the subtleties of his time. His characters are unmistakably honest and his use of color is delicate. These combine to give his paintings a charm that few artists have achieved. Frost's subjects were generally hunting, fishing, and golf scenes. Range $3,000 to $18,000.

Philip R. Goodwin *(1882–1935)* was a student of Howard Pyle, and his work shows the strong influence of Pyle's discipline. His work is strong and bold, with north woods scenes a favorite. He was an excellent portrayer of animal life. Range $1,000 to $8,000.

Owen Gromme was born and raised in the abundant wildlife area of Wisconsin. His consuming curiosity about animals, birds, and natural objects, combined with an innate compulsion to draw, rewarded him with a position with the Milwaukee Public Museum, where he eventually assumed the position of Curator. His many awards include one for the 1945–1946 Federal Duck Stamp design. He works primarily in oils. His subjects include every facet of wildlife. Range $3,000 to $15,000.

David Hagerbaumer is a watercolorist who specializes in wildfowl and upland game birds. Range $1,200 to $4,500.

"Departure Time—5 A.M." Tom Hennessey.

Eldridge Hardie's game-fish paintings are an accurate view into many fresh-water habitats, for both the knowledgeable biologist and the avid fly-fisher-man. His unique style of showing both the above-water and below-water scenes gives a special feeling for the fish's environment. While he is best known for his fish paintings, he is equally proficient in both waterfowl and upland watercolors. Range $500 to $2,500.

Tom Hennessey is truly a sportsman's artist, relying heavily on his varied outdoor activities to produce classic hunting and fishing scenes. His art is in the style of Ripley and Pleissner, depicting sportsmen in favorite outdoor scenes, such as salmon fishing on the Restigouche, sea-duck shooting off his native Maine coast, quail shooting in Georgia, or big-game fishing in the Gulf Stream. Range $750 to $2,500.

John F. Herring, Sr. *(1795–1865)* was a prolific artist, yet known for his careful attention to detail. For over a quarter of a century, he painted almost all the famous race horses of his time. Herring's horses, somewhat exaggerated, often appear overly elongated; he subscribed to the theory that length of the back is directly related to the speed and stamina of the horse. Range $8,000 to $60,000.

James Hill *(1839–1922)*, a contemporary of A. F. Tait, was especially competent in his renderings of game birds. His work reveals Audubon's influence, but his paintings depict his subjects more convincingly because they are more lifelike. Range $1,500 to $8,000.

"Ruffed Grouse." David Maass.

Winslow Homer *(1836–1910)* enjoyed early success as a Civil War battlefield artist and later turned his attention to Adirondack and Canadian woodland scenes. His paintings are an authentic documentation of that period, strong and well-composed, with effective use of tone and color. He was a prolific artist who captured the mood not only of the North Woods but also of seascapes from New England to the Caribbean. Homer is an artist of permanent importance. Range $6,000 to $450,000.

Lynn Bogue Hunt *(1878–1960)* was a prolific artist, yet maintained consistent high quality in his work. Early work as a taxidermist greatly contributed to his thorough anatomical knowledge, and almost all his works are of wildlife. Some of his finest works appeared in sporting magazines and as illustrations in books. Range $300 to $5,000.

Francis Lee Jaques *(1887–1969)* painted brilliant wildlife renderings that are truly representative of nature at its best. Jaques, a self-taught artist, spent 20 years as a staff artist for the American Museum of Natural History. Range $3,000 to $30,000.

J. D. Knap painted almost exclusively in watercolor and is best known for his sensitive renderings of waterfowl. He was an award winner for the Federal Duck Stamp design in 1937. Range $200 to $1,500.

Robert Kuhn is a contemporary American artist whose works cover virtually everything sporting from upland gunning to African big game. His style is soft and pleasing. Range $4,500 to $10,000.

Lee LeBlanc was an artist, animator, and photographic head of several movie studios in Hollywood. He did not concentrate fully on wildlife painting until a few years ago. Upon retiring from Hollywood, he won the 1973 Federal Duck Stamp design award, which pushed him into national prominence. A prolific artist, his works have a unique softness that gives animation to his oils and watercolors. Range $1,500 to $6,000.

David Lockhart is familiar with most of the areas of the country. The scenes he paints — lands, lakes, and seas — are as diverse as the subjects he selects. His paintings reflect the work of an inveterate sportsman who captures the nostalgic mood of the setting. Range $1,000 to $4,000.

David Maass's oils of game birds in their natural habitat are among the finest available. Relying strongly on proper lighting, his subjects have a realism that is often imitated, but never copied. Maass won the 1974 Federal Duck Stamp design award and now enjoys international recognition and an enviable position in the ranks of America's foremost wildlife artists. Range $3,000 to $10,000.

Henry McDaniel's love of fishing is very evident in his paintings. His watercolors are colorful, yet soft, and the details of his subjects are beautifully executed. Whether it be a trout stream or a tail-walking salmon, he handles it with equal facility and realism. Range $1,100 to $2,500.

Edwin Megargee painted oils of dogs and upland shooting. His dog portraits are some of the finest. Range $800 to $2,500.

Tara Moore's extensive travel — Kenya, Zambia, Nepal, and the jungles of the Amazon — has contributed greatly to her ability as an artist. Dedicated research, self-discipline, and a unique skill have given her remarkable stature as an artist. Although she paints many species of wildlife, from African elephants to Eastern Shore Canada geese, her most recent efforts in capturing mischievous puppies is most appealing. Range $750 to $2,500.

Gustav Muss-Arnolt *(1858–1927)* was an expert in depicting bird dogs in action. His art epitomized classic gun dogs, superb working animals staunchly holding point in flawless conformation. He was not too prolific an artist, and his work is difficult to find. Range $3,000 to $12,000.

"Erie Marsh." Ogden M. Pleissner.

Edmund Osthaus, a German-born artist, is best known for his portraits of famous gun dogs. A field-trial devotee, he traveled throughout the country, capturing on canvas the best bird dogs of his time. Range $4,000 to $20,000.

Roger Tory Peterson is known for, among other things, his precise illustrations in the well-known series "Birds of America." His work is painstakingly accurate and anatomically correct. Range $1,500 to $10,000.

Ogden M. Pleissner (N.A; A.W.S; R.S.A.) is without question, one of America's finest living artists. His contribution to the sporting scene is virtually unequalled. From Scottish highlands, to salmon rivers of Canada, to New England bird covers, to Southern waterfowl marshes, his paintings accurately record the elusive moments of the sportsman's world. Although an avid sportsman, Pleissner's sporting art is only a portion of his efforts. His landscapes and still-life paintings are equally important. Range $3,500 to $20,000.

Alexander Pope *(1849–1924)* was a master draftsman and is best known for his still-life paintings. A student of the *trompe l'oeil* school, he commanded superb technical dexterity; every detail is precisely depicted. His subjects usually contained the elements of a successful hunt—hat and coat, powder horn, rifle, and dead game. Range $5,000 to $30,000.

Maynard Reece is a versatile painter of fish, fowl, and big game who travels extensively and continues to add to his vast collection of research material.

He has won the Federal Duck Stamp competition five times, and his diversity and colorful brush work have brought great recognition to the popular artist. Range $3,000 to $30,000.

Joyce Hagerbaumer Reed is a self-taught artist who has been a biological illustrator. Encouraged by her famous artist father, David Hagerbaumer, she has developed a style that is truly distinctive. Her watercolors are finely detailed studies of the abundant wildlife that surrounds her. Range $400 to $1,500.

Frederic Remington *(1861–1909)* was one of the finest artists this country has produced, and his prodigious outpouring of art has enriched us with his picturesque portrayal of the Old West. He had little formal art training, but his natural ability, and the vigor and authenticity of his subject matter, won him immediate recognition. Range $5,000 to $100,000.

Chet Reneson paints only subjects he has personally experienced. His travels to the wheat fields of Saskatchewan, the salmon rivers of Ungava, the trout streams of Wyoming, and the waters of the Bahamas enable him to capture the essence of the theme he paints. He is an avid fan of Winslow Homer, who has been a strong influence on his work. His works are strong and aggressive, and his colorful style is distinctly his own. Range $500 to $3,000.

A. Lassell Ripley *(1896–1969)* was extremely versatile in subject, style, and medium. He was an excellent portrait painter and a superb landscape and still-life artist, but undoubtedly some of his finest work was generated by his love of the outdoors. A sportsman all his life, his hunters, dogs, and quarry are very believable, and the viewer is easily drawn into the scene. Range $1,000 to $15,000.

Carl Rungius *(1869–1959)*, a German artist, migrated to America in 1894. His fascination with big game so possessed him that he turned all his energies to their pursuit with both gun and sketch pad. For more than 50 years, he wandered throughout North America, primarily in the Rockies, where his efforts produced some of this country's finest examples of wildlife art. Range $6,000 to $50,000.

Charles M. Russell *(1864–1926)* had a career similar in many ways to Remington's. Both had little formal art training, and both spent their early years living in the West. Russell had a special fascination with Indians and lived with them for a time. Hence, his Indian paintings have an authenticity that is unrivaled. Today, his original works are eagerly sought by museums and private collectors. Range $5,000 to $100,000.

"Sneak Box." Chet Reneson.

John Ruthven is a leader of the movement fostering conservation and protection of endangered species. He is often called the "Twentieth Century Audubon" and uses the same techniques as his famous predecessor. He studies his subject thoroughly — its habitat and its habits — making sure that every detail to be used later in the painting is correct. Range $5,000 to $15,000.

William J. Schaldach paints watercolors of upland game and fish. His loose style has a very "homey" feeling. Range $500 to $2,500.

Charles Schrevogel *(1861–1912)* shows the strong influence of Remington's and Russell's historical school of popular Western art. His paintings are carefully composed, and he possessed an immense technical facility. His love of the West and its inhabitants is clearly reflected in all his art. Range $4,000 to $75,000.

George Schelling captures the essence of both the power and the menace of the fiercest predators of the ocean depths and the exquisite beauty of a leaping game fish. His interest in painting wildlife, rugged landscapes, and seascapes has taken him throughout the United States, Mexico, and Canada. Range $500 to $10,000.

David Shepherd is a contemporary oil painter whose specialty is African big game. Having spent years studying them and their habitat, he is able to capture their moods. Range to $25,000.

Peter Skirka is an artist of tremendous ability, and his big-game scenes successfully capture the mood and excitement of his subject. A former art teacher, his creative efforts in wildlife art were motivated by a trip to Kenya to study African antelope, the subject of a book that he illustrated. His first love is big cats, but the subject of his work is extremely varied, and he brings the same degree of skill to every subject he paints. Range $6,000 to $15,000.

Eric Sloane is best known as an artist of rural America. Throughout his career, he has done some sporting work. Range $1,200 to $20,000.

Ken Smallwood is an outstanding artist whose paintings are truly representative of great moments in stream and field. To admirers of fine sporting art, his dramatic and finely crafted oils are most appealing. Range $1,800 to $3,000.

George Stubbs *(1724–1806)* was probably the first English artist whose inspiration came directly from nature. His search for realism was an obsession. At an early age, he studied anatomy and became so proficient that he often lectured on the subject. A self-driven perfectionist, he eagerly sought both live and dead models for his animal studies. His popularity as an animal artist earned him many commissions from the finest judges of horses. Stubbs' work is considered by many to be the finest of his period. Many of his works have been published as engravings. Possibly the most interesting to sportsmen is the "Spanish Pointer," 1768. Stubbs' work is difficult to obtain, being much in demand. Range $12,000 to $200,000.

Gary Swanson has worked as a taxidermist for natural history museums, which gave him knowledge of animal anatomy that has proven invaluable to his art career. His paintings are superb, precise recreations of big-game animals he has studied around the world. Range $3,000 to $20,000.

Arthur F. Tait *(1819–1905)* was an Englishman who journeyed to America in 1850, bringing with him a great artistic talent and an insatiable love for the outdoors. For more than 30 years, Tait hunted, fished, and camped in the Adirondacks, recording in detail the life of the sportsman. He was a superb draftsman, and his paintings celebrate a robust outdoor life and the wildlife with which he shared it. Range $3,000 to $20,000.

Milton C. Weiler was truly a sportsman's artist. His watercolors have a unique

"Pick Up Time at Barnegat Bay." Watercolor by Milton C. Weiler.

charm, loose and yet tight in style. His hunting and fishing scenes are very collectible. Since his death in 1974, his paintings have risen sharply in value. Range $3,000 to $5,500.

Wayne Willis is an ardent conservationist and sportsman. His oils portray a vividness and realism to which sportsmen can easily relate. He has a unique ability to create a certain dimensional quality in his game birds so that they appear to fly off the canvas. Range $2,500 to $6,000.

GALLERIES

Ackermann, New York City

Arts Unlimited, San Antonio

J. N. Bartfield, New York City

The Crossroads of Sport,
New York City and Wellesley, Massachusetts

Dean's, Atlanta

Grand Central Art Galleries,
New York City

Kennedy Galleries, New York City

Kerrs, Los Angeles

The Old Print Shop, New York City

Petersen Galleries, Beverly Hills

Sporting Life, Washington

Sports Art, New Orleans

Sportsman's Edge, Ltd.
New York City

SELECTED BIBLIOGRAPHY

Allen, Douglas. *Frederic Remington's Own Outdoors*. Dial Press, 1964.
Biographical Sketches of American Artists, 4th edition. Michigan State
    Library, 1922.

Clark, Roland. *Pot Luck*. New York: A. S. Barnes, 1945.

Elman, Robert. *The Great American Shooting Prints*. New York: Knopf, 1972.

Frost, A. B. *A Book of Drawings*. New York: P. F. Collier & Son, 1904.

Goodrich, Lloyd. *The Artist in America*. New York: W. W. Norton, 1967.

Nivel, Ralph. *Old English Sporting Prints and Their History*. London: The Studio, Limited, 1927.

Patterson, Jerry. *Antiques of Sport*. New York: Crown, 1975.

Reed, Walter. *The Illustrators in America*. Reinhold, 1966.

Thomas, Joseph. *Hounds and Hunting Through the Ages*. Garden City, NY: Windward House, 1933.

Chapter 2 ❧ Prints and Etchings

ALLAN J. LIU

Sporting prints are as much a part of the American scene as hot dogs and apple pie, and the history of their production in this country is almost as long as the history of the American field sports they depict. Yet as recently as five years ago, there was no demand for them among collectors; like many other items now considered antiques, they were taken for granted and were always available.

But times have changed. A few generations of spring housecleanings have taken their toll. Prints done in very large editions in the last century, and even early in the present century, to satisfy a popular demand for inexpensive sporting art were a glut on the market for decades, but now are being recognized as rarities. For example, the A. B. Frost, 1895, *Shooting Portfolio* was done by Scribner's in an edition of 2,500 — but today I would guess that no more than 25 intact portfolios in excellent condition exist.

Prints include woodcuts, etchings, and engravings. They can be either one color — usually black — or multicolored; colored prints can be further divided into those that are hand-colored and those that are printed in color. Prints come in all shapes and sizes — sometimes as calendars or advertisements. They may be unsigned or signed, unnumbered or numbered, unlimited or limited; some may even be remarqued, which means that the artist has added a small original sketch to the margin. All of these variables — and, of course, rarity and objective quality — affect the value of a print.

If you are starting a print collection, the best way to protect your investment is to choose a reputable dealer, one who will guarantee authenticity and condition, and tell him your interests. Follow your own taste, and buy the best you can afford — buy one fine print rather than three or four mediocre ones. Beware of the multitude of contemporary prints flooding the market today; these are fine if you are buying them simply because you like them, but how many of them will be in demand in half a century? Since the contemporary artist is still in business, if he has a successful edition he is apt to follow it up with another.

Take note of all the prints you come across as you go through dealers' stocks and ask plenty of questions. Before long you will have acquired a working knowledge of print valuation—the significance of publisher, printing process, quality of paper, size of edition, and all the other finer points.

You can make a helter-skelter collection, just buying whatever appeals to you, but it is more interesting and in the long run a wiser investment to build a collection in specific areas. You could collect the works of a single artist. You could specialize in Derrydale editions. You could collect etchings only, or woodcuts only, and so forth. You could restrict yourself to a certain period, or to a certain activity—freshwater fishing, fox hunting, or whatever activity you like.

CARING FOR YOUR COLLECTION

If a print is worth framing, it's worth framing right. According to Laurence F. Jonson, who runs The Art Shop and Gallery in Davenport, Iowa, the most destructive and avoidable abuse of paperborne art is caused by improper framing and improper handling during framing. Framers must be selected with as much care as the prints themselves. Many framers do beautiful, creative work and are fine craftsmen, but through ignorance of proper material usage, are guilty of introducing destructive elements to the art works they should be protecting. The use of woodpulp boards, sulphite-core mats, pressure-sensitive tapes, animal glues, contact papers, corrugated boards, and spray glues should be avoided as assiduously as trimming or lining art works or writing on their borders.

Questions to ask your framer include whether he uses museum standard procedures. These should include:

1. Mat and backing should be 100 percent cotton fiber museum board.
2. Print should be mounted with rag hinges or plastic flanges and vegetable glue.
3. If a colored mat is used, it should be undermatted with a rag board extended at least ¼ inch from the lip of the colored mat.
4. If a print is "floated," a fillet should be inserted between the glass and the print.
5. Hinging material should be weaker than the print support, so that if put under stress, the hinges will give first.
6. The print should always be attached to the backing board, not the window mat.

These are the major safeguards to insist upon. For further information, you might want to get hold of *A Guide to Collecting and Care of Original Prints* (New York: Crown, 1967), by Carl Zigrosser and Christa Gaehde, and *How to*

"Journey's End." Roland Clark.

Care for Works of Art on Paper (Boston: Museum of Fine Arts, 1979), by Francis W. Dolloff and Roy L. Perkinson. And when you hang a framed print, make sure it will not be exposed to high humidity, sunlight, or fluorescent light, all of which will cause the print to deteriorate in one way or another.

Prints can be framed in special ways. Some framers make constructions with prints. They mount trout and salmon flies around angling prints. Grouse-hunting prints are framed with the grouse's tail feathers fanned out.

If you don't frame all your prints, you should store them flat in a dry place. Serious collectors use blueprint cabinets such as are found in architects' and engineers' offices; the wide shallow drawers are ideal.

CURRENT VALUES OF SPORTING PRINTS

The following list of values is up to date at the time of writing, but with inflation unchecked, they are apt to be out of date rapidly. Relative values should stay about the same, except in the case of recently released editions. All values are given for a print in excellent condition, with full margins and no stains, or foxing, or folds. An asterisk next to the number of copies means that the edition was numbered and signed by the artist. Blank entries occur where the information is unknown or unavailable.

	Year of issue	Publisher	Edition size	Current value
ROBERT ABBETT				
Down Wind	1973	Crossroads & R. Abbett	500*	$300
Luke	1973	Sportsman's Edge	500*	75
Gray Water, Black Lab	1974	Crossroads	500*	200
Windfall		Sportsman's Edge	550*	500
First Season	1975	Greenwich Workshop	1,000*	300
Partners	1976	Sportsman's Edge	500	150
Setter and Woodcock	1976	Sportsman's Edge	500	150
Setter and Grouse	1977	Sportsman's Edge	500	160
English Setter Family	1978	Sportsman's Edge	750	190
HARRY C. ADAMSON				
Winging in—Pintails	1971	Wild Wings	450*	$500
Wild Bounty—Black Ducks	1972	Wild Wings	450*	500
Oxbow Sorlery—Mallards	1973	Wild Wings	480*	400
Arctic Citadel—Dall Sheep	1974	Wild Wings	580*	200
Greenhead Exodus—Mallards	1974	Wild Wings	580*	200
JOHN J. AUDUBON				
Birds of America	1827-38	Havell		

(Volumes upon volumes have been done on the man and his works, and deservedly so. This edition is the collectible one. The last price I've heard of was about $600,000 at auction for the complete portfolio. The Havell Edition is an elephant folio containing 435 hand-colored prints.)

	Year of issue	Publisher	Edition size	Current value
AL BARKER				
etchings			50	$200
FRANK W. BENSON				
etchings				$200–500
RICHARD BISHOP				
etchings			signed	$150–250
			unsigned	20–50

(A prime mover in Ducks Unlimited. Market for his etchings not high since many of his editions are unlimited.)

		Year of issue	Publisher	Edition size	Current value
RALPH L. BOYER					
Fathers of American Sport	(set of 6)	1931	Derrydale	250*	$350
After a Big One		1936	Derrydale	200*	400
An Anxious Moment		1937	Derrydale	250*	500
etchings					200
REX BRASHER					
prints					$75–200
PAUL BROWN					
American Polo Scenes	(set of 4)	1930	Derrydale	175*	$3,500
The Meadowbrook Cup		1931	Derrydale	250*	2,000
Hoick! Hoick! Hoick!		1937	Derrydale	250*	600
Pressing Him		1937	Derrydale	250*	600
Music Ahead		1939	Derrydale	250*	500
Kennel Bound		1941	Derrydale	250*	500

(One of America's top equestrian artists.)

	Year of issue	Publisher	Edition size	Current value
DR. EDGAR BURKE				
Canada Geese	1941	Derrydale	250*	$400
The Vanguard		Frank J. Lowe	250*	225
GEORGE CATLIN				
signed prints				$400
RAYMOND CHING				
Kestrel	1978	Russell Fink	850	$100
Treasure Chest Wrens	1979	Russell Fink	850	100
ROLAND CLARK				
The Alarm	1937	Derrydale	250*	$1,200
Down Wind	1937	Derrydale	250*	450
Sanctuary	1938	Derrydale	250*	450
The Scout	1938	Derrydale	250*	450
Winter Marsh	1939	Derrydale	250*	750
Dawn	1939	Derrydale	250*	350
A Straggler	1940	Derrydale	250*	600
Calm Weather	1940	Derrydale	250*	750
Taking Off	1941	Derrydale	250*	750
Dropping In	1941	Derrydale	250*	800
Mallards Rising	1942	Derrydale	250*	2,000
Pintails Coming In	1942	Frank J. Lowe	250*	600–1,000
Open Water	1943	Frank J. Lowe	250*	350–650
Fairhaven	1943	Frank J. Lowe	250*	800–1,200
The Rendezvous	1944	Frank J. Lowe	250*	200–500
The Raider	1944	Frank J. Lowe	250*	250–400
Seclusion	1945	Frank J. Lowe	250*	150–250
Visitors	1945	Frank J. Lowe	250*	300–600
Tranquillity	1946	Frank J. Lowe	250*	150–250
Journey's End	1946	Frank J. Lowe	250*	800–1,200
etchings				200–400

(Noted for his waterfowl, Clark painted birds the way a hunter sees them. "The Alarm," a single black duck, is the best of this species I've seen.)

	Year of issue	Publisher	Edition size	Current value
GUY COHELEACH				
Jungle Jaguar	1973	Regency House	5,000*	$115
Clouded Leopard	1973			90
Charging Elephant	1974			100
ARTHUR COOK				
Backwaters—Duck		Art Cook	600*	$35
The Traveler Rests—Arctic Tern	1974	Wild Wings	450*	50
After the Storm—Pheasants	1975	Art Cook	350*	50
PETER CORBIN				
Chance to Double	1980	Orvis	250	$300
CURRIER & IVES (c.1850-1895)				
Small Folio				$200–500
Medium Folio				1,000–2,000
Large Folio				2,000–8,000

(A good sporting art collection must have a Currier or two in it. For the angler, two of the most famous are Tait's "Trout Fishing, an Anxious Moment" and Palmer's "The Trout Stream." Any collector in this area should have the reference book, *Currier and Ives Sporting Prints* [New York: Public Library, 1931], by Harry Peters.)

	Year of issue	Publisher	Edition size	Current value
MONTAGUE DAWSON				
Rolling Home	1925	Frost & Reed	250	$750–1,500
Racing Clippers	1926	Frost & Reed	250	750–1,500
Searching the Seas		Frost & Reed		
Lord Nelson's Flagship "Victory"	1926	Frost & Reed	250	750–1,500
Flying Cloud	1926	Frost & Reed	250	750–1,500
The Golden Hind	1927	Frost & Reed	325	750–1,500
Boundless Ocean	1928	Frost & Reed	250	750–1,500
Homeward Bound	1928	Frost & Reed	250	750–1,500
Southerly Wind – The Waimate	1928	Frost & Reed	250	750–1,500
Happy Days	1929	Frost & Reed	250	750–1,500
Chasing the Smuggler	1930	Frost & Reed	250	750–1,500
Picking Up the Pilot		Frost & Reed		
The Cutty Sark	1930	Frost & Reed	250	750–1,500
Twilight Shadows	1931	Frost & Reed	275	750–1,500
Mist of Morning	1932	Frost & Reed	250	750–1,500
A Winning Tack	1933	Frost & Reed	250	1,200–1,500

"The Trout Stream." Currier & Ives hand-colored stone lithograph.

	Year of issue	Publisher	Edition size	Current value
Sails of Evening	1934	Frost & Reed	250	750–1,500
Neck and Neck	1935	Frost & Reed	250	1,200–1,500
A Following Wind	1936	Frost & Reed	250	750–1,500
White Clipper	1937	Frost & Reed	250	750–1,500
Wind and Sun	1937	Frost & Reed	250	750–1,500
The Silvered Way	1938	Frost & Reed	250	750–1,500
Narvk Fjord (The Altmark)	1940	Frost & Reed	No Proofs	
A Stretch to Seaward	1940	Frost & Reed	250	750–1,500
The Run Home	1941	Frost & Reed		
The North America—Far Horizon	1941	Frost & Reed	250	750–1,500
"Caught"—The Doomed Bismark	1941	Frost & Reed	No Proofs	
Breaking Out the Royals	1943	Frost & Reed		
Fine Weather and a Far Wind	1946	Frost & Reed	100	1,800–2,100
Evening Gold—The Red Jacket	1947	Frost & Reed	250	750–1,500
The Homecoming	1947	Frost & Reed	150	750–1,500
Racing Wings	1950	Frost & Reed	150	750–1,500
Ocean Racers	1954	Frost & Reed	200	1,200–1,600
Royal Racers	1954	Frost & Reed	200	1,200–1,600
Eight Bells—Belaying the Anchor	1955	Frost & Reed	200	2,500–3,000
Days of Adventure	1957	Frost & Reed	200	1,500–2,000
The Golden West	1958	Frost & Reed	200	1,200–1,500
Summer Breezes	1961	Frost & Reed	250	1,000–1,250
The Thermopylae Leaving Foochow	1962	Frost & Reed	250	1,500–2,000
Racing Home—The Cutty Sark	1963	Frost & Reed	300	4,000–6,000
Ariel and Taeping	1964	Frost & Reed		
24" × 30"			500	1,000–1,500
29" × 36"				2,000–2,750
U.S.S. Constellation	1966	Frost & Reed	200	500–1,000
The Java and Constitution	1966	Frost & Reed	500	1,200–1,700
Horn Abeam	1967	Frost & Reed	150	3,500–4,500
Up Channel—The Lahloo	1968	Frost & Reed	500	750–1,200
The Tall Ship	1969	Frost & Reed	1,000	750–1,000
The Rising Wind	1969	Frost & Reed	500	800–1,100
The Gallant Mayflower	1970	Frost & Reed	500	500–1,000
Crescent Moon	1970	Frost & Reed	500	750–1,000
Pieces of Eight	1971	Frost & Reed	500	750–1,000
Smoke of Battle	1972	Frost & Reed	500	750–1,200
In Full Sail	1972	Frost & Reed	500	600–1,000
Night Mist	1973	Frost & Reed	500	600–1,000
Pagoda Anchorage	1973	Frost & Reed	500	600–1,000
Battle of Trafalgar	1973	Frost & Reed	750	1,500

(An English artist. His love of wind and sea and sailing ships lives in his work.)

J.&T. DOUGHTY
hand-colored prints $75-125

(First American colored sporting prints. The book *Cabinet of Natural History and American Rural Sports Illustrated* came in three volumes. Many of these books have been cut up, so prints are available.)

CHURCHILL ETTINGER
Worn Rock Pool $150
etchings 50-200

JAMES P. FISHER
| Pintail | 1974 | Sportsman's Edge | 450* | $100 |

	Year of issue	Publisher	Edition size	Current value
Wood Duck	1974	Sportsman's Edge	450*	100
Black Labrador	1974	Sportsman's Edge	450*	100
Yellow Labrador	1974	Sportsman's Edge	450*	100

ARTHUR B. FROST

Scribner's Shooting Portfolio (set of 12 complete)	1895	Scribner's	2,500	$12,000
Autumn Grouse				500
Autumn Woodcock				500
Quail – A Dead Stand				500
Quail – A Covey Rise				500
Rabbit Shooting				500
Summer Woodcock				500
Duck Shooting from a Blind				500
Duck Shooting from a Battery				500
Rail Shooting				500
Prairie Chickens				500
English Snipe				500
Bay Snipe				500
A Day's Shooting (set of 6 complete)	1903	Scribner's		4,500
Ordered Off				650
Gun Shy				650
Good Luck				700
Bad Luck				700
Smoking Him Out				600
We've Got Him				600
Chance Shot While Setting Out Decoys	1933	Derrydale	200	1,500
October Woodcock Shooting	1933	Derrydale	200	2,500
Coming Ashore	1934	Derrydale	200	1,500
Grouse Shooting in the Rhododendrons	1934	Derrydale	200	1,500

(Anything with Frost's name on it is worth something, and he's the only artist listed here whose unsigned prints are highly collectible and worth a tidy sum of money. Henry M. Reed's *The A. B. Frost Book*, Tuttle, 1967, is a must for the Frost collector.)

JOHN FROST

Maryland Marsh	1936	Derrydale	150*	$400

ARTHUR FULLER

colored prints				$25–100

GORDON GRANT

Off Soundings	1941	Derrydale	250*	$400
The Weather Mark	1941	Derrydale	250*	400

OWEN GROMME

Wintering Quail	1971	Wild Wings	450*	$800
Brittany on Point	1971	Wild Wings	450*	450
Back to Cover – Pheasant	1971	Wild Wings	450*	125
Late Season – Canvasback	1972	Wild Wings	450*	250
Sunlit Glade – Ruffed Grouse	1972	Wild Wings	450*	350
Wintering Grosbeaks	1973	Wild Wings	600*	200
Blue Jay	1973	Wild Wings	800*	100
Startled Grouse – Golden Retriever	1973	Wild Wings	480*	300

	Year of issue	Publisher	Edition size	Current value
Island Lake Loon	1973	Wild Wings	580*	200
Expectation	1973	Wild Wings	580*	75
Sacred Cranes over Hokkaido	1974	Wild Wings	600*	60
English Setter	1974	Wild Wings	580*	225
Pileated Woodpecker	1974	Wild Wings	580*	75
Tamarack Lake—Canada Geese	1974	Wild Wings	580*	150
California Quail	1974	Wild Wings	580*	60
Hemlock Hideaway	1974	Wild Wings	580*	325
Whistling Swans	1974	Wild Wings	580*	400
Dropping In—Mourning Doves	1974	Wild Wings	580*	100
Edge of the Field—Pointer	1974	Wild Wings	580*	60
The Rascal's Revenge—Owl	1974	Wild Wings	580*	150
Winter Afternoon—Pheasants	1975	Wild Wings	580*	190
Scurrying Greenwings	1975	Wild Wings	580*	60

JOHN GROTH

etchings	$50–250
prints	75–100

"Silver Riffles." W. Goadby Lawrence.

	Year of issue	Publisher	Edition size	Current value
DAVID HAGERBAUMER				
October Evening – Pintails	1963	Frost & Reed and Sportsman's Gallery	400*	$600–1,000
Placid Marsh – Black Duck	1964	Frost & Reed and Sportsman's Gallery	400*	500–800
Woodcut Covey – Quail	1965	Frost & Reed and Sportsman's Gallery	400*	500–750
Foggy Morning – Mallards	1965	Frost & Reed and Sportsman's Gallery	400*	400–700
Portfolio of 4 Prints	1967	Frost & Reed and Crossroads of Sport	400*	200–450
Green Wing Flurry	1969	Venture Prints and D. Hagerbaumer	600*	150–275
Autumn Ruffs – Grouse	1969	Venture Prints and D. Hagerbaumer	600*	150–300
The Narrows – Wood Duck	1971	D. Hagerbaumer	450*	150–250
Double Rise – Wood Duck	1971	D. Hagerbaumer	450*	150–250
The Shanty	1972	D. Hagerbaumer	450*	
Thru the Pines – Mourning Doves	1972	D. Hagerbaumer	450*	100–300
Hill Country Gobblers	1972	D. Hagerbaumer	450*	100–300
Gathering Storm – Pintails	1972	D. Hagerbaumer	450*	75–150
Over the Ridge – Pheasants	1973	D. Hagerbaumer	450*	125–300
Minus Tide – Cans	1973	D. Hagerbaumer	450*	
Timber Potholes	1973	D. Hagerbaumer	350*	100–200
Hog Ranch Point	1974	D. Hagerbaumer	350*	
Sink Box Gunning	1974	D. Hagerbaumer	350*	
Twin Island Marsh	1974	D. Hagerbaumer	450*	
The Old Duck Camp	1974	D. Hagerbaumer	450*	
Mixed Doubles	1978	D. Hagerbaumer	450	350

(A fine contemporary artist, his "Over the Ridge – Pheasants" is one of the best pheasant prints around.)

	Year of issue	Publisher	Edition size	Current value
GERARD HARDENBERG				
prints not signed				$50–150
ELDRIDGE HARDIE				
Set of 4 Trout (with flies)				$150
Brown Trout & Light Cahills	1973	E. Hardie	450*	50
Brook Trout	1974	E. Hardie	450*	50
WINSLOW HOMER				
Canoe in the Rapids (unsigned)				
Leaping Trout		Anglers Club		$350

(Despite his renown, he did not sign his prints, which explains the low prices.)

	Year of issue	Publisher	Edition size	Current value
LYNN BOGUE HUNT				
series of sporting birds done for du Pont, unsigned				$200
etchings				100–250
D. W. HUNTINGTON				
prints, not signed				$100
EDWARD KING				
Saratoga Racing (set of 4)	1928	Derrydale	80*	$800
The Aiken Drag	1929	Derrydale	80*	200
Hunt Race (set of 4)	1929	Derrydale		
American Hunting Scenes (set of 4)	1929-1930	Derrydale	250*	1,000

	Year of issue	Publisher	Edition size	Current value
Belmont Terminal Lithographs (set of 2)	1929	Derrydale		100
American Shooting Scenes—Quail Shooting	1929	Derrydale		300
Hunting Lithographs (set of 2)	1929	Derrydale	250*	450
Woodcock Shooting—In the Birches	1930	Derrydale	350*	100
Quail Shooting—The Briar Patch	1930	Derrydale	350*	100
Diana Goes Hunting (set of 4)	1930	Derrydale	250*	300
Rochester	1932	Derrydale	250*	100
A Glorious Burst	1932	Derrydale	250*	250

S. A. KILBOURNE

Fish Portfolio	1876			$35–200 each

MARGUERITE KIRMSE

The Fox	1931	Derrydale	250*	$800
The Hounds	1933	Derrydale	250*	600
etchings				75–200

HANS KLIEGER

signed, limited prints				$50–200

J. D. KNAP

Daybreak		Frank J. Lowe		$100–225
The Inlet		Frank J. Lowe		100–225
Reflections		Frank J. Lowe		100–225
All Clear		Frank J. Lowe		100–225

LES KOUBA

signed, limited prints				$25–75

BOB KUHN

The Soft Touch	1973	Art Unlimited, Inc.	1,500	$80
Jaguar and Egret	1974	Emerson Hall	100*	60
Sunshine and Shadow	1975	Tryon Gallery, Ltd.	500	70

W. GOADBY LAWRENCE

Rising Mists	1946	Frank J. Lowe	300*	$400
Silver Riffles	1946	Frank J. Lowe	300*	1,000

(Although his speciality is big-game fishing, "Silver Riffles" is one of the nicest trout scenes around.)

LEE LeBLANC

Ruffed Grouse				$45
Bobwhite Quail				45
Arkansas Mallards			400*	
Honkers at Horkon			400*	45
A Noble Pair—Wild Turkey	1974		580*	60
A Stately Pair—Mallards	1974		580*	60

DAVID LOCKHART

Dixie Idyl			50*	
Covey Point Quail			480*	$60

MICHAEL LYNE

Away			500*	$90
VIP			500*	90
Hurdle Race			500*	90

	Year of issue	Publisher	Edition size	Current value
Point to Point Impression				150
The Grand National – Canal Turn				100
DAVID MAASS				
Canvasback	1966	Crossroads	50 remarqued	$750
			400 signed	500
Grouse	1966	Crossroads	50 remarqued	550
			400 signed	300
Coming In, Canada Geese	1969	Crossroads		300
Mallards	1971	Venture		100
Quail	1971	Venture		100
Misty Morning, Woodcock	1972	Wild Wings	450*	800
Back Bay Mallards	1973	Wild Wings	600*	250
Breaking Weather – Canada Geese	1973	Wild Wings	580*	300
Misty Morning, Grouse	1973	Wild Wings	580*	650

"Grouse in Snow." David Maass. Note the remarque in the lower-left corner.

	Year of issue	Publisher	Edition size	Current value
Breaking In, Bluebills	1973	Wild Wings	450*	250
Among the Pines, Quail	1973	Wild Wings	600*	250
Misty Morning, Wood Duck	1974	Wild Wings	580*	400
The River Flats, Pintails	1974	Wild Wings	580*	200
On the Move, Canvasback	1974	Wild Wings	580*	200
Ridge Line, Ruffed Grouse	1974	Wild Wings	580*	275
Autumn Birch, Woodcock	1974	Wild Wings	580*	175
Misty Morning, Mallard	1975	Wild Wings	580*	350
Dusk in the Bay, Canada Geese	1975	Wild Wings	600*	250
Misty Morning, Quail	1975	Wild Wings	580*	350
DU—Artist of the Year Print: The King of Ducks—Canvasback	1974	Ducks Unlimited	600*	400
Grouse in Snow			40 remarqued	900
			signed	300
Canvasback				700
Greenwing Teal			40 remarqued	700
Canada Geese				700

ALDERSON MAGEE

Coachman's Conquest—Brook Trout	1975	Sportsman's Edge	450*	$200

HENRY McDANIELS

Fishing the Dry on the Upper Conn.	1973	Anglers Club	400*	$300
An Unnamed Pool	1974	Crossroads	325*	100

EDWIN MEGARGEE

Pheasant Shooting	1930	Derrydale		$300
Woodcock Shooting	1931	Derrydale	250*	300
Grouse Shooting	1931	Derrydale	250*	300
American Cock Fighting Scenes (set of 4)	1932	Derrydale	250*	1,600
Closing In	1939	Derrydale	250*	125
Golden Retriever in Action	1972	West Surf		35

GARY NEEL

October Flight	1974	Crossroads	375*	$60

EDMUND OSTHAUS

dog prints			unsigned	$20–50

ROBERT F. PATTERSON

The America and Defenders of the America's Cup	1935	Gosden Head	260*	$6,000

ROGER TORY PETERSON

Great Horned Owl	1974	Mill Pond	750*	$700
Bald Eagle	1974	Mill Pond	950*	400
Ruffed Grouse	1975	Mill Pond	950*	375

(Primarily an artist in the style of Audubon.)

OGDEN M. PLEISSNER

Atlantic Salmon Fishing	1939			$800
Downs Gulch		Anglers Club	300*	750
Casting for Salmon	1949	Sportsman's Gallery & Bookshelf		800

	Year of issue	Publisher	Edition size	Current value
Beaverkill Bridge	1953	Anglers Club	221*	1,500
Leaping Sea Trout	1957	Frost & Reed		350–700
The Bridge Pool	1957	Frost & Reed		200–600
West Duncan, Clove Valley		Clove Valley Club		600
Grande River, Upper Malbraie	1959	Frost & Reed		600–900
Driven Grouse, Glancie Beat	1959	Frost & Reed		600–900
October Snow	1959	Anglers Club	350*	600–900
Blue Boat on the Saint Anne				1,500
Raising Salmon	1961	Sportsman's Gallery & Bookshelf		600–850
Lye Brook Pool		American Museum of Flyfishing	400*	300–450
June Trout Fishing	1967	Theodore Gordon Flyfishers	350*	300–450
Grouse Shooting				300–700
Trout Fishing				1,000–1,400
Quail Hunters	1973	Crossroads	425*	400
Hillside Orchard, Grouse Shooting	1975	Crossroads	275*	550
Woodcock Shooting	1976	Crossroads	275	425
Battonkill				550
Head of the Pool				450

(A member of the National Academy, his "Beaverkill Bridge" and "Blue Boat" are musts for any angling collection.)

ALEXANDER POPE

Upland game birds and waterfowl	1878			$200

GORDON POWER

signed prints				$150

ROGER PREUSS

Snow Geese	1964	Wildlife of America	100	$650
Canada Geese at Sunrise	1969	Wildlife of America	400	1,000
Waiting for Mom	1970	Wildlife of America	400	450
Whitetail Deer in Springtime	1973	Wildlife of America	450	375
Black Ducks at Twilight	1974	Wildlife of America	560	700

MAYNARD REECE

Mallards	1964	Maynard Reece	250*	$600
Bobwhites	1964	Maynard Reece	250*	600
Mallards – Pitching In	1969	Maynard Reece	500*	550
Edge of the Hedge Row – Bobwhites	1970	Maynard Reece	1,000*	650
Against the Wind – Canvasback	1972	Maynard Reece	550*	400
Marshlander Mallards	1973	Ducks Unlimited	550*	600
Pheasant Country	1973	Maynard Reece	600*	350
Feeding Time – Canada Geese	1973	Maynard Reece	550*	175
Wood Ducks	1973	Mill Pond	550*	200
Late Afternoon – Mallards	1973	Mill Pond	450*	250
Quail Cover	1974	Mill Pond	750*	300
Snow Geese – Blue Geese	1974	Mill Pond	750*	175
Winging South – Canada Geese	1974	Mill Pond	750*	225
Courtship Flight – Pintails	1974	Mill Pond	950*	150
Snowy Creek – Mallards	1974	Mill Pond	950*	175
Mallards – Dropping In	1974	Mill Pond	950*	125
Solitude – Whitetail Deer	1974	Mill Pond	950*	125

	Year of issue	Publisher	Edition size	Current value
A Burst of Color — Ringneck Pheasant	1974	Mill Pond	950*	150
Early Arrivals — Mallards	1974	Mill Pond	950*	100
The Sandbar — Canada Geese	1974	Mill Pond	950*	75
The Passing Storm — Canvasbacks	1974	Mill Pond	950*	75
Flooded Oaks — Mallards	1974	Mill Pond	850*	250
Afternoon Shadows — Bobwhites	1975	Mill Pond	950*	325
Hazy Day — Bobwhites	1975	Mill Pond	950*	350

JOYCE HAGERBAUMER REED

	Year of issue	Publisher	Edition size	Current value
Backwater Teal	1974		450*	$100
Wintering Doves	1975		450*	100

FREDERIC REMINGTON

	Year of issue	Publisher	Edition size	Current value
prints			signed	$2,500
prints			unsigned	75–150

CHET RENESON

	Year of issue	Publisher	Edition size	Current value
On the Flats	1976	Sportsman's Edge	200	$400
In the Keys	1979	Sportsman's Edge	300	200

LOUIS RHEAD

	Year of issue	Publisher	Edition size	Current value
prints			signed	$50–125

A. LASSELL RIPLEY

	Year of issue	Publisher	Edition size	Current value
Gunning in America	1947	Field & Stream		$50–275
Grouse Cover	1952	Frost & Reed		800–1,200
Pheasants in the Corn Field	1952	Frost & Reed		800–1,200
Covey by the Cabin	1957	Frost & Reed		800–1,200
The Turkey Blind	1957	Sportsman's Gallery and Bookshelf, Frost & Reed		500–800
Mallards Coming In	1963	Frost & Reed		150–350
Woodcock Cover	1963	Frost & Reed		500–850
End of the Grouse Season	1966	Frost & Reed		250–550
A Turkey Drive	1966	Frost & Reed		200–450
etchings			signed	150–250

(Sporting art at its best showing scenes with gun in hand.)

PERCIVAL ROSSEAU

	Year of issue	Publisher	Edition size	Current value
prints			signed	$200–400
prints			unsigned	50

CARL RUNGIUS

	Year of issue	Publisher	Edition size	Current value
etchings				$250

(North American big game is his subject.)

JOHN N. RUTHVEN

	Year of issue	Publisher	Edition size	Current value
Canvasbacks			1,000*	$200
Cinnamon Teal			1,000*	
Ruddy Ducks			1,000*	200

WILLIAM J. SCHALDACH

	Year of issue	Publisher	Edition size	Current value
American Game Birds — Woodcock	1931	Derrydale	250*	$800
Eastern Brook Trout	1974	Theodore Gordon Flyfishers	300*	150
etchings			signed	100–350

(His etchings of upland-game hunting are especially important.)

	Year of issue	Publisher	Edition size	Current value
MANFRED SCHATZ				
Mallards	1978	Russell Fink	500	$250
Lynx	1978	Russell Fink	500	100
Brief Interlude — Red Fox	1979	Russell Fink	500	200
Wing Majesty — Canada Geese	1979	Russell Fink	500	80
Out of the Mist — Mallards	1980	Russell Fink	500	60
Winter Fox	1980	Russell Fink	500	60
Wolf Pack	1980	Russell Fink	500	125
OLAF SELZER				
prints			signed	$50–200
DAVID SHEPHERD				
Wise Old Elephant			unsigned, unlimited	$95
Elephant at Amboseli			unsigned, unlimited	240
African Children			unsigned, limited	700
African Children			signed, limited (1,800)	2,200
Baby Kudu		Solomon & Whitehead	unsigned, limited	400
Baby Kudu		Solomon & Whitehead	signed, limited (1,800)	2,200
Old George Under His Favorite Baobab Tree			unsigned, limited	650
Old George Under His Favorite Baobab Tree			signed, limited (1,800*)	2,200
Lion Majesty		Solomon & Whitehead	500*	1,900
Elephant and the Ant Hill			850*	650
Tiger Fire			850*	2,400
The Big Five	1974	Solomon & Whitehead	850*	1,500
Elephant Heaven	1975	Solomon & Whitehead	850*	210
DONALD SHOFFSTALL				
etchings			signed	$50–200
NED SMITH				
Big Red	1979	Sportsman Specialties	600	$200
Thunder King	1981	Sportsman Specialties	600	200
JOHN STOBART				
South Street — N.Y. 1874	1967	Kennedy Galleries	250	$1,200
South Street — N.Y. 1880	1975	Maritime Heritage Press	950	1,500
EDWARD S. VOSS				
The Hartford Fox	1943	Edward S. Voss	400*	$350
FRANKLIN B. VOSS				
Foxhunting in America — Over the Open	1939	Derrydale	250*	$750
Foxhunting in America — On a Fresh Line	1939	Derrydale	250*	750

	Year of issue	Publisher	Edition size	Current value
Foxhunting in America—Working it Out	1941	Derrydale	250*	750
Tally Ho		Frank J. Lowe		
ARTHUR WEAVER				
Play on 12th Green, Augusta			250*	$250
View of 18th Green, Pebble Beach	1974	Robert J. Perham	750*	300
Cypress Point		Robert J. Perham	750*	50
WALTER WEBER				
Snow Geese	1974	Russell Fink	550*	150
MILTON C. WEILER				
Classic Shorebird Series	1969	Winchester Press	1,000	$20
Classic Decoy Series	1969	Winchester Press	1,000	40
Pick Up Time—Barnegat Bay	1970	Winchester Press		200
Atlantic Salmon Fishing on the Matapedia	1972	M. C. Weiler		700

"Atlantic Salmon Fishing on the Matapedia." Milton C. Weiler.

	Year of issue	Publisher	Edition size	Current value
Plate from *Upstream and Down*	1973	Derrydale	60*	200
Upper Twin Pool—Henryville	1973	Henryville Conservation Club	125*	600
Virgin Water	1973	American League of Anglers	500*	150

(Fishing collectors should have "Henryville" and "Matapedia." Classic Decoy Series already a classic—and those prints signed by Weiler bring $25 more.)

LEVEN WEST
etchings $40–175

DEALERS IN SPORTING PRINTS AND OTHER ART

Drew Holl
The Crossroads of Sport
5 East 47th St.
New York, NY 10017

William Webster
Wild Wings, Inc.
Lake City, MN 55041

Sportsman's Edge, Ltd.
136 East 74th St.
New York, NY 10021

Russell A. Fink
9843 Gunston Rd.
Lorton, VA 22079

Lee Talcott
The Orvis Co., Inc.
Manchester, VT 05254

Harold Whitman
The Bedford Sportsman
Bedford Hills, NY 10507

Petersen Galleries
9433 Wilshire Blvd.
Beverly Hills, CA 90212

Chapter 3 ❧ Photographs

MARGOT F. CONTE

Webster's *Dictionary* defines photograph as "a picture, image or likeness obtained by photography; extremely faithful, minutely detailed or mechanically accurate reproduction or representation." Because of the many excellent photographers today, people are becoming more and more aware of what nature has to offer. Outdoor photography has existed since the days of glass negatives and H. K. Job, William Dawson, and William Finley, the pioneers in wildlife and bird photography. With the technical advances in film and other aspects of photography, nature photography has come into its own during the past few decades.

Positions and observations depicted by artists have been questioned many times. "Does the bird have the proper number of flight feathers?" "Bears don't fish that way." "You wouldn't see a moose in that setting." However, in photography, with photographers spending hours in natural habitats, the moment, stance, and attitude are captured and recorded, and there can be no question about their authenticity.

Descriptions of animals and birds date back to the earliest books. Writers were describing flocks of cranes, rookeries, migrations, hunts, but it was not until this century that actual movements, flights, and behavioral patterns were documented on film. An English photographer named Muybridge (in 1875) shot the first instantaneous pictures of a horse at a gallop, which brought to light facts that the human eye was unable to detect. In 1893, Louis Boutan took the first successful underwater photographs. In 1907, Dr. P. Gromier brought back pictures from Africa of animals in a completely wild setting. Oliver Pike, the first truly professional nature photographer, made a film called, "In the Kingdom of the Birds," in England at the turn of the century. This was the beginning of wildlife photography as we know it today.

Wildlife photography is one of the most difficult forms of the craft. It takes much technical preparation, as well as research and knowledge of the particular species being photographed. The physical hardships can be enormous— carrying heavy equipment into the bush in extreme weather; hours, days, weeks, maybe months (maybe never) of waiting; and timing and luck. All of these ingredients are essential to the final picture. A picture does not (as a rule) "just happen." Film and motors can freeze, (as can the photographer), and extreme heat can cause a completely different set of problems.

The photographer must know when the migrations occur or he will have made the trip for naught. In knowing that waterfowl "bark" before they take off and by studying their behavioral patterns, that marvelous picture of geese running across the water (in a matter of seconds) or raising up with wings outstretched is achieved, instead of a picture of a bird just sitting on the water. Animals have set patterns, just as people do, and there is no doubt that the wildlife photographer who has done his or her homework will be the one whose pictures are most sought after.

In the early days of photography, everything was shot in black and white, and early nature photographers such as Allan Cruickshank and Eric Hosking are known for their extraordinary images. Now that color film has become more sophisticated, most of the nature and wildlife photographers prefer to use color film, not only for esthetic reasons, but also for identification purposes (especially with birds).

The use of black and white or color film is a personal decision of the photographer, many times based on technical reasons: for instance, black and white film has the most latitude, especially under trying, shooting conditions. I personally prefer color film and believe that in wildlife photography, it is the only way to go. There is a certain golden color seen on the plains in Africa that can transport the viewer from his print right back to that wonderful moment at about eight or nine o'clock in the morning in Kenya.

WHAT TO COLLECT

At this point in this relatively young field, it would be difficult to give a breakdown on what to collect and what will appreciate in value. There is no question that the very early photographs will command high prices; not because they are in the sporting art field, but because they are old photographs. It is best to become familiar with some of the more well-known photographers and decide what you like and want to collect. In the past few years, many of the fine galleries, dealers, and museums, including the Museum of Modern Art, have been collecting and selling early photographs for thousands of dollars. Turn-of-the-century photography is considered one of the hottest new investments on the market. Sotheby Parke Bernet conducts regular auctions at which record prices are broken with each succeeding auction. Wildlife photography, just as wildlife art of a few years ago, is the newcomer. It is just starting to be recognized, and many books and portfolios on nature and wild-life have become collector's items. Three outstanding ones are the following.

John S. Dunning — "Birds of the Tropics" — A Yale graduate and a field collaborator at Cornell's School of Ornithology. A beautiful photographic book on neotropical birds. Dazzling portraits. It is rapidly becoming a much sought-after book.

Crawford Greenwalt — "Hummingbirds" — Scientist-photographer with an unequalled reputation in this area. This book is a triumph and has captured precisely the actions and colors of hummingbirds. In 1960, this book was published at $25. Now, if you can find a copy, it costs over $400.

Edgar Queeny — "Prairie Wings" — A pen-and-camera flight study that was done on 16mm film in the 1940s. It holds a strong place in black-and-white photography, and is still competing with today's 35mm photography. The original book is commanding a high price.

The list of photographers involved in wildlife and nature photography is growing every day, the competition getting stronger, and the work more and more imaginative. Although it is precise documentation of nature as we see it, three or four photographers can photograph the same subject and the results will be three or four totally different images. Many photographers specialize in various aspects of wildlife — birds, African wildlife, underwater creatures, and so forth. Following is a list of several outstanding wildlife and nature photographers.

Allan Cruickshank has produced more than forty thousand negatives covering almost 550 species of North American birds (black-and-white Panchromatic film). His first published work was "Wings in the Wilderness" (1947). His wife, Helen, a fine photographer in her own right, is carrying on where her late husband excelled.

Eric Hosking has completed over 50 years of nature photography. Roger Tory Peterson has been quoted as saying that Hosking is one of the "world's greatest bird photographers." He has been able to combine technique, artistry, and portraiture. He has progressed from a Brownie camera to today's modern equipment, and very few people would argue that he is certainly the tops in his field.

Roger Tory Peterson has done some marvelous photographic work with birds although he is not generally thought of by many as a photographer. Since he is primarily known as a naturalist, ornithologist, and artist, his photographs would certainly be an unusual acquisition.

Frederick Kent Truslow took up photography, using 35mm color film. In 1954 at the Audubon camp in Maine, he met Cruickshank and became fascinated with photographing birds. He then moved to Florida, where he specialized in the birds of southern Florida and became one of the greatest bird photographers of our time.

These persons are among the finest of nature and wildlife photographers. Here are some others, with a short note on each.

Jen and Des Bartlett. "The Flight of the Snow Goose." All forms of wildlife.

Erwin Bauer. Naturalist. "Hunting with a Camera." Many articles.

Stanley and Kay Breeden. Numerous articles on wildlife.

Dennis Brokaw. Nature.

Fred Bruemmer. Wildlife, the Arctic region, birds. Former newspaper photographer.

Jane Burton. One of today's leading animal photographers. Europe, Africa, and Asia. Often teams up with her father, Maurice Burton.

Maurice Burton. Zoologist, formerly with the British Museum of Natural History.

James Carmichael. Teaches nature photography in Florida.

Patricia Caufield. Many large-format books on the American wilderness and the Okefenokee Swamp.

David Cavagnaro. Biologist and entomologist. Close-ups of nature, including spiderwebs, dew, natural abstract patterns, and insects.

Stephen Dalton. "Borne on the Wind." Technically magnificent, stop-action, detailed photography. Inflight studies of insects at one millionth of a second.

Thase Daniel. Outstanding nature photographer.

Tui DeRoy. Nature photographer specializing in the animals and birds of the Galapagos Islands.

Douglas Faulkner. Underwater microphotography. Diver, scientist, naturalist, and artist. Probably one of the best underwater photographers in the world.

Jeff Foote. Biologist. Mammal behavior.

M. Philip Kahl. Contributions to all the top nature magazines. Specializes in magnificent color. Birds primarily.

Leonard Lee Rue, III. Magazines, books. All forms of wildlife.

Nina Leen. *Life* staff photographer. Studies on bats. "America's Vanishing Wildlife."

Les Line. Editor of *Audubon Magazine*. Nature and birds.

Norman Meyers. "The Long African Day."

Eliot Porter. Naturalist. Birds, wildlife. A protégé of Alfred Stieglitz.

WHERE TO BUY AND SELL

As mentioned earlier, many galleries and dealers, as well as auction houses, are starting to handle wildlife and sporting photographs. In 1978, The Waterfowl Festival in Easton, Maryland, began a counterpart to the Federal Duck Stamp Contest. A photography contest was held, open to anyone who wanted to enter, as long as the subject matter was birds. It was won by Archie Johnson of Virginia Beach, Virginia, and the winning photograph has already become a collector's item. The prints have been sold in a limited edition, at an issuing price of $50.

Flea markets sometimes are good places to find photographs, and many times you can write directly to a photographer, or his agent, requesting a print of a photograph from a magazine or book. Most galleries and shows, even street shows, are in the business of selling photographs. But don't expect to be able to buy them at the same price as your Kodak prints.

Although the cost of printing *should not* determine the price of a photograph, most professional photographers either print their own work or have it professionally printed at custom labs. This fact has to be taken into consideration, as well as their time, other expenses, and the many hours spent trying to achieve that image.

I remember a particular photograph of mine that took two long, difficult, and frustrating years to get exactly the way I wanted. It is a picture of two cygnets sitting on their mother's back (a mute swan). This event only happens for a couple of days early in a cygnet's life, for as soon as the cygnet puts on a little weight, its mother won't let it up there. Two at the same time, with mute swans, is a real bonus. It is *only* allowed by the mother when she feels safe and relaxed. So, one, I had to find a swan with babies. Two, it had to be on a fairly large body of water (because they only behave this way when cruising). Three, I had to sit without moving, to observe from 6 A.M. until dark, because only the mother knew when this would happen, *if* it happened. Four, several times it did happen, but even with the longest of lenses, they were just too far away for a good picture. Five, just when all the circumstances were right, a car pulled up and the nervous mother dumped the babies off her back to be ready to defend them if necessary. And that was the end of my picture for the first year that I tried. After two weeks, the cygnets had gotten too heavy. So, I had to wait until the next year and go through the same kind of vigil with the hope of better luck.

The following year, on just about the last possible day (as the babies were getting chubby and the mother less enthusiastic), I got my picture. I have no idea how many rolls of film and weary hours were involved. The picture was great and has been used in several magazines and exhibited at shows. Yet, when a woman once asked her husband to buy it for her, his reply was, "Oh, it's cute, but I can get that with my Instamatic." Well, possibly he can, and I wish him well. But I think it is highly unlikely unless he is willing to spend some time and energy. This endeavor was really a fairly easy one—there was no arctic wind, no mountains to climb, no scaffolds to build. It really just took patience. Wildlife and nature photography is a combination of love, knowledge, and just plain hard work.

HOW TO DISPLAY PHOTOGRAPHS

Photographic images differ from most other art forms in that you can choose the size of the image you want. Unless there is a limited edition (which is usually printed in one size), many photographers will let you order a size that would be suitable for your home or office.

There are many ways to display photographs. Most museums and galleries prefer a "museum mount," which is either a dye transfer (an extremely costly manner of printing) or a "C" print (less expensive and the most popular form of custom printing performed by custom laboratories). These prints are mounted on acid-free ragboard and placed under ultraviolet-repellent glass.

Another process (a nonsilver pigment process) produces carbro prints, which are nonfading, permanent, full-color pigment photographs. This method sometimes is used for archival prints. According to Ken Lieberman of Stewart Color Labs, carbro prints are ideal for deluxe, limited edition photographs. They will not fade although the original color may change over the years.

Whether your prints are Kodak printed, "C" prints, dye transfer, or carbro, they can be shown in a museum box mount (the photograph has been sprayed so that no glass is necessary), or under ultraviolet-repellent glass. They should never be in constant direct sunlight and should be treated the same way you would treat watercolor paintings.

INSURING YOUR PHOTOGRAPHS

Photographs can be insured under a homeowner's policy in the same way that other valuables are insured. If you have a particularly valuable print or a limited edition, you may want to insure it on a floater to your insurance policy. The best thing to do is to discuss it with your insurance agent. Always keep your sales slips and proof of ownership.

Chapter 4 ❧ Wildfowl Decoys

THOMAS A. WINSTEL and ALAN G. HAID

D ecoy collecting is not a recent activity in North America. Decoys have been found, in the Lovelock Caves of Nevada, that date back more than 1,000 years. The care taken by their makers in storing these decoys reflected the value placed on their maintenance.

The first extensive book on decoy collecting, *Wildfowl Decoys* by Joel Barber, was published in 1934 (Windward House). William J. Mackey, Jr. published his book, *The American Bird Decoy*, in 1965 (Dutton). The book is a revelation of decoys and the men who carved them and was a culmination of 40 years of research, writing, and photographing of the makers and their decoys. Mackey has been the major contributor to the prominence of the waterfowl decoy.

Goose. Ira Hudson, Chincoteague Island, Virginia. (Photo courtesy Allan Kain)

In the early 1950s, decoy collectors from various regions began trading among themselves. The carving of decoys accompanied this trading, and the birth of the "contemporary" carver who fashioned wood destined for the mantle rather than the marsh or bay took place.

A decoy on the shelf now rivals the American turkey at Thanksgiving as a demonstration of American traditionalism. The decoy justly deserves this attention for nowhere in the world is there such a waterfowl concentration and migration as that found in North America. Although European and Asian countries experimented in making decoys and a few can be found today, they are insignificant when compared with the numbers produced on our continent.

Although a multitude of wooden decoys were made, many were destroyed in the hearths and stoves of America's homes and hunting camps and replaced with plastic, rubber, and even canvas decoys. Fortunately, many of the wooden decoys that are treasured today were packed away for safekeeping or stored on the mantel as an example of grandpa's handiwork. A few survived the elements in boat houses, and today there are still some great old wooden decoys to be found in a hunter's rig.

FINDING DECOYS

Collecting decoys is fairly easy for those persons who live along the coast. But if you are a resident of a land-locked city, the collecting is more difficult. Following are some sources for finding decoys.

Antique shops are the best source. Although most antique store proprietors are not very knowledgeable about the make, condition, and history of the decoys, this is changing as the value of the decoy increases. Many valuable old tollers are sitting in antique stores today, but along with these are a great number of new decoys that appear to be old. Caution should certainly be used by the decoy collector. Flea markets are also a good source of decoys, depending on their proximity to waterfowl hunting. The East Coast, West Coast, Illinois River, and most of Louisiana are fertile areas. The most pleasurable and fruitful source, however, has been fellow collectors who often have an extra decoy or two for trade or sale. Also, many important historical facts concerning the construction of the decoy or its maker can be learned during the transaction. An extensive list of decoy collectors, including their addresses and telephone numbers, has been compiled by Gene and Linda Kangas in their book, *The National Decoy Collectors.* The book may be ordered by sending a check for $10 to National Decoy Collectors Guide, 6852 Ravenna Rd., Concord Township, OH 44077.

DECOY SHOWS

Decoy shows are increasing in popularity each year and have become congregating places for decoy collectors. Following is a list of some of the shows, the person currently in charge of arrangements, and the approximate time of year the show is held. These shows are of great interest because a wide variety of decoys are exhibited and offered for sale. If a particular decoy interests you and you find the decoy's style, appearance, and condition acceptable, get a second opinion from someone other than the seller. Often decoys can be honestly, but inaccurately, described with regards to maker, or to repair of defects, and a knowledgeable collector can be an asset in confirming your decision or perhaps correcting some fact about the decoy. An experienced collector's advice is good insurance in evaluating a decoy's condition because the untrained eye often overlooks a repair or touch-up.

February The Long Island Decoy Collectors Association
Stony Brook, Long Island
Amel Massa
56 Park Avenue
Babylon, NY 11702
(516) 587-3915

Minnesota Decoy Collectors Show
Minneapolis–St. Paul, Minnesota
Bob Michaelson
4702 White Oaks Road
Edina, MN 55424
(612) 922-2163

The Northeast Decoy Collectors Meet
Babylon, New York
Amel Massa
c/o Wildfowler Decoys
56 Park Avenue
Babylon, NY 11702
(516) 587-7974

March The Ohio Decoy Collectors & Carvers Association
Sandusky, Ohio
Bill Green
P.O. Box 29224
Parma, OH 44129
(216) 885-0596

The Wisconsin Decoy Collectors Show
Fond du Lac, Wisconsin
Bill Brauer
2106 Lakewood Beach
Fond du Lac, WI 54935
(414) 921-2711

April   Midwest Decoy Collector's Association
Oakbrook, Illinois
Gene Konapasek
1100 Bayview Road
Fox River, IL 60021
(312) 639-9392

June   Pacific Flyway Waterfowl Festival
Santa Rosa, California
Jim Kergan
1559 W. Foothill Drive
Santa Rosa, CA 95404
(707) 542-0235

July   Bourne Decoy Auction
Hyannis, Massachusetts
Richard Bourne
(617) 775-0797

Clayton New York Decoy & Wildlife Art Show
Clayton, New York
Arthur Knapp
P.O. Box 292
Clayton, NY 13624
(315) 686-3039

New England Decoy Collectors Association
Hyannis, Massachusetts
Robin Starr
11 Josselyn Avenue
Duxbury, MA 02332
(617) 934-2044

September   The Louisiana Wildfowl Carvers & Collectors Guild
Waterfowl Festival
Charles Frank, Jr.
Suite 303

615 Baronne Street
New Orleans, LA 70113
(504) 866-6709

MidAtlantic Waterfowl Festival
Virginia Beach, Virginia
Bill Walsh, Jr.
P.O. Box 651
Virginia Beach, VA 23451
(804) 428-8549

Midwest Decoy Contest
Pointe Moville
Jim Foote
Route 3
Rockford, MI 49341
(313) 676-8180

October   Spring Valley Decoy Show
Spring Valley, Illinois
Joe Tonelli
720 West Cleveland
Spring Valley, IL 61363
(815) 664-4580

Ward Foundation Wildfowl Carving and Art Exhibition
Salisbury, Maryland
Knute Bartrug
707 Cooper Street
Salisbury, MD 21801
(301) 742-3638

November Easton Waterfowl Festival
Easton, Maryland
Lou Satchell
c/o Waterfowl Festival
Easton, MD 21601
(301) 822-4567

BOOKS ON DECOYS

Acquiring a knowledge of these wood sculptures and their carvers is accomplished in several manners. Many good books are available: *Factory Decoys* by John and Shirley Delph, Schiffer Publishing Limited, Box E, Exton, Pa. 19341; *American Bird Decoys* by William J. Mackey, Jr., E. P. Dutton and Company, 1965; *The Art of the Decoy* by Adele Ernest, Bramhall House, New York, 1965; *Decoys of the MidAtlantic Region* by Henry A. Fleckenstein, Jr., Schiffer Publishing Limited, 1979; and a soon-to-be-released book on decoys of the Mississippi Flyway by Alan Haid, also available through Schiffer Publishing. The new edition of *The Decoys and Decoy Carvers of Illinois* by Paul Parmale and Forrest Loomis is now available through Northern Illinois University Press, De Kalb, Illinois. Its illustrations and text on decoys and decoy carvers are exceptional. During the early 1960s, Hal Sorenson (312 Franklin Street, Burlington, IA 52601) printed decoy collector's guides and later had them bound in book form. They are still published.

CHARACTERISTICS OF DECOYS

The old decoys varied greatly in their form, style, and paint pattern. The type of water the decoys were hunted over often dictated the size and shape of the decoy. For this reason, the decoys of Michigan have broad, flat bottoms enabling them to ride the waves of Lake Michigan without overturning. The old Illinois River decoys are characterized by their small, slender, hollow bodies to ease the burden of the hunter who had to carry them on his back to a blind that may have been a half-mile trek to a slough or prairie pothole. The decoys used on the Eastern Seaboard are heavy bodied and sturdy to withstand the constant boating required for transporting them to and from off-shore blinds. These regional characteristics often inspire the collector to obtain decoys having other unique forms and painting. One of the most popular decoy makers was the Mason Decoy Factory of Detroit, Michigan. Its catalogs were distributed throughout the United States, and today the famous Mason Decoy is still found from coast to coast.

The evaluation of a decoy consists of several steps. The most important factor is eye appeal. For this reason, many decoys whose maker's name has been lost to history are still very important because of their fine form and/or lavish painting. Originality of painting and/or construction is also a prime consideration because a repainted decoy loses considerable merit when compared with another decoy, by the same carver, that has retained its original paint. Restoration of a decoy may improve its appearance, but again, in a value sense, the restored decoy with a bill or tail repair is not as valuable as a similar, unrestored decoy would be. Many carvers produced their decoys for a dollar or two dollars a dozen in the old days, and it's not uncommon to find an outstanding decoy by a maker who created an example of waterfowl realism that stands head and shoulders above other decoys carved on a hurried day. For this reason, the collector should remember that decoys are to be valued for their rarity as well as their quality when comparing and evaluating decoys by the same maker. An example of this is often encountered when the collector has the choice of acquiring either a merganser or a blue bill. Mergansers are a racy, sleek bird and not very palatable. Therefore, the decoy maker did not make many merganser decoys. The blue bill, however, is found from coast to coast and was a staple in the diet of early Americans. Many decoys of this species exist today, and for this reason the value of a blue bill is quite low as compared with the scarce merganser. The blue bill does, however, offer the collector the opportunity to display the variation in decoys of the same species that may be found throughout the country.

VALUES OF DECOYS

Following is a price list for decoys according to carver groups. The prices are often the values placed on the decoys by the seller. The pricing also assumes that the decoys are in original paint and structurally sound. The variation in price reflects the quality variables, such as condition of paint and style that exist in decoys by the same maker. The prices are not based on auction results because these prices do not reflect commission costs incurred by the seller.

Carver and decoy	Value
MAINE	
George R. Huey, Friendship, Maine	
Goldeneye	$300–500
Red-breasted Merganser	500–750
Willie Ross, Chebeague Island, Maine	
Red-breasted Merganser	$800–1,200
August A. "Gus" Wilson, South Portland, Maine (1864–1950)	
Black Duck	$400–1,200
Goldeneye	400–600
Mallard	500–1,200
Scoter (Regular)	

Pintail. Charles Walker, Princeton, Illinois, circa 1935. (Photo courtesy Allan Kain)

Carver and decoy	Value
Scoter (Monhegan Island style)	800–2,000
Red-breasted Merganser	1,000–2,000

NEW ENGLAND

H. Keyes Chadwick, Oak Bluffs, Martha's Vineyard, Massachusetts (1868–1959)	
Black Duck	$300–500
Bluebill Drake	200–400
Redhead Drake	300–500
Red-breasted Merganser Drake	800–1,500
A. Elmer Crowell, East Harwich, Massachusetts (1862–1951)	
Black Duck (oval stamp)	$600–900
Redhead Drake (oval stamp)	600–900
Pintail Drake (oval stamp)	900–1,500
Mallard Drake (oval stamp)	900–1,500
Red-breasted Merganser Drake (oval stamp or no stamp)	1,000–2,000

Carver and decoy	Value
Bluebill Drake (oval stamp)	600–1,000
Brant (oval stamp)	600–900
Canada Goose (oval stamp)	1,200–1,800
Joseph Lincoln, Accord, Massachusetts (1859–1938)	
Black Duck	$1,200–1,800
Pintail Drake	1,500–2,200
Goldeneye Drake	800–1,200
Widgeon Drake	1,000–1,500
Scoter	1,200–1,800
Wood Duck Drake	2,000–5,000
Brant	1,200–1,800
Canada Goose	1,200–1,800

CONNECTICUT

Benjamin Holmes, Stratford, Connecticut (1843–1912)	
Black Duck	$900–1,500
Scoter	1,000–1,600
Bluebill	750–1,400
Charles E. "Shang" Wheeler, Milford, Connecticut (1872–1949)	
Black Duck	$2,000–3,500
Canvasback	2,500–3,800
Bluebill	1,500–2,700

NEW YORK

Frank Coombs, Alexandria Bay, New York (1882–1958)	
Black Duck	$150–200
Redhead Drake	175–225
Redhead Hen	125–175
Bluebill Drake	150–175
Bluebill Hen	100–150
Canvasback Drake	185–250
Canvasback Hen	175–200
Chaucey Wheeler (circa 1900–1925)	
Black Duck	$250–350

Carver and decoy	Value
Redhead Drake	275–325
Bluebill Drake	200–300
Bluebill Hen	175–250

DELAWARE RIVER

Classic Blair (circa 1870)

Mallard Drake	$1,000–1,500
Mallard Hen	900–1,400
Black Duck	800–1,200
Pintail Drake	1,000–1,700
Widgeon Drake	1,000–2,000
Widgeon Hen	800–1,600
Teal Drake	1,050–2,500
Teal Hen	800–1,500

John Dawson

Black Duck	$400–800
Pintail Drake	1,000–2,000
Redhead Drake	500–700
Bluebill Drake	250–450
Widgeon Drake	800–1,200
Widgeon Hen	500–700

John English

Goldeneye Drake	$450–600
Goldeneye Hen	400–500
Black Duck	350–550

John McLaughlin

Pintail Drake	$300–500
Pintail Hen	250–400
Black Duck	200–400
Bluebill Drake	175–300
Bluebill Hen	150–250

NEW JERSEY

Henry Grant

Black Duck	$250–350
Bluebill	175–250
Goose	250–350

Carver and decoy	Value
Brant	275–375
Roland Horner	
Black Duck	$400–600
Bluebill	300–500
Brant	600–800
Merganser	800–1,500
Harry Shourdes	
Redhead	$500–1,500
Goose	750–1,500
Black Duck	500–1,200
Old Squaw	1,000–2,500
Bluebill	500–1,000
Merganser	1,000–1,600

CHESAPEAKE BAY AND MARYLAND

Henry Lockard	
Redhead Drake	$80–130
Redhead Hen	100–150
Bluebill Drake	60–120
Bluebill Hen	75–150
Canvasback Drake	75–125
Canvasback Hen	100–175

Ward Brothers Goose, Crisfield , Maryland, circa 1935.

Carver and decoy	Value
Madison Mitchell	
Pintail Drake	$75–150
Pintail Hen	50–125
Bluebill Drake	70–120
Bluebill Hen	40–90
Canvasback Drake	75–125
Canvasback Hen	50–100
Ward Bros, Crisfield, Maryland (1920–1940)	
Pintail Drake	$900–1,750
Pintail Hen	700–1,500
Canvasback Drake	800–1,500
Canvasback Hen	600–1,500
Bluebill Drake	700–1,500
Bluebill Hen	500–1,100
Black Duck	800–1,600

VIRGINIA

Carver and decoy	Value
Charles Birch, Willis Wharf, Virginia (1868–1956)	
Black Duck	$300–500
Bluebill Drake	200–400
Brant (Hollow Inletted Bill)	600–1,000
Canada Goose (Hollow Inletted Bill)	800–1,200
Swan (Hollow Inletted Bill)	1,500–3,000
Nathan F. Cobb, Jr., Cobb Island, Virginia (1825–1905)	
Black Duck	$800–1,600
Bluebill	600–1,200
Redhead	800–1,500
Brant	1,000–1,500
Brant (swimming, head and neck)	1,000–2,000
Canada Goose (swimming, head and neck)	1,000–1,500
Canada Goose (swimming, head and neck)	1,000–2,500
Miles Handcock, Chincoteague, Virginia (1880–1974)	
Pintail Drake	$150–200
American Merganser Drake	200–300
Brant	150–200
Canada Goose	200–300

Carver and decoy	Value
Ira Hudson, Chincoteague, Virginia (1876–1949)	
Black Duck	$200–400
Bluebill Drake	150–300
Redhead Drake	200–400
Red-breasted Merganser Drake	500–1,000
Brant	300–500
Canada Goose	400–800

CAROLINA AND BACK BAY

Ned Burgess, Church's Island, North Carolina (circa 1945)	
Canvasback Drake	$100–125
Canvasback Hen	125–150
Bluebill Drake	75–100
Bluebill Hen	50–75
Canvas Covered Geese	75–100

Immature canvasback drake. John R. Wells (J.R.W.), St. Clair Flats, circa 1928.

Carver and decoy	Value
Lem Dudley	
Drake Canvasback	$1,500–2,000
Ruddy Duck	1,000–1,500
Bluebill	500–800
Goose	1,500–2,000
ST. CLAIR FLATS	
Thomas Chambers	
Redhead Drake	$175–250
Redhead Hen	150–225
Canvasback Drake	300–400
Canvasback Hen	250–350
Goose	1,000–2,000
Low-Head Black Duck	250–350
George Warin	
Canvasback Drake	$400–500
Canvasback Hen	300–400
Redhead Drake	250–300
Redhead Hen	200–300
Pintail Drake	900–1,200
Bluebill Drake	300–400
Bluebill Hen	200–300
Goose	1,000–2,000
J.R.W. (John R. Wells)	
Pintail Drake	$600–800
Pintail Hen	500–700
Canvasback Drake	600–800
Canvasback Hen	600–800
Mallard Drake	700–900
Mallard Hen	700–900
Bluebill Drake	600–700
Bluebill Hen	500–650
MICHIGAN	
Ferdinand Bach, Detroit, Michigan (1888–1967)	
Redhead Drake	$1,000–1,500
Bluebill Drake	800–1,200

Green wing teal. Charles Perdew, Henry, Illinois, circa 1933. (Photo courtesy Allan Kain)

Carver and decoy	Value
Canvasback Drake	1,000–1,500
Nate Quillen, Rockwood, Michigan (1839–1908)	
Black Duck	$500–900
Redhead Drake	500–900
Redhead Drake (Low Head)	1,000–1,500
Pintail Drake	800–1,200
Benjamin J. Schmidt, Detroit, Michigan (1884–1968)	
Black Duck	$250–350
Mallard Drake	300–400
Canvasback Drake	250–350
Redhead Drake	200–300
Bluebill Drake	150–250
Canada Goose	300–500

ILLINOIS RIVER

Walter "Tube" Dawson	
Mallard Drake	$200–300

Carver and decoy	Value
Robert Elliston, Bureau, Illinois (1849–1915)	
Mallard Drake	$800–1,200
Mallard Hen	900–1,400
Bluebill Drake	1,000–1,500
Redhead Drake	1,000–1,500
Canvasback Drake	2,000–3,000
Pintail Drake	1,200–1,800
Coot	2,000–3,000
Blue Wing Teal	1,500–2,500
G. Bert Graves, Peoria, Illinois (1887–1956)	
Mallard Drake	$300–600
Mallard Hen	350–650
Pintail Drake	800–1,200
Canvasback Drake	800–1,200
Henry Holmes	
Mallard Drake	$200–400
Pintail Drake	300–500
Charles H. Perdew, Henry, Illinois (1874–1963)	
Mallard Drake	$400–1,000
Mallard Hen	500–1,100
Pintail Drake	900–1,500
Canvasback Drake	900–1,500
Green Wing Teal Drake	1,700–2,500
Charles Walker	
Mallard Drake	$1,000–3,000
Pintail Drake	2,000–5,000
Perry Wilcoxsen	
Mallard	$150–300
Canvasback	150–300
Pintail	200–400

WISCONSIN

August Moak	
Canvasback Drake	$250–300
Canvasback Hen	300–350
Goose	400–600

Carver and decoy	Value
Frank Strey	
Mallard Drake	$150–175
Mallard Hen	125–150
Canvasback Drake	100–150
Canvasback Hen	80–125
Coots	100–125

LOUISIANA

"La France" Decoys	
Mallard Drake	$200–400
Mallard Hen	150–300
Teal	600–900
Pintail Drake	200–400
Canvasback	300–500
Ringneck	250–400

Mark Whipple	
Mallard Drake	$300–500
Mallard Hen	400–600
Teal	700–1,100
Pintail Drake	800–1,200
Canvasback Drake	500–750
Ring Neck	400–600

WEST COAST DECOYS

Bergman	
Mallard Drake	$200–400
Mallard Hen	200–400
Bluebill Drake	400–600
Bluebill Hen	300–500
Teal Drake	500–700
Teal Hen	500–700
Pintail Drake	150–400
Pintail Hen	150–400

Horace Hy Crandall	
Mallard Drake	$400–800
Mallard Hen	400–800
Teal Drake	1,000–1,500

Carver and decoy	Value
Teal Hen	1,000–1,500
Pintail Drake	500–700
Pintail Hen	500–700
Dick "Fresh Air" Jansen	
Mallard Drake	$300–400
Mallard Hen	300–400
Pintail Drake	100–250
Pintail Hen	100–250
Canvasback Drake	300–500
Canvasback Hen	300–500

FACTORY DECOYS

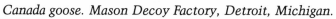

Species	Premier	Challenge	Detroit
Mason			
Mallard	$300–500	$200–400	$100–150
Black	400–800	300–600	150–200
Bluebill	200–400	150–300	75–125
Canvasback	300–600	200–500	100–200
Redhead	300–500	200–400	100–150
Pintail	800–1,600	600–1,400	200–400

Canada goose. Mason Decoy Factory, Detroit, Michigan.

FACTORY DECOYS

Species	Premier	Challenge	Detroit
Canada Goose	1,000–1,600	—	—
Brant	800–1,400	800–1,400	—
Merganser	1,000–3,000	1,000–3,000	200–700
Goldeneye	400–800	300–600	200–400
Blue Wing Teal	600–1,400	600–1,400	200–500
Green Wing Teal	800–1,800	800–1,800	300–600

Dodge

Mallard	$100–200
Black	150–250
Bluebill	75–150
Pintail	200–350
Redhead	100–200
Merganser	300–500
Canada Goose	400–600

Petersen

Mallard	$125–250
Black	150–300
Bluebill	100–250
Pintail	250–400
Redhead	150–300
Canada Goose	500–800

Evans	Standard	Mammoth
Mallard	$125	$200
Canvasback	150	225
Bluebill	100	150
Pintail	250	350
Blue Wing Teal	300	400
Green Wing Teal	400	500
Redhead	150	225
Coot	150	225

CARE OF DECOYS

The care of the decoy on the shelf is often an object of controversy among decoy collectors today. Years ago, collectors advocated varnishing the decoy to preserve its paint. Over time, the varnish yellows, and today decoy collectors believe that this decreases the value of a bird considerably. For centuries, however, artists have varnished their paintings, and with time and exposure, these paintings dating back hundreds of years, have been protected and are often renewed by the removal of the varnish at a later date. The varnish that is applied then is a very thin coating and, hopefully, will protect the painting for another century. Some Michigan collectors believe that the decoy paint should not be coated or treated in any manner.

Humidity, or the lack of it, is a great destroyer of decoys. Many carvers were not very selective in their choice of woods for their decoys, and while decoys may be well-constructed from the finest of cedar, low humidity in a house can quickly cause halves of a hollow decoy to separate and checker the painting with the shrinking that accompanies the ambient condition. Recommended humidity is a constant 50%. Some decoy collectors in the Midwest use a solution called "Furniture Feeder" that includes turpentine, bee's wax, and other chemicals for restoring the luster to the paint of the decoy as well as preserving its stability and texture. Along the East Coast, many notable collectors use a combination of turpentine and a small amount of linseed oil on their decoys every 10 years or so to prevent the paint from drying out.

Good luck in your decoy hunting.

Chapter 5 ❧ Shorebird Decoys

CHARLES WARD

When Newbold Lawrence Herrick, in 1922, placed some of his old shorebird hunting decoys (called snipe stool in those days) up on the shelves of his home in Lawrence, Long Island, little did he realize where it would lead. Along with some mounted species of shorebirds, this early collection has given collectors many hours of enjoyment. The mounted birds were presented to the Tackapausha Museum in Seaford, Long Island, and the wooden snipe stool are now on display in the Waterfowl Wing of the Stony Brook Museum in Stony Brook, Long Island. These shorebird decoys by Bill Bowman of Lawrence, Long Island, and Obediah Verity of Seaford, Long Island, are, without doubt, the finest museum collection of such items anywhere. If one is at all interested in old hunting decoys, one *must* view this group.

While both duck decoys and shorebird decoys came into being in the early part of the nineteenth century, the shorebird decoy was discontinued about 1918 when a law was passed that prohibited the shooting of just about all species of shorebirds. The making and use of duck decoys continues to the present time.

Shorebird decoys, for all intents and purposes, were used almost exclusively on the shores of the East Coast bays between Virginia and New Hampshire. Generally speaking, the more collectible examples come from four major areas.

New England – the coast of Massachusetts, including Cape Cod, Nantucket, Martha's Vineyard, and a small area of the New Hampshire coast. A few have turned up in Connecticut and Rhode Island.

Long Island – the southshore of Long Island, from and including Jamaica Bay on the west to the Hamptons on the east.

New Jersey – the whole coast and bay areas of New Jersey.

The Eastern Shore – from Cape Charles to Chincoteague, Virginia. A few examples have turned up in the Carolinas, but no outstanding shorebird makers have come to light south of Virginia.

It is almost impossible to compile a price list for shorebirds. Any shorebird decoys in good or better condition made by makers such as Cobb, Verity, Bowman, Crowell, Shourds, Dilly, and Lincoln would certainly command a four-figure price. The sky's the limit on fine items. The lowest prices would be for flat decoys, known as "flatties." While these are a great collector's item, they still can be bought for $200 and up. Some fine old primitives are still offered in the low hundreds and are certainly a good investment. Here, too, condition is important.

As far as species are concerned, the most common is the black-bellied plover. Most species of shorebirds would decoy to plover decoys, while plover usually would avoid anything but wooden plover. In order, after plover, are yellowleg, robin snipe or knot, willet, curlew, ruddy turnstone, and sanderling (peep). Most golden plover decoys come from the Northeast area, with Nantucket Island having more than any other place. As far as curlew is concerned, the Eastern Shore of Virginia and South Jersey seem to have produced more than other areas.

Generally speaking, the rarer the species, the more valuable the decoy. But this is not to say that a Bowman plover would not have more value than a primitive curlew by an unknown maker. However, if an Elmer Crowell curlew in good condition should pop up, mortgage the old homestead!

As in all collectibles, condition is important in determining value. Because shorebirds are 60 years old or older, it is hard to find many in mint or even excellent condition. We have to accept, reluctantly, a replaced bill more readily than we would on a duck decoy because of the shorebird's vulnerable construction. As with wooden ducks, repainting takes away much of the value. Old, worn, hardly visible paint is better than a repaint. The sculptural form can help make up for loss of paint. An example would be an Obediah Verity or Elmer Crowell, carved wing, bird versus a Harry Shourds or George Boyd decoy with smooth sides. The former two without paint would retain a great deal more value than the latter two.

Almost every time a fine shorebird decoy is sold at an auction, a new record price is set. Therefore, in examining the well-known carvers from the four areas, I've tried to give a general relative value rather than a current price list. The lowest figure is for good condition examples, while the highest figure is for decoys in excellent to mint condition.

NEW ENGLAND

George Boyd, Seabrook, New Hampshire, 1873–1941

Plover and yellowlegs seem to be the only two species George Boyd carved, but he did a fine job on these. His yellowlegs have a slim gracefulness that

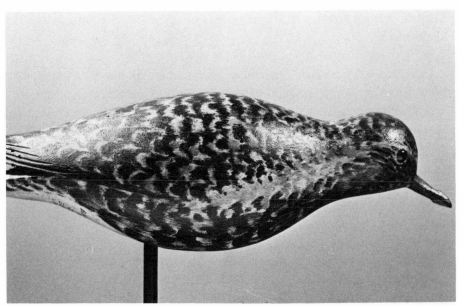

Black-bellied plover in the running position. Elmer Crowell, East Harwich, Massachusetts, circa 1910.

captures the feeling of the bird very well. His plover have a distinctive squarish look that is very appealing. Boyd's short brush strokes used in his painting are feather-like. All this adds up to a product that has increased in value strongly. Range $2,500 to $4,000.

Elmer Crowell, East Harwich, Massachusetts, 1862–1952

Recognized as New England's finest shorebird carver, Crowell's carving and painting were second to none. While his later decorative works made for the tourist trade are excellent, his old gunning snipe decoys are what make the collector's heart beat faster. Not many legitimate old gunning decoys are found in unusual positions. But, to the collector's delight, Crowell carved birds in the feeding position and birds with turned heads. Three Elmer Crowell plover, each in a different position, are pictured on the dust jacket of William Mackey's book, *American Bird Decoys*. These decoys illustrate Crowell's talent at his best. Range $4,000 to $10,000.

Joseph Lincoln, Accord, Massachusetts, 1859–1938

While Joe Lincoln was primarily known for his outstanding duck, brant, and goose decoys, he made a fair amount of excellent shorebirds. No wing carving was used, but his clean style of painting is evident in his snipe. Until recently, there was some question as to exactly which decoys were made by

Lincoln, but it's pretty well straightened out in collectors' minds now. Range $2,000 to $4,000.

Other makers from New England include Charles Thomas, Lothrop Holmes, Franklin Folger, and members of the Burr family. These carvers, while not as prolific as the first three, made excellent and very collectible birds, but their works are too scarce to establish prices.

LONG ISLAND

William Bowman, Lawrence, Long Island, circa 1880

Whenever shorebird collectors gather, the conversation does not go very far before the name of Bill Bowman is mentioned. If any one carver can be called the king, Bowman would most likely receive that distinction. To hold one of his carvings is "like having a live bird in your hand." Since his birds were so finely detailed and delicately carved, many survivors are badly damaged. Slim necks and thinly carved wing tips were more often broken than not. The pride he took in his work is evident by his careful painting and his use of imported German glass eyes obtained from a taxidermist. Bowman's work included just about all the species native to Long Island. On some birds, he even went to the trouble of carving the thigh. It has been written that

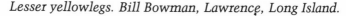

Lesser yellowlegs. Bill Bowman, Lawrence, Long Island.

Black-bellied plover. Bill Bowman, Lawrence, Long Island, circa 1890.

Long-billed dowitcher. Bill Bowman, Lawrence, Long Island.

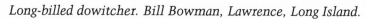

Bowman pitched a tent on the salt meadow near Lawrence, Long Island, and that is where he carved and painted his birds. But I'd have to believe that to produce such consistently fine shorebirds, he had the use of a shop and good tools. In 1922, Newbold Herrick recognized the quality of Bill Bowman's work. It may have taken the rest of us a little longer, but we're learning. Range $10,000.

John Dilly, Quogue, Long Island, circa 1900

Shorebirds by this carver were first called "Jess Birdsall type" decoys by the eminent collector and author Bill Mackey. Then, when a box containing some examples turned up on Long Island with the name John Dilly stenciled on the side, they became "John Dillys." Whoever you were, John Dilly, you were a good carver and an exceptional painter. The painting on these birds is by an artist with no equal in the decoy field. Shaded and feather-painted would be a modest description of a Dilly. They have an almost decorative look. A small percentage of his work had wing-carving, and some have tail-separation. Like Bowman, he used glass eyes when most makers carved the eyes. His work included most shorebirds found in the Northeast, including a couple of curlew. At this late date, it's unlikely that much more information will surface on this carver. Range $4,000 to $10,000.

Black-bellied plover in the feeding position. Obediah Verity, Seaford, Long Island, circa 1880.

Hudsonian curlew and "peep." Obediah Verity, Seaford, Long Island.

Lesser yellowlegs. William Southard, Bellmore, Long Island.

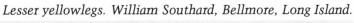

Thomas Gelston, Quogue, Long Island, circa 1910

Much of Gelston's work was hastily turned out and not too interesting, but a few of his birds were outstanding. Most of these were great curlew. It was almost as though he wanted to prove to the world what he was capable of doing. Unfortunately, many of his birds were made of cork and not in the same league with his wooden curlew. Because of this, his cork birds are not very expensive. Range $300 to $10,000

William Southard, Bellmore, Long Island, circa 1880

An in-law of the Verity family, Will Southard was a wheelwright who carved fine yellowlegs from the limbs of trees rather than pieces of lumber. Other than yellowlegs, only one species, a beautiful peep, is known. His painting could be described as a series of dots. Some of his birds were painted by his father-in-law, Smith Clinton Verity. Maybe some day other species of shore-birds by Southard will show up, but until then we'll enjoy his great yellow-legs. Range $3,000 to $5,000.

Obediah Verity, Seaford, Long Island, 1850–1910

If it weren't for Bill Bowman, Obediah Verity would certainly have the number-one spot on Long Island. While his work is totally different from Bowman's, it is no less appealing. In fact, in many folk-art circles, Verity is still in contention for the number-one spot. His chunky birds are beautifully stipple-painted and made to last. As a now deceased old market gunner once put it: "Throw an old Verity shorebird up under the head of the boat and it wouldn't break apart like most of them fancy stool." No question, they were made to last. If for no other reason than that, thank you, Obediah. From tiny peep to robust curlew, Verity carved them all. There were other members of the Verity clan who carved fine shorebirds, but Obediah was the best and most prolific. If one includes odd birds in the shorebird class, his works include great blue heron and common tern. Range $4,000 to $10,000.

Other Long Island carvers include John Henry Verity, Al Ketchum, John Henry Burch, Andrew Verity, Frank Kellum, Capt. Abrem Smith, and Daniel De Mott.

NEW JERSEY

Lou Barkelow, Forked River, New Jersey, circa 1900

Plover, yellowlegs, and peeps seem to be the only species Barkelow carved. His birds have a graceful, distinctive shape and are easily identified as his. Some, but not all, have an "L.B." impressed in the side. Apparently his pro-duction was on a small scale compared with other carvers, and finding one today is very difficult. Range $1,500 to $2,500.

Harry V. Shourds, Tuckerton, New Jersey, 1861–1920

No other area had one carver who dominated his section as did Harry Shourds. He had to be one of the most productive duck and shorebird makers in the

Hudsonian curlew. Harry V. Shourds, Tuckerton, New Jersey, circa 1900.

country. His consistently fine painting overshadowed the fact that his birds did not have the raised wing-carving of a Verity or a Cobb. Uniformity and selection of excellent wood, coupled with his choice of good oil paint, gave today's collector a great item to pursue. Shourds made most species of shorebirds, with his knot and curlew favorites of collectors. His paint was so durable that a great many decoys retain their original paint. Range $2,000 to $4,000.

Others in the New Jersey area include the names of Leeds, Truax, Johnson, Sprague, Parker, and Joe King. Again, too few of these makers' birds have surfaced to establish a price range. A Leeds curlew or ruddy turnstone would certainly bring a four-figure price.

THE EASTERN SHORE

Nathan Cobb, Cobb Island, Virginia, 1825–1905

Time and space won't allow me to do justice to the colorful history of the Cobb family and their patriarch, Nathan Cobb. This has to be the most interesting family as far as history is concerned, in all the shorebird world. Originally from New England, they combined the characteristics of two decoy areas into one excellent product. Nathan Cobb's carvings covered just about all species. His curlew were the finest and were varied enough to please any collector. While many Cobbs are still in good original paint, decoys from this area seem to retain their value to a surprising degree, even with worn, almost invisible paint, which is probably a tribute to their fine carving. Another plus for old Nathan was the fact that he carved birds in the "running position." The letters "A" for Albert, "N" for Nathan, and "E" for Elkenah are found on many Cobb decoys. Range $3,000 to $10,000.

Ira Hudson, Chincoteague, Virginia, 1876–1949

Ira Hudson, one of the top duck decoy carvers in the country, may have produced as many duck decoys as any other carver. His shorebirds seem to be limited to yellowlegs, but what yellowlegs! Very slim necks, and nicely scratch painted would be a thumbnail description of Hudson's birds. Very few have survived the years without having a neck snap off. It seems a shame that a maker of Hudson's caliber and imagination in the duck, brant, and goose areas carved only one species of shorebird. Range $3,000 to $4,000.

William Matthews, Assateague Island, Virginia, circa 1900

Curlew, yellowlegs, and plover seem to be the species Matthews enjoyed carving most. His stylized painting and carving had a folksy look that collectors are quick to appreciate. With paddle-like tails, his birds are almost caricatures of the real thing. Range $1,500 to $4,000.

Luther Nottingham, Cape Charles, Virginia, circa 1900

A game warden, Nottingham chose hardwood for his decoy carvings, which must have made the task difficult and might explain why he produced so few decoys. With fine scratch painting and wing-carving, his work was mostly with curlew. He carved his initials "LLN" on the bottom of his decoys. Range $3,000 to $6,000.

Other Eastern Shore makers turned out adequate decoys, but none as interesting as these. Andrews, Hoff, and Doughty are other shorebird makers from this area. Dave Watson, a fine Chincoteague decoy maker, made a very few shorebirds of an excellent quality, but he stayed with duck decoys primarily.

STARTING A COLLECTION

If you are considering putting together a collection of shorebird decoys, here are a few words of advice. Read whatever you can find on the subject. View as many collections as possible. Most collectors are delighted to show their collections and share their experiences in collecting. Visit any museums with shorebird collections. The Stony Brook Museum in Stony Brook, Long Island, the Shelburne Museum in Shelburne, Vermont, and the American Folk Art Museum in New York City all have fine collections. Decide what area you would like to collect, such as a specific maker, a specific species, or unknown primitives.

When you think you are ready to spend some money, make sure you do so with a reputable dealer. It has been my experience that most people involved with decoys are honest and value their reputation too much to become involved in anything dishonest. Unfortunately, there are always a few exceptions. Be sure there is a clear understanding between yourself and the seller, whether he is a dealer or a collector. You should have return privileges for a reasonable amount of time, such as two weeks, which will give you time to show your purchase to someone who has more experience than yourself. This will enable you to determine if the bird is as represented by the seller. Some buyers abuse the return privilege for a number of reasons, such as the decoy doesn't fit in with the décor of their home or they've found something else they like better. I don't think that these are legitimate reasons for returning anything, and the dealer should not be expected to honor this sort of thing.

BIBLIOGRAPHY

The following books approach shorebird collecting from different views, but all will be helpful. Only the one by Fleckenstein is devoted solely to shorebirds. It is published by Schiffer Ltd., Exton, PA, 1980.

Barber, Joel. *Wildfowl Decoys*. Garden City: Windward House, 1934.

Colio, Quintina. *American Decoys*. Ephrata: Science Press, 1972.

Ernest, Adele. *The Art of the Decoy*. New York: Bramhall House, 1965.

Fleckenstein, Henry A., Jr. *Shorebird Decoys*. Exton: Schiffer Publishers, 1980.

Johnsgard, Paul A. *The Bird Decoy*. Lincoln: University of Nebraska Press, 1976.

Mackey, William, Jr. *American Bird Decoys*. New York: Dutton, 1965.

Sorenson, Hal, editor. *Decoy Collector's Guides*.

Starr, George Ross. *Decoys of the Atlantic Flyway*. New York: Winchester Press, 1974.

Stout, Gardner D., editor. *The Shorebirds of North America*. New York: Viking Press, 1967.

LEGEND

From Joel Barber: *Wildfowl Decoys*.

A long time ago an American Indian had a swell idea. He was a fowler — one whose quarry passed swiftly and beyond range of his primitive weapons. And so he thought to invent a lure, an invitation for all wild waterfowl to foregather at hunter's ambush.

The new device was fashioned in the likeness of duck; an artificial Canvas-back, made of reeds and feathers and colored by native paints. The man cut and tried and tried again. He made one. He made two. Finally there were seven and when tethered on the water, they floated for all the world like a group of wild ducks feeding.

In the distance a swiftly moving flock of birds faltered in the sky. The false Canvas-backs rolled and pitched dully on the water.

Events followed swiftly. The leading birds swung shorewards toward the false ducks on the water. Oncoming trailers followed, telescoping and banking on the turn. There was no disorder. Like magic the line of hurtling birds straightened, gathered speed, drove headlong in and set their wings to halt.

They were over the group on the water.

On shore a bow-string twanged! then again! and again!

For a moment there was hurried confusion; then bending sharply on stiff wings the visitors fled.

And then it came — the long drawn yell of Indian victory; victory for generations of fowlers to come.

Wild ducks had decoyed; were to decoy for evermore. They were never to know and never to understand. For that was a thousand years ago.

Chapter 6 ❧ Contemporary Carvings

EDWARD C. GERMAN

Contemporary carving, wood-sculpting, or wildfowl counterfeiting is designed to attract the hunter or collector and not to lure ducks or other wildfowl. Carving remained in its somewhat primitive state until Lem and Steve Ward, from the Chesapeake Bay area, transgressed from their decoy carving to the carving of decorative decoys. Fame had come to them, and their orders were too numerous to fill. Pressure from the public to carve a duck that could be used to decorate a mantle rather than attract wild game motivated this evolution. The carvings took on pleasing lines and unique paint patterns, and the Wards continuously strived to improve their art in both areas. Steve was primarily the carver and Lem the painter. Around 1950, they began to spend more and more of their time on decorative birds. By 1957, they were no longer carving working decoys since both demand and price made it possible for them to concentrate their efforts exclusively on decorative birds. About 1965, Lem began making highly decorative birds, and this truly was the start of wood-sculpting or wildfowl counterfeiting. The Wards carved the birds with a smooth finish. After the block was sanded and shaped, they carved in the feathers and shaped the bird for painting.

As other carvers began using the techniques of the Wards, more decorative decoys began appearing on the market. In 1948, the first decoy contest was held in Babylon, Long Island. By the middle of the 1960s, these contests were being held throughout the United States. Carvers entered for the prestige of winning and the increased prices that their work could command as a result of winning.

A classic example of Wards' carving is the Canada goose they carved in 1969. When it was purchased in 1969, the cost was $750. Its present value is probably $6,000 to $7,500. Even the old decoy carvings by the Wards have a value in four figures.

The Wards trained Oliver B. Lawson as their protégé, and he immediately became one of the outstanding carvers of the 1960s and 1970s. A classic example by Lawson is a pair of blue-winged teal that was carved in 1971 and sold for $1,000. Lawson does an extremely good job on songbirds, which are invariably on a branch of blooming flowers or a branch entwined with ivy. The de-

Canada Goose. Steve and Lem Ward.

tail is extremely fine, and the work is not only accurate but pleasant to look at. Lawson's carvings are selling for $2,000 to $10,000.

Dave Hawthorne is another well-known carver from the Chesapeake Bay area. As shown in the picture of the preening broadbill, the feathering is unmatched and is done primarily with a paintbrush. In the 1968 edition of *The Decoy Collector's Guide*, Hawthorne said:

> I have carved fish, whales, ducks, shore birds, song birds, game birds, reproductions of trail boards from old ships and old inn signs. I've sent birds from Maine to California, some good and some not so good. The only way to make a good bird is time and plenty of it.
>
> People ask me how I get the feathers on and I tell them — with a brush, feather for feather. This I consider a bird sculpture.
>
> A decoy is something else. I believe a decoy should be rugged and a characterization of the species, so at a glance you know what it is.

This broadbill was purchased in 1972 for $650.

Another example of Hawthorne's work is shown in the picture of the owls.

The center owl is a screech owl done by Hawthorne in 1972, and it cost $650. The owl on the right is a saw whet owl, carved in 1974 at a price of $450. The owl on the left is Herbie Miller's version of a screech owl. Note the radical difference in the carvings of these two birds of the same species.

Hawthorne is also extremely competent in carving shorebirds. The least bittern was carved in 1977 at a price of $1,500, the curlew in 1977 at a price of $1,500, and the jacksnipe in 1979 at a price of $1,200. The semi-palmated sandpiper was carved in 1973 at a price of $250, and the dunlin was carved in 1977 at a price of $450. The lesser yellowlegs was carved in 1968 at a price of $250, and it is easy to visualize that the detail, except for the carving of the tailfeathers, is strictly in the painting. On the other hand, the other birds were carved more recently, and it is also easy to visualize that Hawthorne's detail is not now restricted to painting.

Hawthorne made the hanging dead birds, shown with their "live" counterparts. The woodcock, carved in 1972, cost me $450, and the quail, carved in 1976, cost me $1,500. The dead birds hang in my office, and since they are on the wall, they are safe from the curiosity seeker. Each hanging dead bird cost $600 and was carved in 1981. Hawthorne normally charges from $1,500 to $3,500 for his carvings.

Herbie Miller carved his screech owl in 1978 at a price of $500. He also carved

Blue-winged teal. Tuts Lawson.

a pair of shovelers in 1976 at a price of $1,200. You can observe a carving of the strainers in the ducks' bills, as well as the tongues. All the carvers I have mentioned so far are full-time carvers, but Miller is captain of the police force in Ship Bottom, New Jersey, and his carving is a part-time avocation. His price range is about $1,000 to $2,000.

In 1970, a new carver appeared on the scene. John Scheeler from Mays Landing, New Jersey, went to the Decoy Show in Salisbury, Maryland and became interested in carvings. Within a short time, Scheeler introduced a revolutionary change in the carving of decorative wildfowl—the Foredom power tool, which is similar to the Dremmel power tool used by hobbyists. For a bit, John most often would file the head of a nail to the desired size and grind away at

Preening broadbill. Dave Hawthorne.

Left, *screech owl, Herbie Miller;* center, *screech owl, Dave Hawthorne; and* right, *saw whet owl, Dave Hawthorne.*

Back row, left to right, *least bittern, curlew, and jacksnipe.* Front row, left to right, *lesser yellowlegs, semi-palmated sandpiper, and dunlin. All carvings are by Dave Hawthorne.*

Hanging dead birds and "live" counterparts. Dave Hawthorne. Left, woodcock; right, quail.

the block of wood with a power tool. The tool would become so overheated that John held the tool in an asbestos glove. He then cut the feathers with a knife and also used a burning pen for cutting the barbs in the feathers. The bird was painted two or three times with artist's oils, a very thin coat each time. The pair of pintails was carved in 1971 for a price of $1,000 and entered in the Salisbury Show. It is my recollection that this carving only received honorable mention at the show. Scheeler also entered a pair of lesser scaup, and again they did not get the recognition they deserved because they did not right themselves properly when turned upside down. These lesser scaup were done in 1971 for a price of $300. They are shown photographed in front of Plate 4 from the book, *Birds of the Northern Forest* (paintings by J. F. Lansdowne and text by John A. Livingston). There can be no doubt as to what Scheeler used for his model when carving these birds. The number of people who own Scheeler's work is limited. The prices that I paid for Scheeler's work are misleading. These are two of his very earliest pieces, and they are presently worth perhaps ten times their original cost.

The present state of the art developed about the same time that Scheeler started using his Foredom tool. Gilbert Maggioni started the technique of

Pair of shovelers. Herbie Miller.

Pair of pintails. John Scheeler.

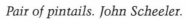

Pair of lesser scaup. John Scheeler.

carving the primary, secondary, and tailfeathers individually and then insert-
ing them into the body of the bird. Only a few carvers today successfully and
artfully use this technique: Gilbert Maggioni, Ocean, Lake and River Fish
Company, Beaufort, South Carolina; Grainger McKoy, Wadmalow Island,
South Carolina; E. Lynn Forehand, 237 Old Drive, Chesapeake, Virginia;
William L. Schultz, Box 752, Rt. 1, Scandinavia, Wisconsin; and Anthony J.
Rudisill, 214 Toulon Avenue, W. Atlantic City, New Jersey.

When Anthony J. Rudisill carved the green herons fighting over a fiddler
crab, he plucked the feathers from the skin of a bird and traced them onto a
paper-thin piece of wood. With this technique, each feather is individually
carved, painted, and inserted into the body of the carving. In the green herons,
there are 30 to 40 individual feathers carved in each wing, a total of approximately 120 to 160 wing feathers and 12 tailfeathers in each bird. Rudisill also
carved a black-bellied plover and a blue-clawed crab emerging from the water.
The grass in the plover carving is made from wood; however, it proved too
delicate and Rudisill began using brass. The baby blue jay is carved from a solid
block, and the feathering is carved right into the wood. Rudisill used acrylic
paints for the herons and blue jay, and watercolors for the plover. The watercolors were sprayed with a clear protective coating. The price of the herons

Pair of green herons fighting over a fiddler crab. Anthony J. Rudisill.

was $10,000, the plover $5,000, and the blue jay $1,750. Rudisill will only do large pieces like the herons on commission, and estimates the price at about $20,000.

Another outstanding example of fine contemporary carving is the ruffed grouse carved in 1978 by James Foote. To the best of my knowledge, Foote is now devoting all of his time to painting and is doing no carving. This bird was purchased in a silent auction from the National Geographic Society at a cost of $2,500.

The green-winged teal carved by Dan Brown from Salisbury, Maryland, won first prize for decorative birds in the National Decoy Contest last year. Brown has won many such ribbons.

Another pair of green-winged teal was carved in 1970 by Bob Kerr from Smith Falls, Ontario, and cost $600. Again, these birds were carved many years ago, and Kerr's prices have increased significantly. Kerr is one of the finest carvers of green-wing teal, and the detail he displays in painting is exceptional. The sleeping male is perfectly balanced on one leg and is not the least bit tippy. The attitude of the female is extremely lifelike.

An avocet, carved in 1976 at a price of $250, and an oyster catcher, carved in 1977 at a price of $225, were both carved by Armand Carney from West Creek, New Jersey.

Birds carved by William H. Cramner of Spray Beach, New Jersey, include the laughing gull carved in the early 1960s, the herring gull in 1974 at a price of $350, and the tern in 1973 at a price of $250. These birds show how the state of the art has progressed. Cramner is an extremely fine carver. When shown the herons carved by Rudisill, he was completely overwhelmed. At the same time, he stated that in a way it made him sad because they clearly demon-

Black-bellied plover and blue-clawed crab. Anthony J. Rudisill.

Baby blue jay. Anthony J. Rudisill.

strated that the "state of the art had reached the point where there is no room left for improvement."

An area of specialized carving that is growing in popularity is miniature carvings. The mallard drake by Gus Stoholm is placed next to a dime. Yet, cover the dime and the bird looks perfectly proportioned and feathered. Stoholm's miniature decoys cost about $450 now, and his miniature flying birds, which are superb, cost about $1,000 each. Miniatures are also great for people who lack space to display a life-size collection.

Ruffed grouse. James Foote.

The price of contemporary carvings with individual feathers is extremely high. The price is, in part, determined by the prize money, particularly at the World Decoy Show held at Ocean City, Maryland, each year. This year, first-prize money for the world championship wildfowl competition in the decorative life-size class is $18,000. The carver receives the money, and the birds are then given to the Ward Foundation and are displayed in the Wildfowl Art Museum at Salisbury State College. This type of carving will bring a price of upwards of $10,000. I have seen pieces priced at $35,000; whether or not they sold for this amount I do not know.

Pair of green-winged teal. Dan Brown.

Pair of green-winged teal. Bob Kerr.

Left, *avocet;* right, *oyster catcher. Armand Carney.*

Left, *laughing gull;* center, *tern; and* right, *herring gull. William H. Cramner.*

Miniature mallard drake. Gus Stoholm.

Living room showing methods of displaying carvings.

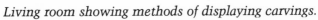

The price of the normal decorative decoy will vary from about $500 to per-haps $4,500, depending on the prestige of the carver and the amount of detail involved. Birds of high quality are not readily available, and a person can wait several years if the artist is commissioned to do a specific bird. Birds by cer-tain carvers cannot be purchased. For example, John Scheeler of Maryland and William Schultz of Milwaukee are under contract to Douglas Miller of Denver, Colorado. I believe each of them carves six birds a year, and they must go to Mr. Miller.

Otherwise, the best places to look for birds are the various exhibits. The World Decoy Show in Ocean City is probably considered the top show. Other outstanding shows are those held in Salisbury, Maryland, in the fall, and Chestertown, Maryland; the Wildfowl Exhibit sponsored by the Academy of Natural Sciences of Philadelphia, in November; the Michigan Show, in Dav-enport, Iowa; and shows extending up and down the Mississippi and as far west as California.

Anyone willing to spend this amount of money should personally view the work of the carver before placing an order. Birds are positioned according to the individual impressions of the carvers. As a result, some of the carvings seem unattractive since they often appear to be in extreme or radical positions.

It would be impossible to compile a complete list of current carvers. A Na-tional Directory of Decoy Collectors and Carvers was compiled in 1978 and 1979, and I believe copies are still available from Gene and Linda Kangas, 6852 Ravenna Road, Painesville, Ohio 44077 at a price of about $15. They had contemplated future editions; however, to the best of my knowledge, none has been released recently.

Contemporary carvings have appreciated in value and probably will con-tinue to do so. However, I have always believed that a collector should collect for the pleasure derived from the collection and not as a form of investment. Should the collectibles appreciate, this is a side benefit but should not be a pri-mary consideration in starting a collection.

The following names were taken from the Philadelphia Wildfowl Exposi-tion, Academy of Natural Sciences of Philadelphia, November, 1980.

CARVERS

Clarence Carlyle Ailes
314 Old Lancaster Road
Devon, PA 19333

Tad Beach
Eastville, VA 23347

George and Olaine Becker
1 St. Regis Drive
Newark, DE 19711

Hans Bolte
301 Scottsdale Drive
Troy, MO 48084

Don Briddell
77 E. Main St.
Dallastown, PA 17313

Dan Brown
209 W. Philadelphia Avenue
Salisbury, MD 21081

Ed and Esther Burns
The Duck Nest
St. Michaels, MD 21663

E. Lynn Forehand
237 Old Drive
Chesapeake, VA 23320

John Franco
31 Locust Street
Assonet, MA 02702

Patrick Godin
242 St. George Street
Brantford, Ontario
Canada

Davison B. Hawthorne
Route 6, Box 409
Salisbury, MD 21801

Jack and Betty Holt
206 Kirk Avenue
Liftwood
Wilmington, DE 19803

Jim Hutcheson
2701 Granbury Circle
Mechanicsville, VA 23111

Julius Iski
5 Laurel Avenue
Bordentown, NJ 08505

Louis L. Kean, Jr.
Route 3, Box 244 A
Mineral, VA 23117

William J. Koelpin
6442 River Parkway
Wauwatosa, WI 53213

Oliver J. Lawson
38 Wynfall Drive
Crisfield, MD 21817

Ernest Muehlmatt
Old Marple Road
Springfield, PA 19064

John Mullican
4005 Cordell Court
Bowie, MD 20715

Chet Piotrowski
480 Mayberry Road
Schwenksville, PA 19473

Tom Pitzen
Stacyville, IA 50476

Robert Ptashnik
168 Redgrave Drive
Weston, Ontario
Canada M9R 3V7

J. Creighton Riepe
7500 Carnaby Court
Richmond, VA 23225

Anthony J. Rudisill
214 Toulon Avenue
W. Atlantic City, NJ 08232

Kenneth Scheeler
3541 N.W. Ave.
Vineland, NJ 08360

William L. Schultz
Box 752, Rt. 1
Scandinavia, WI 54977

John T. Sharp
6949 Rt. 43
Kent, OH 44240

Gus Sjoholm
670 Everdell Ave.
West Islip, NY 11795

James Sprankle
Rt. 1, Kutalek Rd.
Kirkwood, NY 13795

Mark Taddonio
2355 Sutton Rd.
York, PA 17403

Don Vassallo
5 Old Ham Court
Tavistock
Wilmington, DE 19803

William Veasey
16 Gill Drive
Robscott Manor
Newark, DE 19713

Robert and Virginia Warfield
Jaffrey, NH 03452

Dan Williams
4703 Pleasant Grove Rd.
Reisterstown, MD 21136

Joan Wolf
846 Wissahickon Ave.
Cape May, NJ 08204

Chapter 7 ❧ Federal Duck Stamp Prints

WILLIAM B. WEBSTER

In the late 1920s and 1930s, millions of acres of wetlands were drained for farming use. With those marshes went the future of the great flocks of ducks and geese that once blackened the sky in their semiannual migratory flights. Market hunters, with a ready list of waiting customers, further endangered the massive flocks. And then Mother Nature joined the onslaught with a severe drought in the breeding areas that lasted several years. Those marshes hit hardest were in the north-central states, which were the largest breeding grounds in the continental United States.

It was obvious that our country was rapidly losing its waterfowl. To preserve them, Congress enacted the Migratory Bird Conservation Act of 1929. This law authorized the acquisition of sanctuaries, and established a Migratory Bird Conservation Commission to consider areas for purchase or lease. However, it failed to provide a stable flow of funds for the continuing purchase of wetlands. Largely through the efforts of Pulitzer prize-winning political cartoonist, J. N. "Ding" Darling, conservationists pressed Congress for annual funds. On March 16, 1934, Congress passed the Migratory Bird Hunting Stamp Act, which required every hunter, 16 years of age or older, to buy and have in his possession a signed, federal duck stamp while hunting waterfowl. Just prior to this enactment, President Roosevelt had very wisely appointed Darling as Chief of the Bureau of Biological Survey, predecessor of today's U.S. Fish and Wildlife Service. "Ding" was fittingly given the task of creating and designing the first of this annual series, which was to become known as the Federal Duck Stamp. What followed would be the longest running annual series of any federal stamp program ever published. Darling's small sketch depicting a pair of mallards was the beginning of what was to be the most significant contribution ever made to the conservation and propagation of this country's waterfowl. That same pencil sketch helped establish a most rewarding hobby of both artistic and monetary value – the collection of federal duck stamps and duck stamp prints.

It was a rush job from the beginning. The engravers had approved proofs by July, and the stamps were in the hands of every post office throughout the country by August 14, 1934, in time for opening day of the duck season that fall. That

1940 federal duck stamp design by Jaques, shown matted with the stamp. (Photo courtesy Sportsman's Edge, Ltd.)

first year, 635,000 stamps were sold at $1 each. To date, total sales of federal duck stamps exceed $210 million (over 2½ million stamps annually), providing funds to acquire 2½ million acres of prime waterfowl habitat. No wonder J. N. "Ding" Darling was appropriately given the title, "the best friend ducks ever had."

Until 1949, only a handful of the nation's top wildlife artists was asked each year to submit a design for the stamp. That year, because an increasing number of designs were submitted by hopeful artists, the contest was opened to any wildlife artist who wished to compete. This is the only art competition sponsored by the federal government and by 1981 has grown to over 1,500 entries.

The concept of having prints made of the winning entries was not conceived until 1936. Ed Thomas and Ralph Terrill, working in the Abercrombie & Fitch Book and Art Department, followed a suggestion by Dr. Samuel Milbank to frame the stamp with a print of the winning design. Thomas contacted Richard Bishop, who designed the 1936 stamp, and asked for an etching. Bishop was quite willing to do this but, unlike his previous pieces, it was printed in an unlimited edition. To this day the number of prints made is unknown.

From this unique idea of framing a print along with its corresponding stamp, the most collectible, longest-running, consecutive stamp/print art program was initiated. Little did anyone realize at the time what a great influence this would have on collectors and wildlife enthusiasts. By 1944, through the encouragement of Terrill, "Ding" Darling (1934 artist), Frank W. Benson (1935 artist), and E. R. Kalmbach (1941 artist) published prints of their designs, bringing the series up to date. Since that time, each winner has published prints of his winning entry.

In those early years, winning artists published their design primarily for prestige in the small world of wildlife art; little was realized in monetary gains. While the editions were small, with fewer than 100 in 1935, edition sizes increased slowly in the 1940s and 1950s. As late as 1962, Edward Morris' design numbered fewer than 300; and as recently as 1959, 23 of the first 26 could still be purchased at the original offering price of $10 to $15 each. Today it is believed that there are fewer than 55 complete collections from 1934 to 1980, each valued at $70,000 to $100,000. These same prints and stamps, purchased at the original issue price, would have required an investment of less than $1,700.

The enthusiasm for collecting prints and stamps as a series did not really gain momentum until the mid-1960s. By 1969, the edition size had grown to 750; and by 1970, the collecting of duck stamp prints really blossomed. Ed Bierly, winning the design competition for the third time, decided to increase the edition to 1,000 and to publish his striking watercolor of Ross' geese in color. Previously all prints had been in black and white. Printing in color now played a major role in the demand for duck stamp prints, attracting many new collectors, and the editions sold out very quickly.

The first color duck stamp print was attempted in 1955. In that year, Stanley Stearns won the competition with a design featuring three blue geese in flight. But because of unfortunate delays in getting the original artwork back from the engravers working on the stamp, the project was doomed because of lack of time. Prints had customarily been available for sale by July, so there was great pressure on Stearns to complete the project. This was his first attempt at the etching process, and it did not go well. Finally, on September 6, 1955, he wrote the following to Ed Thomas: "As you can see, I've been experimenting with multi-color and have tried as many as three colors. I've found it takes too much time in planning, etching and printing. I have not gained control of the multi-color process and feel it will just take a lot of etching to get anywhere with several colors." So, with this disappointment in the first attempt at color, collectors had to wait 15 more years before the first color print, and the popularity that grew with it.

In 1974, with demand now far exceeding the supply, David Maass announced that he would publish as many prints of his winning entry as were ordered by a specified date. Since then all edition sizes have been determined in this manner; and the 1980 design has grown to an unprecedented 12,950 prints.

Over the years some designs have been issued in first, second, and third editions to satisfy continuing demands. Consequently, the ultimate collection is one print of each edition; a full series up to the present date would consist of 76 prints. It is believed that there are only two or three complete collections in existence. From a collector's standpoint, however, one print of each year's design would total 47 prints, and there are approximately 54 of these full sets in existence.

For those who might wish to own a complete collection, the chances are not good. However, many persons now collect only color prints, starting with Bierly's Ross' Geese, 1970. And while not unreachable, even this smaller collection becomes increasingly difficult because of the growing interest in duck stamps and duck stamp prints.

Collectors can buy and sell duck stamp prints and obtain appraisals at any of the following dealers, all of whom specialize in duck stamp prints: Wild Wings, Lake City, Minnesota; Sportsman's Edge, Ltd., New York City; Russell Fink, Lorton, Virginia; Crossroads of Sport, New York City; Petersen Galleries, Beverly Hills, California; and The Bedford Sportsman, Bedford Hills, New York.

The best way to display the prints is framed with the stamp, using rag mat board and, generally, a ⅜-inch black molding. Frame size is normally 16½ inches by 16⅞ inches. Whether or not the artist signs the stamp is a matter of personal taste. Many people prefer that the artist sign the stamp; others prefer to have the signature only on the print. The stamp is usually worth more after the artist dies. Duck stamp prints should be insured for their replacement value.

Little attention has been given to the significance of this outstanding series of collectible stamps and prints and the impact it has had on the broader field of wildlife art in general. However, with the increased public awareness of the artistic merits of America's wildlife artists, we are recording for posterity truly fine examples of sporting art. As succeeding generations have always been the beneficiaries of noteworthy art, the wildlife artists of our era will someday be thanked for preserving on canvas and board our world of birds and mammals as found in their natural habitat.

VALUES OF FEDERAL DUCK STAMP PRINTS

Year	Artist/Design	Edition	Value
1934	DARLING (Mallards)		$4,000
1935	BENSON (Canvasbacks)		6,500

Printer's proof of 1971–1972 federal duck stamp design by Maynard Reece.

Year	Artist/Design	Edition	Value
1936	BISHOP (Canada Geese)		850
1937	KNAP (Greater Scaup)		2,500
1938	CLARK (Pintails)		3,500
1939	HUNT (Green-Winged Teal)	1st	6,000
		2nd	5,500
1940	JAQUES (Black Ducks)	1st	6,000
		2nd	5,000
		3rd	3,000
1941	KALMBACH (Ruddy Ducks)	reversed	3,600
		regular	1,100
1942	RIPLEY (Wigeon)		1,000
	Signature, Mrs. Ripley		450
1943	BOHL (Wood Ducks)	1st	900
		2nd	400
1944	WEBER (White-Fronted Geese)	reversed	4,000
		1st	2,200
		2nd	750
1945	GROMME (Shovelers)		5,500
1946	HINES (Redheads)	1st	1,700
		2nd	150
		2nd (RAP)*	250
1947	MURRAY (Snow Geese)		2,000
1948	REECE (Buffleheads)	1st	1,100
		2nd	950
		3rd	600
		4th	400
1949	PREUSS (Golden Eyes) (RAP)*		3,000
			2,400
1950	WEBER (Trumpeters)	1st	1,100
		2nd	400
1951	REECE (Gadwall)	1st	1,000
		2nd	650
1952	DICK (Harlequins)		1,100
1953	SEAGEARS (Blue-Winged Teal)		1,100
1954	SANDSTROM (Ring Necks)		1,100
1955	STEARNS (Blue Geese)	1st ed., 1st pr.	1,100
		1st ed., 2nd pr.	1,100
		2nd	600

Year	Artist/Design	Edition	Value
1956	BIERLY (Mergansers)	1st pr.	850
		2nd pr.	650
1957	ABBOTT (Eiders)	1st	1,100
		2nd	200
1958	KOUBA (Canada Geese)	1st	1,100
		2nd	800
1959	REECE (Labrador Dog)	1st	1,600
		2nd	1,000
		3rd	700
1960	RUTHVEN (Redheads)	1st	800
		2nd	450
		3rd	450
1961	MORRIS (Mallards)		1,000
1962	MORRIS (Pintails)		1,000
1963	BIERLY (Brant)	1st pr.	800
		2nd pr.	650
1964	STEARNS (Nene Geese)	1st	1,100
		2nd	500
1965	JENKINS (Canvasbacks)	1st	750
		2nd	400
		3rd	150
1966	STEARNS (Whistling Swans)	1st	1,000
		2nd	400
1967	KOUBA (Old Squaws)		750
1968	PRITCHARD (Mergansers)		1,000
1969	REECE (Scoters)		900
1970	BIERLY (Ross' Geese) (RAP)*	1st	3,000
			2,000
		2nd	150
1971	REECE (Cinnamon Teal)		4,500
1972	COOK (Emperor Geese) (RAP)*		3,800
			2,400
1973	LEBLANC (Steller's Eiders) (RAP)*		1,800
			1,500
1974	MAASS (Wood Ducks)		950
1975	FISHER (Canvasback Decoy) (RAP)*		1,000
			850
1976	MAGEE (Canada Geese)	scratch board	1,400
			700

Year	Artist/Design	Edition	Value
1977	MURK (Ross' Geese) (RAP)*		500
			400
1978	GILBERT (Hooded Merganser) (RAP)*		700
			350
1979	MICHAELSEN (Green-Winged Teal) (With Etching)		450
			250
1980	PLASSCHAERT (Mallards)		200
1981	WILSON (Ruddy Ducks)		125

*(RAP) REMARQUE

Chapter 8 ❧ State Duck Stamp Prints

ALFRED F. KING, III

State duck stamp prints have been accepted as a "collectible" since 1971. Nineteen states have issued duck stamps for which there are prints. At least two more states plan an initial duck stamp for 1981. As time goes on, more states will probably do the same. And as in the case of federal duck stamp program, virtually all the revenues go toward the purchase of wetlands.

This is the first Maryland state duck stamp, 1974–1975, by John W. Taylor. (Photo courtesy Sportsman's Edge, Ltd.)

I recommend acquiring the initial print for each state. The purist may wish to try to have every print issued, but it becomes an unwieldy collection. You may wish to acquire a full set of prints for the state in which you live.

The initial state duck stamp print of each state is the one to collect. The first of any series is very often the one that carries the greatest premium, and many collectors are late in collecting it. It becomes difficult to acquire, which increases its value. I believe that eventually the complete set of initial state duck stamp prints will be as unique and historically important as the federal duck stamp print collection.

Of course, all duck stamp prints should be framed to museum standards. See chapter on prints and etchings.

Following is a list of the dealers most capable of handling your requirements for state duck stamp prints:

Russell A. Fink
P.O. Box 250
Lorton, VA 22079

The Depot; Midwest Marketing
RR 3, Box 100
Sullivan, IL 61951

Alfred F. King, III
Sportsman's Edge, Ltd.
136 East 74th St.
New York, NY 10021

First Illinois state duck stamp, 1975–1976, by Robert F. Eschenfeldt. (Photo courtesy Sportsman's Edge, Ltd.)

VALUES OF INITIAL STATE DUCK STAMP PRINTS — WITH STAMP AND FRAME

Year	State	Artist		Edition	Offering Price	1976 Price	1981 Valuation
1971	California	Johnson		500	$60	$75	$400
1972	Iowa	Reece		500	60	970	3,500
1974	Maryland	Taylor		500	60	170	1,400
1974*	Massachusetts	Weiler		Less than 50	—	—	1,750
1975	Illinois	Eschenfeldt		500	70	115	800
1975	Massachusetts	Hennessey		500	60	70	400
1976	Michigan	Warbach		500	60	—	450
1976	Indiana	Bashore		500	65	—	400
1976	Mississippi	L. & G. Perkins		500	70	—	550
1976	South Dakota	Kusserow		500	100	—	700
1977	Minnesota	Maass		Not numbered	103.50	—	675
1978	Wisconsin	Gromme		5,800	103.25	—	250
1978	Montana	Urdahl	signed	1,300	104	—	200
			remarqued	200	129	—	550
1979	Tennessee	Elliot	signed	1,979	103	—	300
			pencil remarqued		153	—	400
			watercolor remarqued	50	228	—	500
1979	Florida	Binks	signed	1,000	103	—	450
			remarqued	250	253	—	600
1979	Missouri	Schwartz	signed	2,000	104	—	300
			remarqued		175	—	400
1979	Nevada	Hayden	signed	1,990	102	—	500
			remarqued	500	202	—	650
1979	Alabama	Keel	signed	1,750	105	—	250
			remarqued	250	255	—	400
1980	Delaware	Mayne	signed	1,980	130	—	250
			remarqued		205	—	350
1980	Oklahoma	Sawyer	signed	1,980	129	—	250
			remarqued		279	—	400

*Technically not a duck stamp print. Issued as part of the classic decoy series by Winchester Press. Chosen as the initial 1974 Massachusetts Duck Stamp. Weiler died before a print could be made. Weiler signed fewer than 50 of the Lincoln Wood Duck Decoy Prints from the classic decoy series. A welcome addition to any initial state duck stamp print collection.

Chapter 9 ❧ Wildlife Stamp Prints

RUSSELL A. FINK

At one time, the only stamp print available to collectors was the federal duck stamp print. However, as the federal duck stamp print collection gained in value and popularity, state governmental agencies, nonprofit foundations, and even a few private individuals and organizations began to view this phenomenon in print collecting as a tremendous source of extra funds. Many of them failed to understand, however, that the collector, and only the collector, ultimately determines the success or failure of every stamp-print program.

California issued its first duck stamp in 1971; Iowa followed in 1972. Since then to the time of this writing, 17 more states have adopted similar programs. In some collecting circles, they are considered almost as important as the federal duck stamp prints.

Enter the individual efforts, and nonprofit conservation organizations. The first to promote a stamp-print program was the time-honored firm of Abercrombie & Fitch. In 1974, they offered the original National Fish Stamp and Print, with a sizeable percentage of the proceeds earmarked for The National Recreation and Parks Association, Trout Unlimited, and the International Salmon Foundation, an organization dedicated to the welfare of various species of fish. The print was offered in two sizes, 15¾ inches × 22¾ inches and 6¼ inches × 9¾ inches. The first print and stamp featured a "Squaretailed Trout," another name for the brook trout. The second was an Atlantic salmon. For various reasons, the program got off to a rather poor start, and midway through the second year, it became obvious that it was going to fail. At the end of the second year, the concept was abandoned, and what few prints did sell, faded into obscurity. Exit the private entrepreneur.

About this time, several states began holding contests for their trout stamps. Naturally, the winning artists assumed that a print of their trout stamp design would be as sought after by collectors as the duck stamp design. However, it didn't work out that way. The trout stamps have enjoyed moderate success on a local level, but on a nationwide basis they just don't have the appeal to the collector or sportsman that the bird stamps do. The secondary market in them is not very strong, and consequently they are not in demand by the serious collector.

In 1976, Tom Rodgers, executive vice-president of the National Wild Turkey Federation, decided to give the other-than-duck-stamp prints another try. He telephoned me one day and told me that he was going to launch the National Wild Turkey stamp and print program. To increase the chances of success, he wanted to work out as many "bugs" as possible beforehand. He asked for my help as a collector and major dealer in federal and state duck stamp prints. The primary purpose of the program is to provide funds each and every year to improve all conditions for wild turkeys throughout the United States, so that their numbers will increase naturally. Although the primary goal is directed toward the wild turkey, many other wild creatures are beneficiaries of a habitat-improvement program. I knew that the cause was certainly worthwhile, and the potential for widespread collector interest was strong. I agreed to assist him in any way I could.

We spent the better part of two days analyzing the success of the federal and state duck stamp prints and the failure of the salmon stamp print. Although there is no sure way to predict which prints will be winners and which will fail, a few factors are common to all prints that continue to bring high prices. The single most important factor is *scarcity*. As long as the demand outstrips the supply, prices and interest will continue to rise. Some other determining factors are competence and reputation of the artist, subject matter, quality of the design, and technical quality of the print itself. The more of these factors that can be incorporated into a print, the better the chances are that it will be a collectible print.

The first Wild Turkey Stamp Print was well received by collectors, and the program got off to a flying start. Designed by Russ Smiley, the print featured "Osceola," the Florida subspecies of the wild turkey. The print was 7 inches × 10 inches and was issued in an edition of 1,000 signed and numbered copies plus approximately 50 artist's proofs. It sold out rapidly, and by the time the 1977 print was issued, the market value on the 1976 print was well established at $600. Currently, the value of this print is $2,200.

In 1977, Chuck Ripper's design was chosen as the winning entry for the first wild turkey stamp contest. It featured "Silvestris," the eastern strain of wild turkey, walking through snow-blanketed, eastern hardwood forest. Although some collectors from the southern states had trouble associating turkeys and snow, the print sold extremely well. When all the orders were tallied, the edition was closed at 1,500 signed and numbered copies and 100 artist's proofs, an increase in collector interest of a whopping 50 percent.

Since that time, the Wild Turkey Stamp Print has gained modestly, but steadily, in popularity. In 1978, 1,600 copies of Richard Amundson's "Intermedia" were sold to collectors, and the following year, Ken Carlson's winning entry of the western wild turkey, "Merriami," increased collector activity to 1,900 copies, 600 of which were remarqued.

At this writing, the edition for the 1980 Wild Turkey Stamp Print by Walter Wolfe has just closed at 1,400 signed and numbered, plus 600 remarqued prints. This collection of prints is well-established and should continue to gain in popularity. A complete set of Wild Turkey Stamp Prints is currently selling for about $3,300.

The next major stamp-print program to break into the market was the Ruffed Grouse Stamp Print. The powers that be within the Ruffed Grouse Society reasoned that with so many wildlife-art contests determining the design for a stamp and print, their program should be a bit different. They decided to control the quality of the artwork used for their stamps by selecting the artists in lieu of an open contest. It was a wise decision indeed, for the first Ruffed Grouse Stamp Print (1979) by Jim Foote was selling for $800 before the second one (by veteran wildlife artist David Maass) was even issued. It has been an overnight success with print collectors. There is every reason to believe that this collection will become an important part of the collecting of wildlife art.

The Foundation for North American Wild Sheep was quick to pick up on the success of the Ruffed Grouse Society's program. Before the ink was dry on the first Ruffed Grouse Stamp Print, the directors of the Foundation for North American Wild Sheep announced that they were launching their own stamp-print program that would feature the four subspecies of North American wild sheep: Rocky Mountain Bighorn, Desert Bighorn, Dall, and Stone. The first print is a reproduction of a fine oil painting of Rocky Mountain Bighorns by artist Gary Swanson. The image size is 6½ inches × 9 inches, a size used for many of the duck stamp prints, wild turkey stamp prints, and ruffed grouse stamp prints.

The success of the program could not be predicted because this was the first stamp-print program for mammals. However, demand immediately outstripped supply, and by the time the print was released, it was selling for $300.

The Long Island Wetlands and Waterfowl League issued their first stamp and print in 1977, and it has been fairly well received by collectors. Many collectors who collect the first of state duck stamp prints have included it in their collections as sort of an "honorary" state print. After the first year, though, its popularity has centered in and around the Long Island area. The proceeds from the sale of the prints and stamps are used to improve habitat for all waterbirds on Long Island.

At this time, several other stamp-print programs are in the planning or development stage, among them the deer stamp print and the striped bass stamp print. Undoubtedly, the trend toward stamp-print programs will continue to grow as long as success stories such as the Wild Turkey Stamp Print, the Ruffed Grouse Stamp Print, and the Wild Sheep Stamp Print occur. Many new collectors will enter the field either because they like the art and/or because they are attracted to the speculation aspect of print collecting.

However, the collector must use caution and a great deal of discretion when deciding which prints to purchase and at what price. First, be certain that the art is of collectible quality. If the design is the result of a contest decided by a panel of judges, do a little research on the contest. Get the answers to the following questions: Was the contest open to all wildlife artists? How many judges were there? Who are they? Are they qualified to select good art over bad? How many nationally known artists entered the contest? Which ones? If the answer to any of those questions tends to dampen the collector's enthusiasm to purchase, then he should think twice about purchasing the print at all. However, if he wants to pursue it a little further, contact the major reputable wildlife art dealers in the nation. If the major dealers are not handling the print, then the market for possible resale is severely limited. The more dealers who handle the print, the better the chances for success of the program.

The combination stamp-prints are fun to collect and can often be profitable. It is important that the collector not allow the profit motive to obscure his vision. He should, first and foremost, enjoy his collection. After all, that is what art is all about.

MAJOR SOURCES OF WILD TURKEY STAMP PRINTS

Russell A. Fink
P.O. Box 250
Lorton, VA 22079

Sportsman's Edge, Ltd.
136 E. 74th Street
New York, NY 10021

Wild Wings
Lake City, MN 55041

Midwest Marketing; The Depot
RR 3, Box 100
Sullivan, IL 61951

MAJOR SOURCES OF RUFFED GROUSE STAMP PRINTS

Russell A. Fink
P.O. Box 250
Lorton, VA 22079

Sportsman's Edge, Ltd.
136 E. 74th Street
New York, NY 10021

Wild Wings
Lake City, MN 55041

Collector's Covey
15 Highland Park Village
Dallas, TX 75205

Chandler's
217 Howard Street
Petoskey, MI 49770

Midwest Marketing; The Depot
RR 3, Box 100
Sullivan, IL 61951

MAJOR SOURCES OF WILD SHEEP STAMP PRINTS

Russell A. Fink
P.O. Box 250
Lorton, VA 22079

Collector's Covey
15 Highland Park Village
Dallas, TX 75205

Wild Wings
Lake City, MN 55041

SOURCE OF ORIGINAL FISH STAMP PRINTS (ATLANTIC SALMON)

Bob Hines
2505 Key Blvd.
Arlington, VA 22201

Chapter 10 🙟 Federal Duck Stamps and Postage Stamps

LEO SCARLET

Postage stamps were first issued in 1840, and from the very beginning there was a keen interest in collecting them. The very nature of their use and the extensive variety of colors and designs captivated an audience that extends to every country in the world and to all walks of life. During the past 30 years, there has developed a rapid upsurge of interest in collecting stamps based on special themes. This is known as "topical" collecting. Collections are formed concentrating solely on single topics, such as religion, medicine, guns, sports, the Olympics, and the like. There is an organization of philatelists, the American Topical Association, that carefully lists all the various stamps issued throughout the world and breaks up all these lists into the various topics.

A collection of stamps specializing only in sports can be a fascinating project. Most countries issue stamps commemorating major sports events or sports of the country. In the United States, many collect duck-hunting stamps, which are not postage stamps but are issued, with payment of a license fee for duck hunting, by the U.S. Department of Interior, Fish and Wildlife Service. They were first issued in 1934 and are issued yearly, with a different design each year. All designs used are paintings or drawings by well-known artists. Forming a complete collection of duck stamps can be quite a challenge.

Many duck stamps were printed in colors, and all are beautiful. Any hunter would immediately appreciate their beauty and recognize the type of duck. Among the famous artists who painted the originals are J. N. Darling, Frank Benson, Roland Clark, Maynard Reece, Edward J. Bierly, and Stanley Stearns. The scarcest stamp is the 1935 issue (canvasback ducks) painted by Frank Benson. A decent unused single stamp will cost $150, and a used (signed by hunter) stamp is worth $35.

Less than ten years ago, one could obtain a complete set of duck stamps for about $100. Today, you would be lucky to find a complete set for less than $900. Some collectors make up a fascinating collection of stamps on the original license. Most states have hunting stamps for individual game and fish. There are many hundreds, and obviously the only way to pursue the collection of these

Covers (envelopes) advertising arms companies. The upper one was printed by Winchester for one of its dealers, Hunnewell in Maine. (Photo courtesy Matthew Vinciguerra)

is to work out a reciprocal arrangement with hunters in other states, or seek out a dealer for assistance.

A serious factor enters the pricing of stamps — condition. A stamp that is torn, creased, or discolored will cost less than one in pristine, fresh condition. Unfortunately, there is no easy way to learn these variations. It is simply something you learn from experience. Any stamp dealer will be happy to help in this area.

Another aspect of collecting is the collecting of covers (envelopes) that picture the various topics. Late nineteenth-century and early twentieth-century businesses often used envelopes with designs, some in color, and many are intricate and interesting. Among the most difficult to locate these days are covers advertising different guns and ammunition. A collection of such covers is fascination itself. These can be obtained for moderate prices. Selling prices range from $20 to $50 depending on scarcity.

The identification of stamps is really a simple matter with the use of the *Scott Standard Postage Stamp Catalog*. It is published annually and lists every stamp issued by every country in the world, even making a brave attempt to price each stamp. Catalog values should serve only as a relative guide, since prices in the open market are too volatile. Strangely, values of stamps seem to move only upward. This is truer today than ever before because so many people are turning to stamps as an investment or as a hedge against inflation. Some stamps are quite rare. One stamp actually sold for $280,000 at a public auction! Fortunately, one can form an interesting collection with a modest expenditure of money.

Stamps can be purchased from several thousand stamp dealers located throughout the country. The American Stamp Dealers Association will be glad to supply the names of dealer members nearest you. See the proper pages in your telephone directory. Stamp dealers advertise regularly in local newspapers and in several national weekly stamp magazines. Public auctions and regular exhibitions are held at regular intervals. Visit one of these. You will find it worthwhile. You will find most stamp dealers to be helpful and cooperative. They know you need help, and it is to their advantage to win you as a customer.

REFERENCE SOURCES FOR STAMPS

American Stamp Dealers Association, 595 Madison Ave., New York, NY
10022. (Lists all stamp dealers in U.S. and other parts of the world.)
American Topical Association, Jerome Husak, exec. secretary, 3306 N. 50th
St., Milwaukee, WI 53216. (Period lists of stamps broken down by topic.)
Duck Stamp Data, U.S. Government Printing Office, Washington, DC 20402.

Linns Weekly Stamp News, P.O. Box 29, Sidney, OH 45365.

Meekels Magazine, P.O. Box 1660, Portland, ME 04104.

Minkus Stamp Catalog, Minkus Publications, 116 W. 32nd St., New York, NY 10001. (Similar to Scott's. Sold by Gimbel's chain in over 40 department stores.)

Scott Standard Postage Stamp Catalog, Scott Publishing Co., 530 Fifth Avenue, New York, NY 10036. (Lists all stamps issued in the world since 1840.)

Stamp-list catalog sold at major post offices.

Stamps Magazine, 153 Waverly Place, New York, NY 10014.

United States Postage Stamps, U.S. Government Printing Office, Washington, DC 20402.

United States Stamps & Stories, United States Postal Service. Published by Scott Publishing Company, New York, NY.

Western Stamp Collector, P.O. Box 10, Albany, OR 97321.

CURRENT VALUES OF DUCK STAMPS

Year	Designer	Depiction	Unused	Uncancelled*	Used
1934	Darling	Mallards	$ 263	$ 158	$ 63
1935	Benson	Canvasbacks	394	236	103
1936	Bishop	Canada Geese	206	124	53
1937	Knap	Broadbills	122	73	20
1938	Clark	Pintails	122	73	20
1939	Hunt	Green-Winged Teal	84	50	19
1940	Jaques	Black Ducks	84	50	15
1941	Kalmbach	Ruddy Ducks	84	50	15
1942	Ripley	Widgeon	84	50	15
1943	Bohl	Wood Ducks	63	38	15
1944	Weber	White-Fronted Geese	53	32	12
1945	Gromme	Shovelers	34	21	9
1946	Hines	Red Heads	34	21	6
1947	Murray	Snow Geese	38	23	6
1948	Reece	Buffleheads	47	28	6
1949	Preuss	Golden Eyes	47	28	6
1950	Weber	Trumpeter Swans	47	28	6
1951	Reece	Gadwalls	47	28	6
1952	Dick	Harlequins	47	28	6
1953	Seeger	Blue-Winged Teal	47	28	6
1954	Sandstrom	Ring Necks	47	28	6
1955	Stearns	Blue Geese	47	28	6
1956	Bierly	Mergansers	47	28	6

Year	Designer	Depiction	Unused	Uncancelled*	Used
1957	Abbott	Eider Ducks	47	28	5
1958	Kouba	Canada Geese	47	28	5
1959	Reece	Labrador Dog	70	42	5
1960	Ruthvan	Red Head Family	70	42	5
1961	Morris	Mallard Family	88	53	5
1962	Morris	Pintails	113	68	5
1963	Bierly	Brant	119	71	5
1964	Stearns	Nene Geese	119	71	5
1965	Jenkins	Canvasbacks	113	68	5
1966	Stearns	Whistling Swans	113	68	5
1967	Kouba	Old Squaw	113	68	5
1968	Pritchard	Mergansers	48	29	5
1969	Reece	Scoters	50	30	5
1970	Bierly	Ross' Geese	40	24	5
1971	Reece	Cinnamon Teal	40	24	5
1972	Cook	Emperor Geese	35	21	5
1973	LeBlanc	Stellers Eiders	25	15	5
1974	Maass	Wood Ducks	25	15	5
1975	Fisher	Canvasback Decoy	15	9	5
1976	Magee	Canada Geese	15	9	5
1977	Murk	Ross' Geese	15	9	5
1978	Gilbert	Merganser	15	9	5
1979	Michaelsen	Green-Winged Teal	15	9	5
*no signature on face; no gum on back			$3438	$2061	$540

Chapter 11 ❧ State Duck Stamps

RUSSELL A. FINK

A spinoff of collecting the state duck stamp prints is collecting the stamps themselves. At first glance, it would seem that collecting the stamps rather than the prints would be sort of a "poor man's duck stamp print collection." That's not exactly the case. Some of the state stamps have brought prices that equal or exceed the highest price ever paid for any single, federal duck stamp.

If one had purchased just the first duck stamp of each of the states that have issued duck stamps (20 at the time of this writing), the total investment would be about $60. Today, one each of the first stamp of each of the 20 states would cost $700. A complete set of state duck stamps through 1981 sells for about $1,800.

The 1972 California (second of the California series) is without question the rarest of the state duck stamps. Sales have been documented at $600 each; unconfirmed reports of higher figures crop up occasionally. These stamps are so scarce that when Paul Johnson, designer of the stamp, tried to purchase 500 of them (one for each of the prints in the proposed edition), he could only secure 20 copies. Consequently, the edition of prints for the 1972 California turned out to be 12 regular prints, five remarqued prints, and three artist's proofs.

The market in state duck stamps is far more complex than that of the federal duck stamp. Only one federal duck stamp is issued per year, whereas, at present there are 20 state stamps issued per year. The face value of a collection of one each of the state stamps is nearly $75. The equivalent investment in federal duck stamps would be only $7.50. Stamp dealers and print dealers alike are reluctant to stock large inventories because of the sizable annual investment and the relatively poor track record of many other state-issued stamps (fishing stamps, big-game stamps, small-game stamps, and the like). None have been anywhere near as popular as the state duck stamps. In addition, as more states adopt the duck stamp program, the annual investment to stock only one each of the state stamps per year could easily triple.

Another drawback that discourages dealers in philatelic items from carrying any inventory at all of state duck stamps is the degree of difficulty in obtaining the stamps. Federal duck stamps can be purchased in any first-class post office, and they are readily available each year. State duck stamps, on the other hand, must be ordered from individual state agencies, which are usually part of a department of natural resources. First, one must ascertain the price of the stamp. This can be an irritating obstacle because some states impose an administrative fee over and above the face value of the stamp. For example, the Minnesota duck stamp has the face value of $3. However, the purchaser must pay $3.25 for each stamp. Unless the exact price per stamp is determined in advance, any remittance sent to the state will be returned with instructions to send more money.

Having hurdled the first obstacle, the next thing the purchaser will encounter is that many state agencies will not accept personal or business checks as payment. Remittance must be in the form of money orders or cash. Everyone knows the risks of sending cash through the mail, so regardless of advice dispensed by those particular states, a money order is the only sensible method of payment. Money order fees are high in comparison with a check, and they are not transferable except by the original intended recipient. If a money order is returned for any reason, the purchaser must redeem it at the post office and start over with another money order.

Indiana requires that separate checks be issued for each year's stamps desired. The face value (and actual cost) of the stamp is $5. So if you wanted five 1976 stamps, three 1977 stamps, one 1978 stamp, and two 1979 stamps, you would have to send four separate money orders—one for $25, one for $15, one for $5, and one for $10.

The purpose in pointing out the problems involved in securing state duck stamps is not to ridicule the state agencies that administer the sale of the stamps, but to explain the unusual effort and expense that must be expended by the purchaser. Any dealer who perseveres and ultimately builds up a viable inventory of state duck stamps must raise the price of those stamps to adequately cover his expenses and allow for a fair profit. In some cases, this may very well mean that he must sell the stamp for ten or fifteen times the original face value.

State duck stamps come in a large variety of shapes and sizes. The first Mississippi stamp (1976) is a computer card complete with coded punch-out holes. It measures 3¼ inches × 2½ inches and carries a photograph (not artwork) of a wood duck drake. For a number of very good reasons, Mississippi officials changed the format the second year to a size that is rather standard for a duck stamp and is continuing along those lines.

California was the first state to issue a duck stamp (1971). It was of standard size but was printed on peel-off self-adhesive paper. It was convenient for the hunter to peel the stamp off the wax paper back and stick it on his hunting license, but self-adhering stamps have never been popular with collectors. They changed the design to a standard stamp in 1980. Another unique feature in the

California collection is that, in 1978, the state officials changed the stamp denomination from $1 to $5 halfway through the season. Thus, there are two stamps for 1978, each with the same design but different denominations.

Tennessee managed to incorporate the worst of both worlds in its first stamp (1979) — a rather cumbersome size (3¼ inches × 2⅜ inches) and a peel-off format. It is the only state still using peel-off paper for the stamp.

The smallest of the state duck stamps is the one issued by Montana. It measures $1\frac{1}{16}$ inches × 1⅜ inches and is slot-perforated. The first duck stamp issued by Montana didn't even have a duck illustrated on the face; it was a painting of a sage grouse, a favorite gamebird in Montana.

About half the state duck stamps are slot-perforated, and the other half are pin-hole perforated. By and large, the stamps that are pin-hole perforated are more popular with collectors. They seem to possess a little more "class." Perhaps it is the similarity to the postage stamps that we use everyday that makes it appear that they were produced by a professional agency.

An unusual regulation written into the entry form for the Massachusetts duck stamp contest, and an unusual amount of foresight on the part of the officials who established the regulations, has resulted in the Massachusetts duck stamps being highly prized by collectors. The theme each year must be a decoy by a Massachusetts maker. This very interesting subject matter has strong appeal to the hunter and decoy collector. The stamps are of average size, nicely printed, and pin-hole perforated. These qualities appeal to the stamp collector. All in all, the Massachusetts collection is as nice as any.

Collecting state duck stamps is gaining rapidly in popularity and prices are beginning to reflect the demand. In comparison with the federal duck stamp, state stamps are few in number. With so small a supply, a little demand goes a long way to raising prices.

There are only two dealers who seem to have a sizable inventory of state duck stamps. They are:

Carlo Vecchiarelli
2134 Hillside Drive
San Leandro, CA 94577

Richard T. Houk
30 Devon Hill Lane
Granite City, IL 62040

Houk has begun publication of an album for state duck stamps, but at the time of this writing it is not available for review. However, he does have a pamphlet about state duck stamps that is priced at $2.

Chapter 12 ❧ Sporting Firearms

NORM FLAYDERMAN

There have been few fields in the past 20 years that have grown more rapidly in both devotees and values than the collecting of firearms. The number of books written and published in the field is in itself indicative of its rapid and popular growth.

It is best for our purposes to define "sporting guns" in the broadest possible sense: all firearms designed for hunting and target-shooting purposes. Obviously many firearms originally intended solely for utilitarian purposes — for example, to put meat in the pot for the frontiersman, settler, or pioneer — could hardly be called sporting guns if the term is defined narrowly. But we will define it broadly; if you do get involved in collecting, you are free to decide for yourself just what constitutes a sporting arm.

TYPES OF COLLECTIONS

Sporting firearms encompass the entire period of arms-making from its very beginnings in the fourteenth century to the present day. Commencing with the increased popularity and manufacture of firearms in the sixteenth century, sporting guns have always been made in a multitude of grades and qualities to satisfy the fancies as well as the pocketbooks of a variety of sportsmen — from those of little means and taste to those possessing great wealth and refined aesthetic judgment (which is not to say that money and taste always go hand in hand).

Considering the countless paths down which one may go in collecting sporting arms, you would do well to select a specific field and confine yourself to that area, at least until you've learned the basics of collecting. If you are already a hunter, you might start by collecting those guns most closely allied to your own particular hunting interest; for example, bird or wildfowl guns, small-game rifles, or big-game rifles. You could collect everything of this type you find, or concentrate further in a particular historical period.

However, to me, one of the most interesting types of collections is the general one that shows sporting arms from their earliest matchlock types right down to modern-day arms, including at least one of every different ignition system — wheellock, flintlock, miquelet, percussion, and breech-loading-cartridge styles. For the neophyte collector, it is a way of acquiring a broad understanding of antique arms and their major changes over five centuries, and he will find that the items he collects are of wide general interest to others also.

For the low budget and neophyte collectors, muzzle-loading percussion-lock half-stock fowling pieces offer a very wide range of material to collect. Shotguns of these types would have been found in almost every country home in Europe and America. Top: Inexpensively made Belgian 12-gauge percussion fowling piece. A type widely exported throughout the world during the mid-nineteenth century and later eras. Easily available on the current market. Retail selling prices $50 to $100. Middle: English percussion 12-gauge fowling piece, circa 1850–1870, showing excellent workmanship, typical of British gunmakers. Back-action-style engraved lock with London maker's name. Retail value $100 to $200. Bottom: American-made by the famed Whitney Arms Company, percussion 12-gauge fowling piece, circa 1866 to 1880. Very likely the least expensive Whitney-made arm of its day as well as on the collector's market. Retail value $90 to $200.

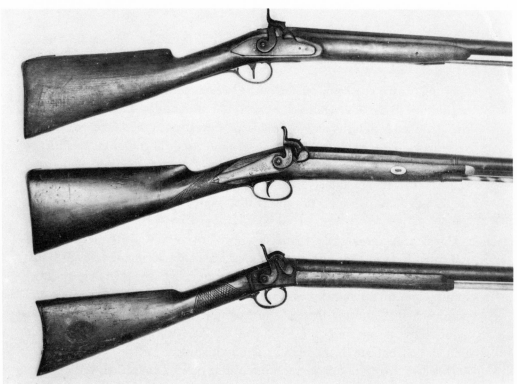

Top: American half-stock muzzle-loading percussion sporting rifle. Classic example of the type made throughout America in the 1840s to 1870s. This is representative of the simpler, more common type with full octagon rifle barrel, double set triggers, and small simple patchbox, and either unmarked as to maker or bearing names of lesser-known gunsmiths. Value at retail $200 to $400. Prices vary considerably depending on both exterior and bore condition. Bottom: Three-barrel American rifle-shotgun. This specimen is a 14-gauge double-barrel muzzleloading percussion shotgun over a .38-caliber muzzleloading rifle and has three exterior hammers. Depending on quality and maker, and of course condition, prices on similar pieces vary from $300 to $1,000. This particular example, in normal worn condition but bearing the California maker's marking, is worth $700. In this particular instance the Western maker adds to its desirability.

It is worth digressing for just a moment on this last point of "wide general interest." One of the greatest satisfactions in collecting is being able to communicate your enthusiasm, for the items you have gathered, to completely unknowledgeable, even uninterested, noncollectors, and to see them show a genuine interest. If you have an esoteric collection—and firearms collections can be very esoteric; the placement of a screw or a variation in a maker's mark may affect value by many hundreds of dollars—you will find it very difficult to share your enthusiasm with a casual visitor to your gun room. Your collection will be of interest only to another dyed-in-the-wool advanced collector or student. But general collections that show a progression of arms through a long era of history lend themselves quite beautifully to an interesting, attractive display that is easily understood by the non-gun person. You will be amazed how easy it is to give an interesting tour through your collection if you keep it of this more general, broad scope. The more highly specialized and detailed your collection becomes, the less interesting it is to the public at large.

I do not mean to disparage highly specialized collectors and ones interested in technical variations, for such pursuits also offer much and have added greatly to the field of gun collecting. It can be easily seen, though, that the more you become involved in detail and fine points, the more you lose your audience. Thus, depending on your own needs and gregariousness, it is worth keeping in mind how much and with whom you would like to share your collecting.

Surprisingly, of the hundreds of books written on the subject of firearms and gun collecting, and the tens of thousands of arms collections there are in the world, there are relatively few that could be considered as devoted solely to "sporting" or "hunting" guns as their major theme. The same is true of the many fine museum collections throughout the world. Although hunting and sporting arms are prominently shown in every arms museum and are by no means relegated to second place in importance, there are less than a handful of museums (one is the wonderful Musée de la Chasse of Paris) whose primary emphasis is the evolution of hunting and hunting weapons. Such arms are certainly actively sought and collected, but regrettably they are generally disassociated from their original hunting/sporting intent, with major emphasis and stress placed on either craftsmanship and artistry, technical features and variations of manufacture, or representation of a type used during a specific era of history. This observation is not intended to reflect detrimentally on the arms or on collecting itself, but merely again points out the fact that collecting often forces the collected items into a context other than that for which they were originally designed.

Thus if you collect sporting arms and show them as closely paralleling the history of sporting and hunting itself, you will be in relatively untrodden territory. Instead of merely collecting firearms and firearms history, you will have the opportunity to broaden your knowledge and share your interest in sporting and hunting history as well. The two, after all, go hand in hand.

Two major categories, each offering limitless possibilities, are muzzle-loading arms and breech-loading arms. Each of these categories is easily subdivided into smoothbore (single or double barrel) fowling pieces or shotguns; small-bore rifles or large-bore rifles for the whole gamut of game animals; and target rifles. Considerable challenges are offered in each of these fields, and a vast wealth of

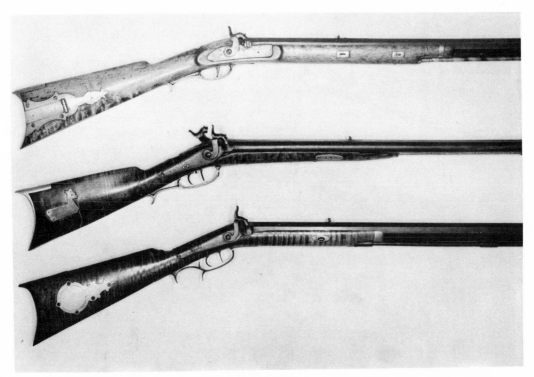

A wide range of half-stock American Kentucky or plains-type rifles of the mid-nineteenth century era are available. Prices vary greatly depending on exterior appearance, maker, and condition. Top: Half-stock Kentucky rifle, beautifully grained birdseye and curly maple stock, all brass-mounted with fancy large patchbox. Retail value $600 to $900. Middle: Side-by-side double-barrel muzzle-loading percussion plains-type Western rifle, circa 1850s. Has a rarity value as a double rifle, and St. Louis dealer's markings on it indicate its actual use on the Western frontier. Retail value $650 to $1,000. Bottom: Fine percussion half-stock sporting rifle with elegantly grained tiger-stripe maple half stock, finely made fittings, and the markings of a famed maker, S. Odell of Natchez, Mississippi, who was known to have sold many arms to emigrants heading west to Arkansas, Texas, and Santa Fe. In this case, quality and historic significance combine to establish a retail value of $1,600.

information on each specific type is readily available for reference. These major categories may be further narrowed by collecting more specialized types, each of which parallels an era or distinct hunting style. A notable example is the American Kentucky rifle. Certainly one of the best-known hunting and sporting arms, it covers the broad spectrum of American history from colonial times through the mid-nineteenth century, undergoing numerous style changes as it

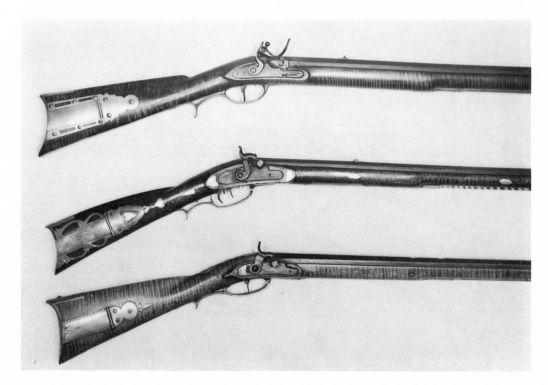

Top: Pennsylvania-Kentucky–style full-stock flintlock rifle displaying some of the classic features of that most eagerly sought after type, undoubtedly qualifying as one of the most handsome of all American guns. The most often encountered and desirable features of these are their fancy brass fittings with large brass patchboxes and stocks of closely tiger-striped, curly maple. Quite rare in original flintlock condition; when so found, prices will begin at $2,050 with the sky the limit for the very fine early ones. Prices vary greatly depending on maker, condition, embellishments, and incised or relief carving. Middle: Pennsylvania-Kentucky–style rifle converted to percussion. Although lessening in importance in this past decade, the matter of originality of ignition system (that is, flintlock or percussion) does decidedly play a role in influencing market value. This particular specimen, because of its well-known maker and numerous fancy inlays, as well as very large pierced-design patchbox, is valued at $1,500. However, this style is often encountered in the collector's market priced from $500 to $2,500 with the values very much established by the outward appearance and condition of the piece, as well as the rarity of the maker. Bottom: New England piece, but fashioned directly after the more famed Pennsylvania-Kentucky rifle. This piece shown in percussion conversion displays the classic style of patchbox found invariably on New England rifles. A few other features about its brass furniture also clearly indicate its New England manufacture. Most often found full-stocked in walnut or cherry. They normally retail in per-

cussion at $500 to $1,000, and in flintlock at $1,500 or more. This particular specimen, quite unusually stocked in very handsomely striped curly maple, commands a premium price.

adapted itself to different hunting, sporting, and target-shooting purposes. Other notable areas for specialization are breech-loading sporting rifles of the American West, covering the second half of the nineteenth century; lever-action sporting rifles; flintlock fowling pieces; single-shot varmint rifles; and big-game double rifles. This last group holds a great deal of fascination for the collector; the guns themselves almost always display the very finest of quality and craftsmanship and exude the aura of romance and excitement associated with African and Asian hunting. A category that is relatively untapped and that certainly offers a very wide potential for future growth is the field of Damascus double-barrel breech-loading shotguns designed for black-powder use.

In each of these fields it is possible to collect an extremely wide range of items; vast differences in style, quality, and appearance exist. Many of these differences are not merely manufacturing variations but were deliberate adaptations to different hunting methods, and the collector will find it of genuine interest to form a collection paralleling them.

BECOMING A COLLECTOR

Guns are costly, to be sure; the sky is really the limit with some specimens. Recent years have seen ever-higher records set for certain types of fine arms, with many reaching the six-figure category. As a generalization, it would be fair to say that all gun prices, antique and modern, have risen sharply over the past decade. But the astronomical figures quoted for the rarest guns should in no way frighten you off; they are the exception and not the rule. There are tens of thousands of guns still available, well within the reach of the average pocketbook. To be sure, in collecting there is expense involved, and at the risk of triteness I cannot help but quote an expression that concisely sums the matter up: "Rich or poor, it's good to have money!" Your taste and your pocketbook will undoubtedly determine the category that you choose to start collecting. If you become proficient at it, and keep your eyes and ears open, you might even be able to turn a profit by buying guns that are not of interest to you personally, selling them at a profit, and turning the profits into your own particular field of specialization. Quite a few important collections have started just that way.

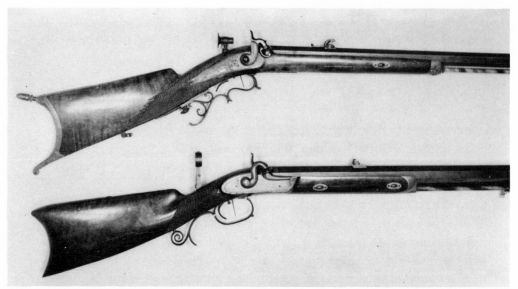

American-made Scheutzen-style offhand target rifles were often made in the mid-nineteenth century by German immigrant gunsmiths. Both of these pieces exemplify some of the best of American quality arms used in the many "Scheutzenfests" popular throughout the country before the turn of the century. Top: New Jersey offhand target rifle displaying the best of quality and workmanship, made by J. Widmer of Newark, weighing 11 pounds with exceptional chiseled and engraved fittings, all silvered finish, and in fine condition. Its retail value is $1,500. Bottom: St. Louis Scheutzen–type rifle by Charles Schaerff. This piece also displays classic lines often found in German rifles of the same era; being valued both for its St. Louis maker's name and its superb condition, it recently listed at $1,250. Other specimens similar to both these pieces may be found in the $500 to $900 range depending on quality and condition.

Knowledge of guns and collecting are the most valuable assets you can acquire; money is secondary.

Myriad are the reasons why people become collectors. Each has its own validity and virtues. If, however, you are contemplating collecting purely on an investment basis, my best advice would be to quit now while you are ahead! If you have read one of those articles in the *Wall Street Journal* or some other publication that reports the skyrocketing prices in antique arms and the big money that has been made or could be made on them, and you are lured into speculative collecting, you might be in for a rude awakening. It is true that many collectors have turned very handsome profits on their antique arms, especially those who have been in the field for several years. A small handful of speculators in recent years have also made killings on a few choice pieces (and a few not so savory characters have made killings on spurious specimens). But speculation failures are rarely found newsworthy. There have been many. It is just not possible to buy antique guns, or for that matter antique furniture, coins, art, or anything collectible, without being armed with some knowledge and a good deal of patience. Few who come into collecting on a purely speculative basis stay long. The very essence of collecting is the acquisition of knowledge, and that takes time. The key requisite for collecting must be a sincere interest in the items themselves, and the ultimate remuneration you should expect is the enjoyment you have had from your collecting activities. Obviously, your money should be well spent; an investment in anything of value should be carefully considered. In the field of firearms, prudent investments have brought very rich returns, and indications are clear that gun values will continue to increase—but go into this field only if you are prepared to open your mind as well as your pocketbook.

All right, you are ready to start. Where do you begin? My very best advice is to buy a few books and read them well. This is, by the way, the least often taken advice! It just takes too much time, and with your money burning a hole in your pocket, you cannot visualize a book hanging on two gun hooks on your wall.

Go slow. Pick up a few basic primers on arms collecting. Any reasonably sized library is bound to have a number of them on its shelves, as will any larger bookseller. There are a few dealers specializing in gun books who issue catalogs of them, and if you happen to visit a gun show, undoubtedly there will be dealers there with a large selection of books on collecting. Just for openers, a good choice would be *The Collecting of Guns* (Harrisburg: Stackpole, 1964), edited by James Serven, which gives a great introduction to the field. A few others you will find worthy are *The Age of Firearms* (New York: Bonanza, 1978), by Robert Held; *The National Rifle Association's Gun Collectors' Guide* (Northfield: Digest Books, 1974), edited by Joseph Schroeder; and *Guns and Collecting* (London: Octopus Books, 1972), by Bailey, Hogg, Boothroyd, and Wilkinson. Although numerous titles are available on specialized sporting arms, there are but a handful available on the field in general, and they are well worth reading: *Hunting and Shooting from Earliest Times to the Present Day* (New York: Putnam, 1971), by Michael Brander; *Sporting Guns* (London: Octopus Books, 1972), by Richard Akehurst; *Hunting Weapons* and *Royal Sporting Guns at Windsor* (London: Her Majesty's Stationery Office, 1968), by Howard L. Blackmore. After thoroughly digesting these primers, you will have acquired at least a basic knowledge of what the field of sporting weapons encompasses and are prepared to get your feet wet...maybe.

Next on your agenda should be visits to museums that specialize in or have good collections of firearms (and there are a number of them throughout the

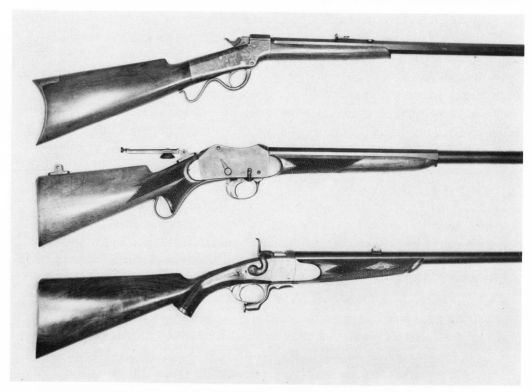

Top: Marlin-Ballard breech-loading "Model #2" single-shot rifle made in a great variety of calibers, barrel lengths, and stock styles. This particular specimen can be found anywhere from $100 to over $750 (if in brand-new condition). The Marlin-Ballard range is so vast, entire collections could be formed around them; the most deluxe specimens with long-range barrels and sights bring well upward of $2,000. Middle: American Peabody-Martini single-shot long-range target rifle made by the Providence Tool Company. One of the more eagerly sought of American single-shots developed for the famed Creedmore shooting of the 1870s–1890s. This piece, in new condition, catalogs at $2,500. There are various sporting, short, and mid-range models of this as well. Priced proportionately less. Condition is highly important and affects value of these pieces. Bottom: Exemplifying the very fine guns of almost every British maker, this breech-loading (falling-block) single-shot .450-caliber sporting rifle is the type that can be found in many grades and styles, sporting to long-range target lengths. Prices range from $1,000 to $1,750 depending very much on condition and embellishments. Prices are considerably lower on guns showing heavy wear.

country); a visit to a gun collector's home; a visit to a gun show that might be in your area or nearby. These need not occur in that order. New horizons will undoubtedly open for you, especially when you visit your first gun show and

At the very top of the list and capturing the imagination (and the pocketbook) of both the hunter and collector are fine-quality double rifles, most notably those of the finer British makers. Prices are very heavily influenced by calibers. Those designed for smokeless modern loads and for which ammunition is still available most often fetch the top prices and are in greatest demand. The earlier outside-hammer black-powder models generally fetch from $500 to $3,000. Prices very much depend on notoriety or the maker and condition. Later specimens such as the two British pieces shown will have values influenced by caliber, condition, and maker. British pieces will fetch higher prices than those of other European countries. Top: Westley Richards double rifle, .300 H&H magnum with original scope. Value $4,000. Middle: Manton, London, double rifle, .470, value $4,000 to $5,000. Bottom: Extremely rare double rifle, .45-70 made by Colt Firearms Company. Although they never achieved great popularity in this country, there were some double rifles made during the black-powder era by lesser-known makers. Their values vary anywhere from $300 to $1,000. This particular piece, by virtue of its being manufactured by Colt, one of the top collecting lines in American antique firearms, and of the fact that but 30 or so of them were made and only a handful known, will fetch, depending on condition and the collector's market, $7,500 to $20,000.

see perhaps several hundred tables with thousands of guns for sale; you will suddenly realize that a new world is just waiting for you. Assuming that you are a cautious individual and that your money is still reposing at the bottom of your pocket, your next step should be to subscribe to a few of the arms periodicals that are regularly issued. I cannot overemphasize the importance of belonging to the National Rifle Association and receiving their very fine publication *The American Rifleman*. Two pure collectors' magazines are *The Gun Report* and *Arms Gazette*, both of which are oriented primarily toward antique arms. There are also a host of other periodicals covering the field of modern weapons. The importance of these magazines to you as a neophyte is not only their wealth of informative arms articles, but the hundreds of advertisements of dealers and collectors all over the country who either offer their catalogs or items for sale. One of the best mediums of exchange in the arms business, especially for antique weapons, is mail order. Of equal importance in these periodicals are the advertisements and listings for all the regularly scheduled gun shows throughout the country. Just about every weekend of the year there are from two to five different shows held somewhere in America; there is every likelihood that some will be close enough for you to attend.

Well, just possibly you are now ready to buy something. If you've been lucky, you have found a mentor in collecting whose opinion you feel you can value (and who is not trying to sell you his guns!), and in making a selection at a show or in a dealer's shop you can get one outside impartial opinion. This will do much to get you started on the right foot. If you are on your own, then you have to use your own discernment, good common sense, and judgment of human nature. A check of the reputation of the party selling it is certainly worth making. Remember, guarantees, whether in writing or not, are only as good as the party giving them.

HOW MUCH IS IT WORTH?

Arriving at a price is one of the most perplexing situations that the new collector encounters. It does take a little bit of experience to understand how it is done—the complexities of it and very often the inequities as well. Basically, the most important factors in determining value are demand, rarity, and condition—in that order. After nosing around a few gun shows and reading dealers' catalogs, you will get the hang of how things are valued and understand why an item that may have been manufactured in very large quantities can often bring five or ten times the price of a far rarer item of which but a handful were made—a classic, pure example of demand setting the price.

The ultimate in an American rarity, an elegant .40 carbine made by the most famed of American frontier gunsmiths, Frank W. Freund, in his "Wyoming Armory" at Cheyenne, Wyoming Territory, circa 1870. Known as his Wyoming Saddle Gun, having a Sharps-type (but completely Freund-made) miniature falling-block action and other features for which Freund was noted, the gun was made in extremely limited quantity with a total of but seven or eight at most believed to be the total manufacture. The few known existing specimens fetch from $7,000 to $15,000 depending on condition and historic association.

Another rule of thumb and advice that you will hear innumerable times, and that is worth repeating here, is to confine yourself as closely as possible to quality and condition. It is far better to have one good piece than a dozen "dogs." This is one of the toughest points to get across to new collectors, especially if they have the pack-rat syndrome. Human nature being what it is, the new collector most often commits all the sins he has been warned to avoid. Those bargains are just so damned hard to pass by in the beginning!

A final rule of thumb on bargains is worth bearing in mind if you are new at the game and are attending an auction. Under no circumstances ever bid at any gun auction (or any other for that matter) unless you have closely examined the item at the exhibition preceding the auction. Further, if you are a novice at it and have no idea of values, you have no business bidding at that auction anyway. Be patient and wait until you know more. There will be more guns and more auctions in the future. When you stand toe to toe and slug it out with other bidders—and that is what auctions are all about—you should at the very least know what you are doing.

This seems a good place to insert the classic "caveat emptor." It has been the case in just about every field of collecting that as prices have risen, so have the numbers of nefarious individuals who are attracted to that particular field. Fortunately, good guys outnumber the bad guys by far; but forewarned is forearmed.

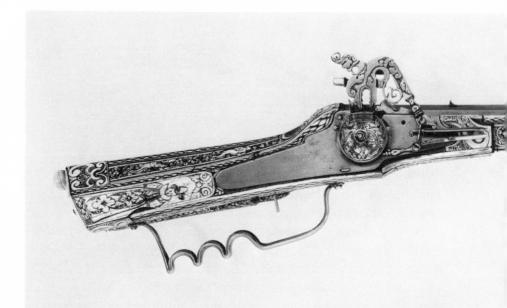

Sixteenth century German wheellock sporting gun. This particular specimen has a part-octagon, part-round smoothbore barrel. A majority of these wheellocks have rifled barrels. Stock inlaid from butt to muzzle with thousands of pieces of ivory and bone in decorative floral and scroll patterns with larger plaques bearing engraved hunting designs. Among the most desirable and certainly handsome of all ancient sporting weapons, these elegantly embellished pieces were made for men of wealth in their day. Great care should be exercised in their purchase as a number of specimens on the market today were made in the nineteenth century for purely decorative purposes; the buyer should be well informed before investing in these pieces. Prices vary greatly depending on importance of maker, quality of workmanship, and condition. Specimens with only the smallest amount of inlay and decorative work start at about $2,000. Heavily embellished specimens similar to this will start at about $7,500 with no limit for the best. Prices have reached well into the six-figure range in recent years. (Photo courtesy Winchester Gun Museum)

A wonderful and certainly practical book that is most heartily recommended is *How Do You Know It Is Old?*, by Harold L. Peterson. Just recently issued, it covers a wide range of antique collecting with considerable material on antique arms.

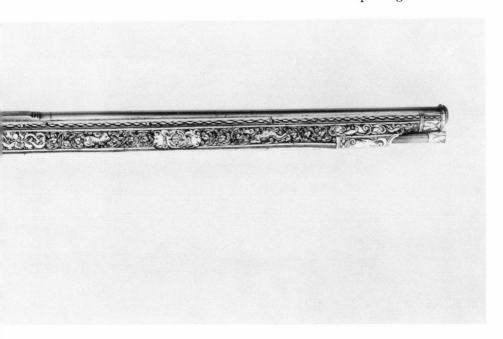

SELLING ITEMS FROM YOUR COLLECTION

As your accumulating activities progress and your collection grows, you will undoubtedly find yourself with pieces that no longer hold an interest for you. A number of methods of selling them are available, depending on the time and effort you wish to spend. You may find that the "book" or advertised price on a specific piece is not always what you can get. In some cases there just might not be any takers at any price. It might very well be that just at this point you get one of your most painful lessons in the fine art of gun trading! But if you have bought wisely, you may well find that a dealer will pay you as high a price as any collector in your area. His own specialized market and access to a national market allows him to know exactly where to place that gun quickly, and in such cases he is willing to pay a premium price for it. He also is usually willing to pay cash immediately for the item; in many private sales you may have to accept trade items in lieu of money.

Should you not realize the price you want through a dealer, you have three other options available. They all take a little time and extra effort, but it might be well spent. The easiest is to take space at a regularly scheduled gun show and display your piece as attractively as possible. You stand a good chance of selling it or trading it, provided, of course, that you have placed a realistic price on it. A second means is by way of auction. There could be both hazard and ex-

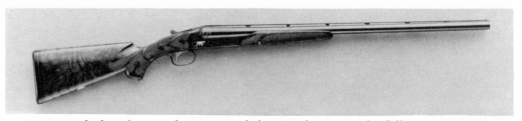

Among the best-known shotguns made by Winchester are the different varieties of the Model 21. The 21 was first announced in the May 8, 1930, price list in Standard Grade with either double or single trigger. A note, however, continued that only Standard-Grade, double-trigger, 12-gauge guns were available immediately, with other styles to be delivered as of April 1, 1931. The original price was $59.50. Current prices—for custom-made guns only—begin at $3,500 for the Custom Grade, go to $5,000 for the Pigeon Model, and up to $7,500 for the Grand American. Although made in all gauges, the .410-bore and 28-gauge guns are the rarest and command the highest prices. Moreover, 20s bring better prices than 12s, which are in turn more desirable than 16s. Top: Model 21 Pigeon Model. Bottom: Model 21 Grand American Model.

pense involved, and you should be well aware, in advance, of the rules of the game. If the auctioneer runs an "open" or "no reserve" auction in which every item must be sold to the high bidder and it happens to be one of those bad days, your piece could be sold for much less than its cost, and on top of that, you have to pay the auctioneer's commission. Should the auction allow you to place a reserve figure on the piece — that is, a price under which they will not sell it — you at least have the opportunity to protect it from being undersold, but usually a commission must still be paid to the auctioneer. This latter method has its strong detractors as well as supporters; probably the key to successful utilization of it is the quality of the other material in the sale and the reputation of the auction house.

The last option, which entails the most time but certainly will reach the widest possible audience, is to advertise your arm in one of the gun-collecting publications. These are widely circulated throughout the United States and abroad, and you certainly stand the very best chance of finding the ultimate specialized collector most actively seeking that particular model. In mail order, however, you must remember there is a considerable time lapse between the placement of your advertisement and its appearance in print—usually a minimum of two months. You must be prepared to answer all inquiries, and you must further be prepared, after shipping the gun, to take it back for full refund (within a reasonable amount of time, of course) if the buyer, after seeing it, does not find it up to his specifications. Not a few well-known dealers in business today started off that way, dabbling in part-time mail order.

There are legal complications in buying and selling firearms of all types and most especially through the mail. You would do well to familiarize yourself with the Federal Firearms Act of 1968, which regulates interstate trade in firearms. Be certain to familiarize yourself with your own state and local firearms ordinances—they can vary greatly from place to place. Generally speaking, anything made before 1898 is free of regulations under the Federal Firearms Act, but this in itself does not cancel any existing state or local laws that might be in effect in your own area. Read the laws themselves (they are readily available) and then check the finer points with your local gun clubs.

PROTECTING YOUR COLLECTION

Since the world is filled with scoundrels, rogues, knaves, and scalawags, not to mention thieves, prowlers, and the light-fingered, you would do well to safeguard your valuable collection. The hazard of fire, of course, is always present. Quite a few articles have been written on the subject of insurance, and it is well covered in Jim Serven's *The Collecting of Guns* as well as in some of the National Rifle Association publications. Generally speaking, if you have accumulated a good collection, you should not merely have it listed under your homeowners policy, but should have it specially covered under insurance policies known as "fine-arts floaters." Any good insurance agent will be familiar with these policies. A number of attractive plans are offered by some of the larger collecting organizations. The key feature of the fine-arts policy is that each and every item in your collection is itemized, valued, and kept on record with the insurance company and agent. When there is a loss, settlements are usually quicker and are usually for the amount on your schedule. Of course, it is necessary to update these schedules as prices rise or as you dispose of or add pieces. Coverage is usually the very broadest and rates the most advantageous.

Appraisals are often important in establishing value. Such valuations are

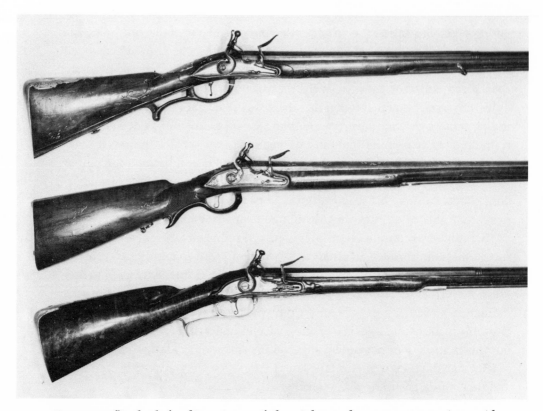

European flintlock fowling pieces of the eighteenth century come in a wide range of values. Top: Austrian full-stock flintlock fowling piece, circa 1750, by noted Austrian maker Marcus Zelmer, Vienna. Displaying the finest in the gunsmith's art, this particular specimen is unusual in being solid-silver-mounted (normally they are found only in brass) and in almost unfired condition as well as bearing the arms of royalty. Its current market value is $4,000 to $6,000. Pieces of lesser quality and distinction, although still displaying fine workmanship, may be found in the $1,000 to $2,000 range. Middle: Another Austrian full-stock flintlock fowling piece of the mid-eighteenth century, with all-wood trigger guard. It displays the finest talents of an accomplished gunsmith, and in superb almost unfired condition, this particular specimen recently sold for $2,500. Pieces of a similar nature although a bit less elegant in quality can still be found in the $700 to $1,500 range. Bottom: Eighteenth-century French gentlemen's flintlock full-stock fowling piece. Displays all the features of the very early eighteenth century and with exquisitely grained burled wood stock as well as heavy gilt-finished chiseled-brass embellishments. This piece, by Claude Niquet, is valued at $5,000. Its price is determined by its superior quality and its exceptional condition as well as its very handsome embellishments. Similar pieces of this same era more simply fashioned (yet of good quality) showing

*normal wear and use, and with fittings less elegant, are more often encountered
and usually sell in the $750 to $1,500 range.*

necessary not only for insurance, but for estate and tax plans, gift and damage
claims, and other purposes. The validity of appraisals depends on the credentials
and background of the appraiser. It is easy to get anybody with the slightest
knowledge of guns to write you an evaluation on your pieces or to pull figures
out of the air for them; all it takes is a typewriter and some paper. However,
remember that those figures are subject to review by quite a few parties who
may accept them or reject them. Credibility is the key word here. There are
major appraisers' associations throughout the United States, and they will be
pleased to give lists of appraisers whose specialty is firearms. A number of the
well-known dealers in the field are also quite well qualified and make it a part
of their usual business routine to perform such appraisals. Appraisals are best
performed by someone who is professionally involved in the field of firearms
and whose specialty includes the exact type of firearms you wish to have eval-
uated. Fees are usually moderate; they are computed according to the quantity
and values of the items appraised.

REPRESENTATIVE PRICES OF RIFLES

Maker and model	Current value
Mossberg bolt-action, slide-action, auto	$25–65
Remington	
slide-action Models 12, 121, 141	75–175
bolt-action Models 720, 721, 722, 760	125–160
Sako bolt-action rifles	200–300
Savage Model 99 lever-action rifles	100–300
Weatherby bolt-action rifles	175–400
Winchester	
lever-action Model 53	225–400
lever-action Model 86	250–750
lever-action Model 94	90–175
lever-action Model 95	225–550
slide-action Model 62	125–200
auto Model 63	150–250
bolt-action Model 70, pre-'64	225–500
bolt-action Model 70, post-'64	125–150
bolt-action Model 43	150–200

REPRESENTATIVE PRICES OF SHOTGUNS

Maker and model	Current value
Baker Batavia	$ 200–350
Beretta Golden Snipe O/U	450
Browning	
Auto-5	200–300
Superposed, Standard Grade	600–700
Superposed, Pigeon Grade	1,000–1,200
Superposed, Diana Grade	1,200–1,400
Superposed, Midas Grade	1,500–2,450
A. H. Fox	
Sterlingworth Grade	200–400
A Grade	400–600
Model B	125–225
H&R single-barrel shotguns	25–35
High Standard pumps and autos	90–145
Hunter Arms double-barreled	200–500
Ithaca	
Field Grade double-barreled	200–325
4E Grade double-barreled	700–800
trap gun, single-barreled, Victory Grade	400–600
pump gun Model 37	75–250
Iver Johnson double-barreled	150–400
Lefever Nitro Special double-barreled	150–250
Marlin Model 90 O/U	200–350
Mossberg bolt-action	25–50
Parker	
Trojan double-barreled	250–750
VHE double-barreled	800–1,000
DHE double-barreled	1,000–1,700
SC Grade single-barreled trap	900–1,500
SB Grade single-barreled trap	1,600–1,800
Remington	
standard pumps	100–250
auto models	100–250
Model 32 O/U	500–900
Richland S/S and O/U	150–250
L.C. Smith Field Grade double-barreled	175–400

Winchester

Model 97 pump gun	150–175
Model 12 pump gun, Standard Grade	250–400
Model 42 pump gun, Standard Grade	250–350
Model 21 double-barreled	800–7,500

Chapter 13 ❧ Modern Sporting Firearms Valuation

HENRY CHRISTMANN

The following is a representative list of sporting shotguns, rifles, and handguns produced from about 1900 to 1960. While most were originally modestly priced, they have attained wide collector status.

Prices are for specimens in original, unaltered, excellent condition. Those in good to very good condition are worth about 30 percent to 50 percent less. Factory-new guns command a premium of 50 percent to 100 percent more. Models that have a lot of engraving must be individually appraised. Factory-engraved guns command high premiums, while customizing that is added by the owner may or may not add to the value. Automatic ejectors add about 30 percent to the value of a fine shotgun. Prices shown for shotguns are for 12-gauge guns. Twenty-gauge guns are worth 75 percent to 100 percent more, while 28-gauge and .410 guns are worth up to three to five times more.

Maker and model	Current value
PISTOLS	
Browning	
.25 caliber automatic	$150
Renaissance Model	300
Hi-Power 9mm	250
Renaissance Model	750
Colt	
Single-action Army .45 Colt	400–800
Camp Perry Single Shot .22	600
Officers Match Model .38	250
Pocket .25 Auto	200
Government Model 1911 .45 caliber	350
Ace .22 caliber auto	500
Woodsman .22 auto	200
Lahti	
Auto 9mm	450

Maker and model	Current value
Luger	
Standard 4 inch 9mm	350
Artillery 9mm	850
Navy Model 9mm	1,500
Mauser	
1898 Auto 9mm	700
Remington	
Vest Pocket .22	300
Derringer	400
Savage	
Model 1902 Auto .45 caliber	1,500
Smith & Wesson	
Spur Trigger .22 revolver	250
Single Shot top break .22	200
Single Action .44 caliber	500
22/52 Target .22	275
Lady Smith .22	700
.44 Hand ejector	400
Straight line	500
.32 caliber auto	500
Walther automatics	
PPK .22	500
PPK .380	400
P38 9mm	450
Webley Fosbery	
.455 caliber auto revolver	350
RIFLES	
BRNO	
Bolt-action .22 Hornet	$600
Model 21 7 × 57	600
Browning	
.22 auto	250
Grade III .22	800
Safari Bolt Action	500
Olympian Grade Bolt Action	1,500
Bar Grade I	400
Bar Grade IV	100

Maker and model	Current value
Mannlichter-Schoenaur (bolt action)	
Carbine	500
.22 caliber bolt action	500
Marlin (lever actions)	
Model 93 Lever	300
Model 94 .44-40	350
Model 97 .22	300
Model 95 .45-70	450
Mauser	
Commercial Sporter bolt action	500
Remington	
Rolling Block Single Shot	300
Model 12A Pump	200
Model 121 Pump	300
Model 25 Slide Action .25/20	200
Model 720A High Power bolt	450
Sako Vixen	
.22 Hornet Bolt Action	375
Finnwolf Lever Action	375
Savage	
99 Lever Action	350
Stevens single-shot rifles	
Favorite .22	150
Walnut Hill .22	450
#44 Center fire	275
#44½ Center fire	375
Schuetzen rifle	1,000
Winchester	
Model 73 Lever ·	500
Single Shot .32-40	400
.22 Windner Musket	300
Model 80 Lever	700
Model 90 Pump .22	300
Model 92 Lever .44-40	550
Model 53 Lever .30-30	600
Model 65 Lever .218	—
Model 94 .30-30	350
Model 64 .30-30	450

Maker and model	Current value
Model 95 .30-06	600
Model 06 Pump .22	300
Model 52 Colt Sporter .22	850
Model 54 Bolt .30-06	275
Model 61 Pump .22	300
Model 70 Bolt .30-06	375
Model 70 Bolt Super Grade	650

SHOTGUNS

Maker and model	Current value
Barker Paragon 12 gauge	$400
Browning	
Auto 5	375
Auto 5 grade 111	1,000
Auto 5 grade IV	1,500
Superimposed O/U	
Standard 1000	1,000
Grade II Pigeon	1,750
Grade III Pointer	2,500
Grade IV Diana	3,500
Grade V Midas	4,500
Charles Daly side by side	
Regent Diamond	4,000
Diamond	3,500
Empire	2,000
Fox side by side	
Sperling Worth	400
Grade A	800
Grade CE	1,600
Grade XE	2,900
Grade DE	5,000
Grade FE	8,500
Francotte	
Box Lock	—
Knockabout	1,800
Grade 25	3,500
Greener side by side	
Empire	1,250
D H 40	2,500
Greifelt O/U	2,000

Maker and model	Current value
Ithaca side by side	
Field	450
#4E	1,500
Single Barrel Trap Victory	1,000
Single Barrel Trap 4E	2,000
Iver Johnson side by side	
Skeeter .410	700
Krieghoff #32 O/U	2,500
Lefever side by side	
DS Grade	400
C Grade	2,000
Merkel O/U	
Grade 200	1,000
Grade 201	1,500
Grade 203	3,200
Parker Brothers side by side	
Trojan	650
VHE	1,250
GHE	2,000
DHE	3,000
CHE	4,000
BHE	5,000
AAHE	7,000
Single-Barrel Trap Guns	
SC	1,500
SD	2,500
Remington	
#32 O/U	800
#32 Premier Grade	2,500
L.C. Smith side by side	
Field Grade	450
Ideal	650
Specialty	900
Crown	3,000
Monogram	5,000
Winchester	
Model 42 Pump .410	500
Model 12 Pump 12 gauge	375

Maker and model	Current value
Model 12 Trap 12 gauge	650
Model 21 side by side	1,500

Chapter 14 ❧ English Game Guns

HENRY CHRISTMANN

High-quality English game guns are very desirable and expensive. Those made during the period 1900 to 1939 represent the highest degree of workmanship and aesthetics in blending wood to metal. Unfortunately, many of the most esteemed firms either merged and lost their identity, or closed, following World War II. Purdey continues to build a fine quality gun, but the majority of the companies no longer produce the type or quality of gun that brought them fame. This chapter deals with the guns made during the golden era.

TYPES OF GUNS

Purdey, Boss, Holland & Holland, and Woodward all made side-lock guns in side-by-side and over-and-under configurations of highest quality. These are the most sought after models. W. W. Greener made some very attractive box-lock guns in the smaller gauges, and Westley Richards' hand-detachable lock gun is very appealing. This gun had a hinged plate on the action bottom, and by pressing a latch and opening the cover, the individual locks could be removed by hand for inspection and cleaning. Extra cased bodies were available and carried in the gun case as spares.

Typical game guns weigh as follows:

12 gauge	6 to 6½ pounds
16 gauge	5½ to 6 pounds
20 gauge	5½ to 5¾ pounds
28 gauge	5 to 5½ pounds
.410	4 to 4¾ pounds

Standard chamber length is 2½ inches. Heavy guns designed for trap, wild fowl, and pigeon shooting will be chambered for 2¾-inch or 3-inch shells. The English have been making guns of this type from the end of the black powder era to the present. It's not unusual to find old guns with steel barrels made between 1890 and 1906 with black-powder proofs only. While these early barrels are probably safe with modern light loads, it is advisable to stay with guns marked "nitro-proof" and with the maximum load of shot indicated. After 1925, the chamber length was added to the barrel markings.

Typical game guns are light in weight and designed for light loads — 1⅛ ounce or less in 12 gauge. Generally 2½-inch chambers can be safely opened up to 2¾ inches, provided you continue to use the recommended light load. While a 1¼-inch load won't necessarily damage the barrel, it is uncomfortable to use and will soon loosen the action and eventually cause splitting of the stock. Some of the larger dealers, specializing in high-grade guns, can furnish English-made 2½-inch shells in most gauges, and it's preferable to use these rather than lengthening the chamber and thereby altering the gun's original condition. Occasionally a gun will be chambered for the 2-inch shell — difficult to come by. These are extremely light guns (5 to 5½ pounds in 12 gauge). Such chambers should not be lengthened under any circumstances.

Purdey's guns are self-openers by design — open the top lever and the main spring pressure opens the gun. Other manufacturers accomplish the same thing with their guns by adding a powerful spring in the forend. Unfortunately guns of this type are difficult to close because the spring must be compressed during closing. Some people like this feature, others call them "hard closing" guns.

THINGS TO WATCH FOR

Always buy guns in at least good, and preferably excellent, original condition. Original guns showing honest and honorable use will always command higher resale value. Expertly re-blued barrels, refinished stocks, and the like are acceptable, but fool no one except the novice. Remember that these guns are 40 to 80 years old, and some wear is to be expected to the blue, stock finish, and action colors. A heavily refinished gun should raise several questions: What was wrong with it? Were the barrels damaged or pitted badly? Was the stock and checkering so worn or abused that it required cosmetic cover-up? You never need apologize for honest wear. Be especially wary of re-colored case-hardened actions. The process requires very high temperatures and invariably warps the frame, requiring the barrels to be re-fitted to the action. Also, the gun's strength will always be in doubt. The new colors never look like the original; and some are downright ugly.

If the chambers have been opened, was it neatly done? A careless job will show tool marks or reamer gouges and, in some cases, an elliptical-shaped forcing cone caused by misalignment of the reamer. Avoid guns that have been taken apart carelessly — burned screws, nicks and dings on the standing breech, and chips of wood missing around the action and side plates. Slightly rough bores are acceptable if reflected in the price, but never consider buying a gun that has deeply pitted bores. Also avoid guns that have barrels with bores enlarged by reaming out pits, bulged barrels, barrels with deep dents, cut off barrels, or guns with the chokes removed from both barrels.

The seller should give a written guarantee as to original condition, including barrel length, choke, finish, chamber length, proof markings, and whether any major repairs were made or are likely to be needed. Ejectors sometimes require timing. Single triggers, as a rule, are troublesome or become so soon after purchase. You are better off with double triggers or the American Miller single type, which has a fine reputation. In general, most repairs to these guns can be completed successfully by many of the leading domestic gunsmiths.

Be sure the gun fits you. Restocking is very expensive. It is best to buy a gun you can use as is.

ACCESSORIES

Most of the guns discussed in this chapter originally had a leather trunk case, either a lightweight V. C. case or the heavier oak and leather case. These cases add a great deal to the value and enjoyment of owning and using a gun. Unfortunately, many of these old cases have been neglected over the years, resulting in rotten leather and frail stitches. It is advisable to invest in a new V. C. case with a canvas cover if you intend to use the case. The case should include the proper accessories—some are really collectibles in themselves—such as a snap case embossed with the maker's name, an ebony cleaning rod with brass fittings, a buffalo horn jug, an oil bottle, a broken shell extractor, and a few specially ground screwdrivers with horn handles. Leather labels with the maker's name can be obtained and affixed to the exterior of the case.

REPRESENTATIVE PRICES OF FINE ENGLISH GUNS

Prices are for 12-gauge guns in excellent condition. Those in good condition are worth about half as much. Twenty-gauge guns are worth 75 percent to 100 percent more, and 28-gauge and .410 guns will bring three to five times as much. All will have automatic ejectors.

Maker and model	Current value
Boss	
Side by side	$10,000
Over and under	15,000
Churchill	
Side by side	$7,500
Box Lock Hercules	4,500
W. W. Greener side by side	—
Box Lock Royal DH 75	$3,000
Box Lock Crown DH 60	2,500
Holland & Holland Royal	$10,000
James Purdey	
Side by side	$13,500
Over and under	16,500
Westley Richards	
Deluxe Side Lock	$10,000
Box Lock Hand-Detachable Lock	6,000
Dickson Round Action	$5,000
Lancaster "Twelve-Twenty"	$8,000
Lang over and under	$7,800
Woodward	
Side by side	$10,000
Over and under	15,000

SELECTED BIBLIOGRAPHY

Burrard. *The Modern Shotgun*. 3 vol. New York: A. S. Barnes, 1961.
Curtis, Capt. P. A. *Guns and Gunning*. New York: Knopf, 1946.
Flayderman, Norm. *Guide to Antique American Firearms*, 2nd ed. Northfield, IL: Digest Books, 1980.
Greener, W. W. *The Gun and Its Development*, (Reprint of 1910 edition). New York: Bonanza Books, 1967.

Greener, W. W. *Modern Breechloaders; Modern Shotguns*, (Reprint of 1870 edition). Forest Grove, OR: Normount Technical Publications, 1971.

O'Connor, Jack. *The Shotgun Book*. New York: Knopf, 1978.

Purdey, T. D. S. *The Shotgun*, 3rd ed. London: A. & C. Black, 1962.

Thomas, Gough. *Shotguns and Cartridges for Game and Clays*. Transatlantic, 1976.

Wahl, Paul. *Gun Traders Guide*. Chicago: Follett, 1981.

Chapter 15 ❧ Cartridges, Shotshells, and Accessories

CHARLES R. SUYDAM

The firearms collections of Louis XIV of France and Henry VIII of England may have been the first to achieve high fame, but since their day, the collecting of "guns," even if not of royal quality, has grown rapidly and widely. Few gun collections, however, delve into the whole field of shooting; most contain only the gun itself and are not concerned with the powder, bullets, bullet molds, and later the cartridges, without which the gun is but an unwieldy club.

Perhaps to fill that void, there have arisen specialty collections of these related items — which frequently and properly contain none of the guns to which they are related. The most developed, organized, and widespread of these is the collecting of cartridges. Powder flasks and powder horns, singly or together, are another field of specialty, followed at considerable distance by the collecting of bullet molds, loading tools, and other accoutrements relating to shooting.

CARTRIDGES AND SHOTSHELLS

"Cartridge" is a term that describes the union of the components of the firearm that make it shoot: bullet, powder, ignition device (primer), and the metallic case that contains them. In addition, those united components used before the development of the modern metallic case are called cartridges: ball and powder in a paper container, from the seventeenth century to about 1865; and the separate-primed foil, skin, paper, or metallic cartridges of the developmental period, 1850–1870. While "cartridge" may also describe the same components for the smooth-bore shotgun, the approved term for this ammunition is "shotshell" — leaving "cartridge" for rifle and handgun ammunition. Thus cartridge collecting may include wooden or metal "cartouches" of the seventeenth century, paper-wrapped charges from the middle of the eighteenth century through the American Civil War, a wide variety of experimental types of the period 1850–1870, paper and metallic shotshells, and the metallic cartridges of war and sport

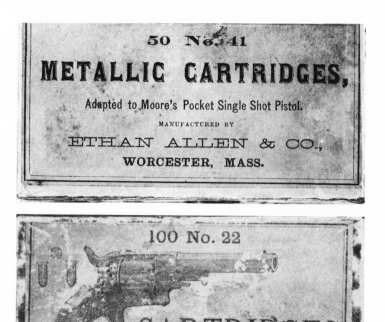

since then. As with firearms, history and the development of the machine age are contained in these small objects.

Cartridges are nearly as ubiquitous as postage stamps and matchbox covers — and as safe, as far as that goes; there is *no* inherent "gunpowder" danger in amassing a collection of sporting rifle, pistol, or shotgun ammunition. Collections vary with the interests and opportunities of the collector. They may be general — as the name implies, a sampling of all types — or specialized: shotshells, "buffalo guns," pinfire, military (both modern and old), auto pistol, and so on. Some collect only one type of cartridge: 9mm Luger, perhaps the most widely made of all centerfire cartridges; or .30-06 USG (one collector has over 1,800 specimens, all different); or .22 rimfire (another collector has nearly 1,500 different *full* boxes).

Shotshells fall into two major categories: metallic shells from the period of the introduction of the breechloader to roughly 1900; and the paper (recently, plastic) shells that essentially replaced the metallic shell (because of lower cost) sometime between 1890 and 1900.

Metallic shells are found in all gauges from 2 to .410 and even in the little .22 rimfire. They are primarily of brass, although early iron cases are known, and there were experiments after World War II in aluminum. Manufacturers' head-

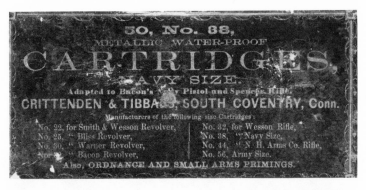

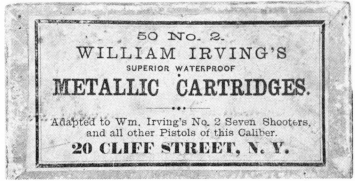

Boxes of cartridges from the early days of their manufacture are rare today and offer one of the more attractive variations of cartridge collecting. Here are rare boxes by Ethan Allen (opposite) and Crittenden & Tibbals and William Irving (above), all made before 1873.

stamps, case-length variations, and some nickel-plated cases, as well as the experimentals, provide a basis for differentiation in the collection. As in other fields, prices for individual specimens vary from 50 cents to $200 or more.

Paper shells have a long history: the Houiller pinfire cartridge of 1846 and the Pottet centerfire of 1855 both used metallic head and paper case. These and other early experimentals developed into the familiar and typical paper-cased shotshell. They were made in sizes from 1 gauge (for saluting cannon and perhaps for punt guns) to the tiny 5.5mm rimfire. After World War II, plastic replaced the paper tube as case material because of greater strength and moisture resistance. Shotshell collecting seems centered in the Mississippi River Valley, where a great abundance of small game made shotguns the natural firearm accessory of farm and village home. Prices range from $200-$400 for a rare Peters candy-striped case to 25 cents or less for a common fired case.

Cartridge collectors are well organized: the International Cartridge Collectors Association (USA) has nearly 500 members worldwide, and the European Cartridge Collector's Club is nearly as large. There are a number of state and

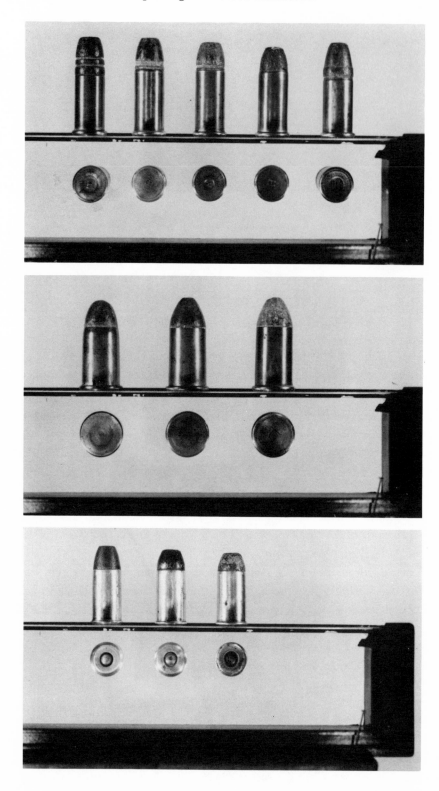

The use of a prismatic reflector makes it possible to record cartridge profiles and headstamps at the same time. Shown are variations of the .44 Henry rimfire (top), the .50 Remington pistol rimfire (center), and unusual variations of the .44 Webley centerfire (bottom) made in the United States.

local collectors' groups in the United States. The Cartridge Collectors Association meeting held each spring near Chicago has as many as 500 participants, and brings collectors from Canada and Europe as well as the United States to its meeting. The state and local groups mentioned above have monthly or quarterly meetings, to which others are invited. Nor is information lacking to assist the cartridge collector: the ICCA and the ECCC put out monthly bulletins, and the ICCA also publishes an annual yearbook. Frank Wheeler, the dean of American cartridge collectors, recently celebrated the twentieth anniversary of his important cartridge column in *The Gun Report* magazine. Nor are book references lacking: The December 1970 ICCA annual contained a 14-page annotated bibliography of over 150 sources having material of interest and aid to cartridge collectors. Since then, other references have been published. Dealers — there *are* specialists who deal only in collectors' cartridges — offer catalogs that have both descriptive material and price ranges.

One of the chief appeals of the cartridge is its relatively low cost in relation to other arms-field collectibles: a large collection can still be formed for less than 50 cents per specimen, and an enormous one for less than $1 per specimen. *The Gun Report* magazine publishes a cartridge price list alternately with a gun price list, in which over 1,600 variations are listed; prices range from 10 cents to $500. A comparison of these lists from their inception in 1965 through the present time will show that cartridges, like other historical items, have been a good financial investment; as interest in cartridge collecting has grown, so has their value.

Another desirable feature of cartridge collecting is that cartridges require relatively little storage space. While display and storage methods vary with the desires of the collector, ranging from shoe boxes to elaborate wall displays, most collectors build or acquire cabinets with shallow drawers having a corrugated bottom, in which the specimens rest securely, yet can be examined and studied easily. Simple sliding bars or a finished wooden panel can conceal the collection. Cartridges are easy to collect, have intrinsic and historic interest, are popular, and have the advantage of requiring relatively little space.

POWDER HORNS AND POWDER FLASKS

From the earliest days of the gun, the admonition "Keep your powder dry" has been of greatest importance, and how to do so has been one of the great problems. Containers of leather, wood, lead and other metals, bone, and horn were all used. By the time guns got to the New World, the commonplace cowhorn had become the most universal powder container. From the elaborate and beautiful map horns of the East Coast and Canada, to the factory-made horns for the Kentucky rifle, to the buffalo horns at the end of the muzzle-loading era, the powder horn accompanied the westward-moving American. There were large horns for military supply; long, winding horns to fit under the arm; small flattened horns to hold fine priming powder (and salt, which must also be kept dry); even crude, unfinished horns that carried grease for the wheels of the Conestoga wagons; the horn was as much a part of the westward movement as it was of the animal on which it originally grew. Kentucky rifles were possibly the first and most famous of American firearms, hence among the first to be romanticized, studied, and collected, and with them the powder horns that fed them.

Horn is not only waterproof; it is soft and easily marked with a knife or pointed object, and, scraped and polished, it offers an ideal surface on which an owner may record the important events of his life. Powder horns from the Colonial period through the Civil War are a prime historical record of their time, and are eagerly sought after by persons who may have little other interest in anything to do with firearms. Major museums have collections and exhibitions of horns. One of the major references to fine horns is *American Engraved Powder Horns*, by Stephen V. Grancsay, Curator Emeritus, Department of Arms and Armor, Metropolitan Museum of Art. It is based on horns in the collection of the Metropolitan.

But these early and elaborate — and expensive — horns are not the only ones of interest. One collection includes a small priming horn, crudely engraved with a deer, a bobcat, and the name "David Tripp" in two places; a Pennsylvania commercial horn (that is, a horn made in a factory between 1830 and 1860 for sale by gunsmiths and suppliers) with an engraved cabin, trees, and Indian teepee, and marked "John Williams Horn 1835"; and a plain smooth buffalo horn with wooden end plug held in place by wooden pegs. These and many more are typical of those still to be found in antique stores and gun shows across the nation and at reasonably low prices. But beware of fakes or newly made horns: these are generally easy to spot by color and a "fresh" look as compared with the dry look of the genuinely old horns.

There is nothing more traditionally American than a Kentucky rifle and its

Items associated with a percussion "Kentucky" rifle: knife and sheath, rare leather cap holder, box of early English percussion caps, cap horn (or salt or flintlock priming horn), powder measures made from cartridge cases, bullet mold, and balls from it. (Photo courtesy Arms Gazette Magazine)

powder horn hanging on the front of a fireplace; lacking the fireplace and the rifle, a couple of old horns can instill the same nostalgia.

Powder flasks, metallic rather than horn, were also used early in the history of firearms, but were uncommon until the development of precision metal-stamping in about 1830. Then matching sides could be soldered together, and a spring closure attached to the top, and carrying rings to the sides—and we have a lightweight, durable, and inexpensive device that can protect powder as well as a horn and be used with greater convenience. From about 1830 to the end of the muzzle-loading period, flasks of copper, brass, zinc, tin, iron, and silver were made in a dazzling array of sizes, shapes, and styles. While probably the best were made in England and France, the United States was not far behind, and all industrialized nations made them. The *magnum opus* on the subject is Ray Riling's 495-page, quarto-sized work succinctly named *The Powder Flask Book*. While not needed to actually start a collection of flasks, it becomes required reading when the collector becomes a student of them. Sales catalogs of collections—still good reference materials—were produced by F. Theodore Dexter of Topeka, Kansas, in 1947 and by Jackson Arms of Dallas, Texas, about 1962, and may still be found in specialty bookstores.

The value of powder flasks seems to be inversely proportional to their size: the smallest ones, to accompany cased sets of pistols and revolvers, are most desirable, and so are U.S. military ones. Fancy rifle-sized ones are next in value, while the large ones for shotguns, carrying a half pound or more, are generally less expensive. Again, the buyer is cautioned to beware of fakes—or reproductions—offered as originals. Perhaps without intending to deceive, many of the old flask patterns have been made from original dies and by the original British makers in recent years to accommodate the growing interest in muzzle-loading shooting. Others have been made in the old patterns, but from new dies. Most can be readily identified by finish or greater weight. As in all collecting, it is a

Indian trade beads and an engraved powder horn on a bearskin hunting pouch. The horn is a factory horn, engraved by the owner and dated 1836. Beads are late but authentic, as is the pouch.

good idea to study many specimens carefully before investing in them and to get a written guarantee from the seller if a high price is involved.

Somewhat related to powder horns and powder flasks are powder cans—the metallic cans in which powder was supplied to both the shooter of muzzle-loading arms, and the reloader of metallic cartridges and paper shells after about 1870. Before that time, black powder was sold in 50-, 25-, and 12½-pound kegs or casks, from which it was distributed by storekeeper, gunsmith, or the leader of a wagon train.

With the coming of the tin can shortly before the Civil War, it became possible to supply powder in 2½-, 1-, or ½-pound cans directly from the powder mills. Painted or printed paper labels on these cans—plus the challenge of finding the rare early ones—makes them an attractive item to accompany a collection of guns. Many of the early powders were given fanciful names, such as Pointer, Pheasant, Grouse, Waidmanns heil, and had appropriate figures on their labels which add to their rarity and interest today. As in other accessory fields, specimens vary in price from a few dollars to several hundred for a specimen that is early, rare, and in good condition.

BULLET MOLDS, LOADING TOOLS, AND OTHER ACCESSORIES

Even as it was necessary to have a container for the powder of a muzzle-loading gun, so it was necessary to have a mold to make bullets for that gun. "Bullet" means, literally, a small ball, and from the first firearms of the fourteenth century to the middle of the nineteenth, bullet and ball were synonymous. The bore size of smooth-bore guns is that of the number of balls per pound of lead: 12 bore = 12 balls to the pound, which have a diameter of about .72 inch. Part of the art of the Kentucky rifle maker was his ability to make a mold of the proper size so that a cloth- or buckskin-wrapped ("patched") ball from it would fit the rifling of the gun he had made. With the development of the science of ballistics between 1830 and 1850, bullets became elongated, cylindro-conoidal in shape, with grooves of varying pattern around the cylindrical part and, frequently, a hollow base that allowed propellant gases to expand that base into the rifling. With the coming of the breech-loading gun and metallic cartridges, there came also the realization that a reloadable cartridge was more economical than one that couldn't be reloaded, and so tools were developed to enable the shooter to reload, at home or in the field. Parallel to the development of reloading cartridges for rifle and pistol was that of the metal-based, paper-bodied cartridge ("shell") for smooth-bore guns that could also be reloaded.

Both bullet molds and reloading tools offer a collecting field: molds for early round balls, both military and civilian; and, molds for the early lead bullets of cartridge rifles and pistols in their wide variety of sizes and shapes. Some of the latter were proprietary — "For Sharps rifles" or "For Smith & Wesson .44 American" — and made by or for the firms named. Others were made by firms specializing in such items. Reloading tools followed the same paths: special tools by and for Winchester rifles, or Marlin, Remington, or Colt; and, those made by such specialty houses as the Bridgeport Gun Implement Company or the Ideal Manufacturing Company. Shotguns had their own accessories: wooden boxes, opening on both sides, for priming and reloading; wad cutters and wad funnels; shot drippers or dispensers for powder; bore scrubbers and cleaning rods; shell extractors, and many others. Military gun tools and instruments are another popular area of collecting.

A few collectors have assembled comprehensive groups of this material, but in general it has been neglected and still offers an opportunity for both inexpensive collecting and extensive research. Reference material is primarily found in original and reproduced catalogs, but there are a few monographs, such as *Early Loading Tools and Bullet Molds*, by R. H. Chamberlain, and a few shorter articles included in general arms reference works such as *Gun Digest* and *Guns & Ammo Annual*.

Engraved horns: a small priming horn, circa 1840, with crude deer and the name David Tripp, resting against a calling horn of circa 1835–1840, masterfully engraved with Diana and her stag, and a fox hunting scene. (Photo courtesy Scott Beinfeld)

Military accoutrements — primarily bayonets, but other items as well — offer another collecting interest in the arms field. Civil War material has been well studied and brings relatively high prices, but militaria from the two world wars is still available in quantity and at "war surplus" prices and offers both a collecting and a studying challenge. Quite a bit of material has been printed on bayonets, but slings, belts, holsters, uniform buttons and insignia, and similar items are relatively untouched and unknown.

To the collector with limited means or limited space, cartridges, powder horns and flasks, loading tools and accessories, and military accoutrements offer a challenging field for acquisition and study.

SELECTED BIBLIOGRAPHY: CARTRIDGES

As mentioned in the text, the ICCA listed over 150 sources of information on collectors' cartridges in their 1970 yearbook; anyone making a collection of cartridges should write to A. D. Amesbury, 4065 Montecito Ave., Tucson, AZ 85711, to inquire about membership and the availability of back issues of the yearbook. In addition, Frank Wheeler, R.R. 1, Box 30, Osborne, KS 67473, publishes a list of cartridge-related books in print and should be contacted for latest materials available. *The Gun Report*, Box 111, Aledo, IL 61231, has the best monthly feature on cartridges in print and the only current-value list published. In addition, the following books will be of value to the collector.

Amesbury, A. D. *Let's Start a Cartridge Collection.* Printed by the author, 4065 Montecito Ave., Tucson, AZ 85711. Introductory monograph.

Barnes, F. C. *Cartridges of the World.* Northfield, IL: Digest Books, 1965. A wide-ranging survey of the cartridge field.

Datig, F. A. *Cartridges for Collectors*, Vols. I, II, III. Los Angeles: Borden, 1965-1967. Drawings and data on a wide variety of cartridges.

Erlmeier, H. A., and Brandt, J. K. *Manual of Pistol and Revolver Cartridges.* Wiesbaden, Germany: J. E. Erlmeier Verlag, 1967. Excellent reference with English and German text, good photos.

Lewis, Col. B. R. *Small Arms & Ammunition in the U.S. Service 1776–1865.* Washington, D.C.: Smithsonian Institution, 1956 and reprints. The basic reference on Civil War and pre–Civil War military ammunition.

Logan, H. C. *Cartridges.* Harrisburg, PA: Stackpole, 1959. A basic and introductory work of great value.

Steward, Frank. *Shotgun Shells.* St. Louis: B&P Associates, 1969. The only reference on shotshells.

Suydam, C. R. *The American Cartridge.* Los Angeles: Borden, 1974 (reprint). The basic reference on rimfires.

White, H. P., and Munhall, B. D. *Cartridge Headstamp Guide.* Bel Air, MD: White Laboratories, 1977. A wide review of headstamps, sporting and military.

SELECTED BIBLIOGRAPHY: OTHER FIELDS

Chamberlain, R. H. *Early Loading Tools and Bullet Molds.* Published by the author, Porterville, CA 1970. A good but brief introduction to the field.

Gavin, Wm. G. *Accoutrement Plates, North & South, 1861–65.* Philadelphia: Riling & Lentz, 1963. Excellent study of this material.

Grancsay, S. V. *American Engraved Powder Horns.* Philadelphia: Ray Riling Arms Books, 1965. Descriptive list of horns in the collection of the Metropolitan Museum of Art, New York City.

Riling, R. *The Powder Flask Book.* New York: Bonanza Books, 1953. The basic and complete reference on this material.

Chapter 16 ❧ Sporting Calendars and Posters

ROBERT F. WOHLERS

Old gun, ammunition, and fishing company advertising has recently become one of the most popular and desirable items for sporting collectors. The posters and calendars for the period 1890 to 1925 are the most sought after and represent some of the finest artwork ever produced in the sporting field.

Starting with a 1923 Winchester calendar purchased 10 years ago, my collection has been narrowed to the posters and calendars relating to the harvesting of waterfowl and fishing. While personally limiting my own collection to those items because of display problems, I do not wish to imply that they are the most collectible. A large percentage of the items are devoted to the harvesting of big game.

About 20 companies distributed this advertising. If you assume that each produced a yearly calendar and two posters during a period of 35 years, a total of 2,100 items would be available.

Some of the outstanding artists were Lynn Bogue Hunt, Phillip R. Goodwin, G. Muss Arnolt, Edmund Osthaus, and Alexander Pope.

The one feature other than the outstanding artwork that makes the posters and calendars so desirable is that they were printed through the process of stone lithography. This process is practically nonexistent today because of the prohibitive cost, and as a result, none of the colors today are so brilliant. Almost all of the items were produced on excellent quality paper. The most desirable old advertising signs are those lithographed on tin. These are all self-framed, and to the best of my knowledge, there were only four or five tin signs distributed by the gun and ammunition companies.

Although the best source of these items used to be antique shops, old hardware stores, and hunting shacks, today they have to be obtained from other collectors and sought out at the numerous antique advertising shows. Several books are available on early advertising, but the gun and ammunition items seem to be the most rare. The value can range up to $1,500 each for the paper items and up to $3,000 for the tin items.

Properly framed, these items make outstanding accent pieces for other sport-

ing collections. All of the items in my collection have been framed and displayed under nonglare glass. To conserve space, I have not matted them but have used a liner within the frame. Once acquired, the items should be framed and properly displayed both for preservation and so others may enjoy them.

A major problem today with these items, as with all antiques, is the number of reproductions. Some of these are properly marked but many have not been,

and the buyer must be aware of this. The wise thing to do is to deal with someone you know and trust. Otherwise, note that the colors of reproductions are
inferior and the quality of paper is poor.

SELECTED BIBLIOGRAPHY

Latham, Sid. *Great Sporting Posters of the Golden Age*. Harrisburg, PA:
    Stackpole Books, 1978.
Klug, Ray. *Antique Advertising Encyclopedia*. Gas City, IN: L-W Promotions,
    1978.
Cope, Jim. *Old Advertising*. Austin, TX: Great American Publishing Com-
    pany, 1980.

Chapter 17 ❧ Western Memorabilia

WILLIAM C. KETCHUM, JR.

Until not so long ago, collectors interested in objects used or produced in the Old West confined themselves fairly much to Indian crafts and artifacts and to the various weapons used by both whites and Indians. Today, however, there are new and exciting areas opening up — areas in which even the newest collector can find a foothold and still not spend a fortune. This comes at a good time, too, for with more Americans moving west and southwest, there is an increasing awareness of the history and importance of these areas and the antiques and collectibles to be found there.

MINERS

The development of the West was to a great extent built on mining, and the riches that came out of such towns as Cripple Creek, Colorado, and Gold Hill, Nevada, were legendary. Today, most of the gold and silver is gone, but the tools and other objects used by the miners survive, and they are highly collectible. There are the picks and shovels used to scratch out the ore-bearing rock, the famous miners' pans employed in scooping sand and water from streambeds in search of the ever-elusive "color," and the canteens and cooking utensils carried into the often-dry foothills by the hopeful prospectors. The "hard rock" miners, those who blasted their way into the very heart of the mountain seeking precious metals, also left signs of their passing: metal or pressed wood "hard hats;" giant pneumatic drills, and much smaller hand drills that were driven into the rock with a sledge hammer; crowbars, or prybars; and a variety of lighting devices from big kerosene lamps to the tiny iron "sticking tommies," — candle holders that had a long sharp point to be driven into a beam or even a stone wall. Once the ore was out and separated (in a variety of large machines such as muckers, jaw crushers, and stamp mills, which are themselves collectible, though too large for most of us to house), it had to be carried about in "pokes" or dust bags, weighed on a set of pocket scales or a fancy brass bullion scale, and assayed for purity, a process that produced many collectible objects, including mortars and pestles, ore splitters, and sifting screens.

Indeed, the mining industry has produced such a variety of interesting objects that almost any collector can find something appealing. For those with lots of room and an interest in the mechanics of the process, there are ore buckets, hoist machinery, supply wagons, ore trains and their engines, and mine elevators. For collectors with less room, there are signs and advertising materials from mines, assayers' offices, and suppliers; deeds to long-abandoned claims; and the extremely attractive stock certificates issued to shareholders in the old mines.

And, happily, most of these objects are still fairly inexpensive. Larger equipment, especially in working order, can cost thousands of dollars, but it is still possible to find a big ore bucket for less than $100, and broken down ore cars and muckers are still rusting away on western hillsides. Smaller and generally more sought-after objects are also often reasonable. Stock certificates and deeds can be had for from $5 to $20, while an early twentieth-century miner's pan may cost $35 to $45, and picks, shovels, and sledges can be found for $20. Lighting devices come in many shapes and forms and at many prices. An ordinary kerosene wall lantern may cost no more than $25, but a rare, miner's tinder box will be closer to $200. "Sticking tommies" are in the $30 to $120 range, while the later fat and carbide head lamps usually cost about $40 to $70. All in all, there is a wide range of both prices and objects, and the material is still there to be found.

MOUNTAIN MEN

Before the miners came, there were the mountain men, the trappers who traded for furs with the Indians or ran their own lines. These hardy adventurers traveled light, but they still left behind some interesting artifacts. Most important, of course, are their weapons—muzzleloading flintlock rifles, wrought-iron trade axes and hatchets, and various gun-loading equipment, including powder horns and bullet pouches. Many such items have long been a part of private collections, and items that are available are seldom inexpensive. A good, early, Northwest Bay trade gun will bring as much as $1,000, while skinning knives trade at about $200, and a good, carved and decorated powder horn will command a figure in the high hundreds. Fortunately though, there are less expensive mementos of that era. Many small-game traps can be found, often for as little as $20 to $40 (though a wicked-looking bear trap can set you back $300). Homemade gut and wood snowshoes can be found for $50 to $200. Fish spears can be found for $30 to $60. Trappers' hats and clothing, often Indian made and decorated, are hard to find but, once located, are frequently inexpensive.

BUFFALO HUNTERS

Related to the mountain men were the buffalo "runners" or hunters (indeed, many of the former turned to killing buffalo when the beaver supply declined). Other than their huge rifles, like the Sharps and the Henry, and the Bowie knife, a sword-like blade-of-all-trades, the commercial hunters left little to mark their passing. They dressed like everyone else, and their cooking or household implements can seldom be distinguished. However, they and other hunters left many trophies, from huge stuffed bison heads, to furniture made of deer, elk, and longhorn-cattle horns. All these objects are quite collectible. Good guns will, of course, bring prices in the $300 to $1,500 range, and Bowie knives may command similar figures, but smaller objects can still be found at modest prices. A good thing to keep an eye out for is the horn furniture, which was often used in hunting lodges. In the East, good pieces will be priced at $500 or more, but it is often possible to find them for far less in the West.

RAILROADS

Another booming category of collectibles is material from western railroading. After the Civil War, transcontinental lines began to link the West Coast and the states east of the Mississippi, and the new form of transportation was the major factor in the development of the western states. Railroading was, and is, big business and has spawned many collectible objects. For those with room to spare, or who are looking for a place to house a restaurant or a store, there are railroad cars and even the old steam engines. Restored examples will bring $30,000 to $60,000, so this is hardly a poor man's hobby.

On the other hand, there are the objects used in the cars, especially the dining cars. Railway silver, glass, and dishware was frequently marked with the name of the line and sometimes even with a picture of a train or station, so it is highly sought. Fortunately though, such wares were produced in great quantity, especially after 1920, and it is possible to obtain ironstone dishes for as little as $10 to $25 apiece. Electroplated silverware goes for $25 to $100. Glassware will bring $15 to $20 for a small glass, or $175 to $250 for a rare blown-glass table ornament. As in all fields, of course, truly rare pieces (such as the Union Pacific historical platter, circa 1890–1900, that sells for $600 to $700) will bring high prices. But dining-car collectibles are still a relatively inexpensive field.

Another area of great interest to many railway buffs is that of the tools and clothing used by the railroaders. Perhaps the area of greatest collector concentration is that of lighting. Trains required many different types of lighting devices, from large marker and switch-stand lights, to engine headlamps, and the various kerosene, candle, electric, and carbide hand-lamps carried by track and line personnel. Again, there is a great price range. Common hand-lanterns with railroad logos will cost $40 to $60, but the same piece in electroplated silver (given to retiring trainmen) will cost $250 to $350. Marker and switch-stand lamps will bring $250 to $750 depending on complexity and condition, and an old engine headlamp (if you can find one) will cost from $700 to $1,000.

Associated collectibles include engine bells at $400 to $600; locomotive number plates ($300 to $700); brake covers and handles (a bargain at $15 to $20); office items such as logbooks ($50 to $75); train design blueprints ($60 to $100); station signs ($70 to $250); station and car furnishings, including oak waiting-room chairs and cast-iron passenger car seats; and the various handcars used in loading freight cars. Furniture — except for the $250 to $300 benches that are now showing up in people's living rooms — is a relatively untapped area.

For those who prefer smaller things, there is a lively interest in the brass and copper buttons used on railway workers' uniforms, the locks and keys used to secure a line's materials, and the many types of advertising materials issued to promote the western lines. At $15 to $20 each, buttons are a good buy as are locks and keys in the $5 to $20 range. Advertising materials are much more diverse and command a great range of prices. A good, early, colored advertising poster will easily bring $500 to $750, while it is possible to find small time-tables, advertising brochures, and bills of lading for as little as $2 to $3.

FINDING WESTERN MEMORABILIA

The ease with which one finds western collectibles depends largely on the field of concentration. Railroad items are popular and well established. As a consequence, there are many specialized dealers in this field, and most antiques dealers will have some items. Likewise, they can be found at most shows and at auctions, particularly in the West. If, on the other hand, you are seeking mining or mountain-men memorabilia, you will probably have to be more adventuresome. Few dealers handle these pieces, so one has to learn what they look like and then seek them out in unlikely places, such as junk and second-hand shops, church sales, and (especially in the mining areas) yard and barn sales. The process is much like treasure hunting and can be just as rewarding, because items found this way are almost always much less expensive than those purchased from dealers — to say nothing of the tales one will be able to tell of how they were found! Another way to discover such elusive treasures is by advertising (a good method with all antiques and collectibles) in publications related to collecting and in small local newspapers in areas where the artifacts were once common. And, remember, sheer luck aside, the collector who usually has the most and the best has generally paid his dues with days of hard work and research, tracking down his wants.

DISPLAYING AND PROTECTING YOUR FINDS

Larger pieces, particularly those of metal, must often be stored in sheds or barns and displayed as they stand. Serious collectors will differ as to whether machinery should be restored and repainted, and that is a matter of personal judgment. Certainly, though, every effort should be taken to avoid rust and damage as well as theft, which is becoming more and more of a problem.

Smaller bulky items may be stored on shelves, in cases, or fixed to a wall. Mining tools look particularly attractive against a white or paneled wall. And the tiniest objects, such as bullet molds, buttons, or locks, can often be shown to advantage under glass, perhaps as an arrangement on a coffee table. There is really no limit other than personal ingenuity as to how such things may be displayed.

Finally, anyone collecting western memorabilia in any quantity will want to think about having it insured against fire, theft, or other calamity. Generally, larger items will be covered by a household policy, while smaller and more valuable pieces may require a fine-arts floater. In any case, insurance company requirements and local laws vary so widely that the only way to be sure that one is adequately covered is to consult a local insurance company or broker.

SELECTED BIBLIOGRAPHY

Beitz, Les. *Treasury of Frontier Relics*. New York: A.S. Barnes & Co., 1977.

Beck, Doreen. *Collecting Country and Western Americana*. New York: Hamlyn, 1975.

Ketchum, William C., Jr. *Western Memorabilia*. New York: Hammond/ Rutledge, 1980.

Klamkin, Charles. *Railroadiana*. New York: Funk & Wagnalls, 1976.

Chapter 18 ❧ Rodeo Bronzes

PATRICIA JANIS BRODER

During the past century, the American rodeo has become a symbol of the American West. The rodeo is a special world filled with excitement, danger, and glory. The heroes of this world are the rodeo riders — independent, competitive, and fearless: the embodiment of the American frontier spirit. Today the rodeo is celebrated as the last stronghold of rugged individualism, dedicated to perpetuating the virtues that built and sustained the American West. The rodeo performer is the symbol of American independence. Receiving no salary, expense money, or guarantee, rodeo performers must pay their own way; in truth, most never earn back their entrance money. Confrontation of danger is a way of life and crippling injuries are an ever-present threat and impending reality. The rodeo is a stage of suspense and heroics where the individual alone must perform, excel, and win. Only those who are in top physical condition and have mental toughness, and good luck, will be victors. It is no wonder the rodeo has been called "the suicide circuit."

The modern rodeo cowboy is the direct descendant of the lone cowhand and bronc buster of the 1860s. The first American cowboys, the first horsemen in North America to work cattle, were the Mexican *vaqueros* of the sixteenth century. The rodeo stock, the cattle and horses, are descended from the Spanish cattle and mustangs that the *conquistadores* brought to the New World in the second half of the sixteenth century. Spanish priests subsequently drove the longhorns to the missions that they established in California, Texas, and New Mexico, and by the eighteenth century, the missions of the Southwest were raising great herds of cattle. A severe drought in the first half of the nineteenth century caused many cattle owners in the Southwest to abandon their herds, which went wild and gradually adapted to conditions of freedom on the range.

As the young American nation grew, the increase in population necessitated an expanding beef industry, and it became economically profitable to round up wild herds and market them for eastern consumption. After Texas joined the Union in 1845, Texans drove great herds of cattle eastward to New Orleans and northeast to Missouri, Illinois, and Iowa. During the Civil War, a lack of manpower and shipping facilities brought a temporary halt to development of the cattle industry; however, once the war was over, the herds of longhorns on the Texas plains were one of the principal assets of the destitute South. During the war years, the herds of cattle in the Southwest had multiplied beyond the capacity of the land to sustain them. To the north lay rich grasslands and to the east the war-starved cities. The building of the railroads, the gold boom in Colorado, and the establishment of Indian reservations also created a great demand for beef, and throughout the Southwest, cowboys began the job of rounding up the longhorns and herding them to railheads in Kansas and Missouri.

The post–Civil War years were the years of the historic cattle drives, romantic in retrospect, but in daily reality long, tedious hours of grueling work. To relieve the boredom, the cowboys competed with their companions and with rival trail hands to see who had the greatest skill in riding and roping. At the railheads, the cowboys celebrated the end of the long drive with wagers and competitions to see who could ride the meanest horses and rope with the greatest ability. It was a time of high spirits for all. Before long, a few towns decided to invite the cowboys to stage their competitions in the town squares. The townspeople loved the color and excitement, and soon communities began to offer prize money to attract more contestants and charged admissions to the spectators to raise the prize money. Many believed that the first rodeo was held in Pecos, Texas, in 1882, when merchants invited the local cowboys to celebrate July 4th by holding a contest.

Today there are hundreds of rodeos each year, and millions of people enjoy the action and spirit of the rodeo. Even though the majority of today's rodeo riders are professional athletes, who specialize in specific events, the original rodeo riders were cowboys, and to all the world the rodeo rider is still thought of as a cowboy. The rodeo calls for bravery, courage, and skill and offers unequalled moments of drama, high excitement, and humor.

Rodeo sculpture, like the rodeo itself, is at once heroic, spectacular, and frequently humorous. To those who love this most popular western sporting event, the combined heroism and humor of the rodeo have irresistible appeal. Rodeo bronzes often bear such descriptive titles as *End of a Short Acquaintance* or *Doubtful Outcome*.

The first sculptures to celebrate the dangers, thrills, and excitement in the competitions between rider and horse were bronzes of bronc riders. The very nature of his work made every cowboy a potential bronc rider. One of the first bronzes of a cowboy riding a bucking horse was Frederic Remington's *The Bronco Buster*, copyrighted in 1895. For Remington, the bronco buster symbolized the story of the American West.

In 1893, two years before Remington's *The Bronco Buster*, Phimister Proctor created a giant plaster of a cowboy on a bucking horse for the fairgrounds of the World's Columbian Exposition in Chicago. It was called *The Cowboy*. Proctor, who frequently served as a rodeo judge, had carefully chosen both horse and rider. The rider was a 6-foot, 3-inch character from Pendleton, Oregon, named

The Bronco Buster. *Frederic Remington. 1905. Height 32½ inches. This is a larger edition of the work copyrighted 1895. (Photograph courtesy Private Collection)*

"Red" whom Proctor had to bail out of jail for horse theft. In 1915, Proctor cast in bronze a small model of *The Cowboy* which became known as *The Buckaroo*. In 1918, a heroic model of *The Buckaroo*, renamed *The Bronco Buster*, was erected in the Civic Center in Denver, Colorado. In 1898, Solon Borglum completed *Lassoing Wild Horses* and *The Bucking Bronco* and in 1901, *One in a Thousand*. America's first cowboy sculptor, Borglum's greatest strength was in his knowledge and understanding of the men and animals of the American West.

The Buckaroo (The Bronco Buster). *Alexander Phimister Proctor. 1915. Height 28½ inches. (Photo courtesy Private Collection)*

Charlie Russell also completed several sculptures of the cowboy in direct competition with the bucking horse. In Russell's sculptures, (i.e. *The Weaver*, *When the Best of Riders Quit*) the horse, not the cowboy, was the hero. Russell wrote of the bronc rider: "An Ingin once told me that bravery came from the hart not the head. If my red brother is right, bronc riders and bulldogers are all

When the Best of Riders Quit. *Charles M. Russell. circa 1920. Height 14½ inches. Collection: Whitney Gallery of Western Art, Cody, Wyoming. (Photo courtesy Harry N. Abrams Inc.*, Bronzes of the American West *by Patricia Janis Broder.)*

hart above the wast band, but it is a good bet there is nothing under there hat but hair."

The prowess and bravery of the cowboy roper and rider remained a favorite subject during the 1920s and 1930s. *The Sun Fisher* and *Scratchin' 'Em* by Sally

One in a Thousand (The Bronco Buster) *Solon Borglum. 1901. Height 43½ inches. (Photo courtesy Mrs. Mervyn Davies)*

James Farnham; *The Cowboy* by Earl Heikka; *Cowboy Roping a Calf* by Clinton Shepherd; *Bronco Buster* by Jo Mora; *Brahma Bull* by Madeline Park; *The Sun Fisher* by R. Farrington Elwell; these are just a few of the hundreds of sculptures which celebrate the bravery, timing, and coordination of the American cowboy. There are even a few Art Deco models, such as, *The Cowboy* by John Held, Jr. Some of the earliest sculpture to portray specific rodeo events were the trophies created by Charles Beil in the 1930s for the Calgary Stampede.

Since 1960, many artists have devoted much of their time and energy to completing sculptures of virtuoso rodeo heroics. Rodeo bronzes depict every aspect of the rodeo and rodeo life. The traditional rodeo events are bareback bronc riding, saddle bronc riding, bull riding, steer wrestling, calf roping, team

Pay Window. *Bob Scriver. 1968. Height 28 inches. (Photo courtesy Graham Gallery, New York City)*

roping, steer roping, and barrel racing. In addition to the rodeo riders and animals, there are sculptures that pay tribute to every participant in the rodeo, including the pick-up man, the rodeo clown, and even the show producer.

Among the contemporary artists who have created individual bronzes and series of bronzes of rodeo performers and animals are Wolf Pogzeba (*Brahma Bull Rider*, 1965; *Bronco Rider*, 1965), Frank Polk (*Bad Time for the Clown*, 1971; *Bareback Rider*, 1969; *Bulldogger*, 1968; *The Calf Roper*, 1970; *Saddle*

Bronc Rider, 1968; *Team Roping,* 1969), Clemente Spampinato (*Bulldogging Contest,* 1955; *Saddle Bronc Rider,* 1953), and Lawrence Tenney Stevens (*Bareback Rider,* 1964; *Barrel Racer,* 1969; *Brahma Bull Riding,* 1962; *The Bulldogger,* 1964; *Calf Roping,* 1965; *Saddle Bronc Riding,* 1970; *Team Tying,* 1963; *Trick Riding,* 1968).

Today there are many contemporary sculptors who are devoted to portraying the excitement and romance of the rodeo. The collector of rodeo bronzes is usually a collector of Western or equestrian art and frequently of both. Many collections include both historic and contemporary sculptures.

During the last ten years, there has been tremendous price appreciation of both historic and contemporary Western art. Today many contemporary rodeo bronzes sell at multiples of their issuing price. Despite the soaring art prices, it is all-important for the collector to buy for personal aesthetic and intellectual enjoyment as well as investment potential. This is particularly true of contemporary art, for only a crystal ball could reveal tomorrow's masters. The collector should learn as much as possible about both the sculptor and the sculpture. Who is the artist? Is he or she living, and where? Has he or she won any major competitions? Is the artist represented in any permanent museum collection? When was the bronze modeled? How many were cast? Was the bronze cast in more than one size? What was the issuing price of the bronze? How does that compare with the current price? It is imperative to buy from reputable sources — established dealers, museum exhibitions and sales, and recognized competitions (for example, The Cowboy Artists of America or The National Academy of Western Art).

Below are listed the rodeo bronzes of five contemporaries who specialize in representations of the rodeo. Because of the limitations of space, this list includes only a few of the many artists devoted to portraying the rodeo world. The information should serve as a guide for future inquiry.

REPRESENTATIVE CONTEMPORARY RODEO BRONZES

Bob Scriver (b. 1914, Browning, Montana; 1980 studio in Browning, Montana)

Title	Date	Height	Edition	Issue price	Current price
The King	1968	19½"	*	$1,500	$4,500
The Producer	1972	22½"	*	2,000	5,200
The Contestant	1968	15½"	*	1,250	4,500
The Cowboy's Working Quarter Horse	1972	16½"	*	2,000	6,000
Saddle Bronc	1971	17"	*	2,000	6,000

Two Champs. *Harry Jackson. 1974. Height 30 inches. (Photo courtesy Wyoming Foundry Studios, Inc., New York City)*

Title	Date	Height	Edition	Issue price	Current price
Bareback Bronc	1971	15½"	*	2,000	5,000
Brangus Bucking Bull	1972	20"	*	2,500	10,000
Rodeo Steer	1969	16"	*	1,250	4,000
Roping Calf	1969	12"	*	950	3,000
Rodeo Queen's Grand Entry	1972	21"	*	1,500	5,800
Let'er Buck	1968	25"	*	2,000	6,500
Two Champions	1972	20½"	*	2,000	6,500
Pay Window	1968	28"	*	4,500	22,000
Steer Jerker	1972	16½"	*	4,500	15,000
10 Seconds Flat	1968	11"	*	950	3,000
Beating the Slack	1968	22"	*	4,500	15,000
Heading for a Wreck	1968	19"	*	4,500	30,000
Twisting His Tail	1968	11"	*	950	4,200
Laying the Trap	1968	20"	*	4,500	30,000
Rodeo's Most Dangerous Game	1972	15"	*	17,500	75,000
National Finals	1972	19½"	*	2,000	6,500
A Short Trip	1972	20"	*	2,000	6,500
Not For Glory	1971	19"	*	4,500	25,000
Re-ride	1968	19"	*	3,500	12,000
Heading for Home	1968	15"	*	2,000	10,000
Tornado	1972	11"	*	1,500	3,500
Freckles Brown on Tornado	1970	21"	*	2,000	6,800
A Twister	1970	22"	*	2,000	6,800
A Hooker	1970	20½"	*	2,000	6,800
A Spinner	1970	18"	*	2,000	6,800
An Honest Try	1968	30¼"	*	4,500	25,000
Bull Riders Best Friend	1972	11"	*	1,500	4,000
The Champ	1973	18½"	*	1,250	4,000
Rodeo's First Event	1980	16½"	100	1,450	1,450
Rodeo's Main Event	1980	16½"	100	1,450	1,450

*Open during artist's lifetime.

Harry Jackson (b. 1924, Chicago, Illinois; 1980 studio in Lost Cabin, Wyoming, and Camaiore, Italy)

Title	Date	Height	Edition	Issue price	Current price
Two Champs (Old Steamboat and Clayton Danks)	—	30"	40	$5,000	$50,000
Two Champs (Painted)	—	30"	20	8,500	45,000
Two Champs II	—	23½"	100	—	11,000
Two Champs II (Painted)	—	23½"	50	—	12,000

Doubtful Outcome. *Grant Speed. 1966. Height 10¼ inches. (Photo courtesy Morgerson Gallery, Chicago)*

Grant Speed (b. 1930, San Angelo, Texas; 1980 studio in Lindon, Utah)

Title	Date	Height	Edition	Issue price	Current price
End of a Short Acquaintance	1965	8¾"	—	$600	$2,500
Fittin' a Hungry Ride	1966	8¾"	—	600	2,500
Doubtful Outcome	1966	10¼"	—	600	2,500

John D. Free (b. 1929, Pawhuska, Oklahoma; 1980 studio in Pawhuska, Oklahoma)

Title	Date	Height	Edition	Issue price	Current price
Where the Money's Made (Calf Roping Event)	1966	7"	30	$1,500	$2,500

Title	Date	Height	Edition	Issue price	Current price
Layin' A Trip (Steer Roping Event)	1966	8"	18	1,300	3,000
Cuttin' One Back (Cutting Horse Event)	1965	6½"	18	900	3,000
Boogered (Saddle Bronc Event)	1965	4"	2	300	1,000
Doggin' (Bull Dogging Event)	1966	4½"	18	600	1,800
Layin' Him Down (Steer Roping Event)	1971	7"	30	1,500	2,000
Bustin' 'im (Steer Roping Event)	1980	7"	50	600	1,800

Don Polland (b. 1932, Los Angeles, California; 1980 studio in Prescott, Arizona)

Title	Date	Height	Edition	Issue price	Current price
Barrel Racer	1978	3½"	350	$350	$700
Calf Roper	1978	3¾"	350	350	700
Bull Rider	1978	5"	350	335	650
Steer Wrestling	1978	4½"	350	650	1,300
Bareback Rider	1978	4¾"	350	335	650
Saddle Bronc	1978	5¾"	350	335	650
Team Roping	1978	4"	350	650	1,300

Layin' A Trip. *John D. Free. 1966. Height 8 inches. (Photo courtesy the artist)*

SELECTED BIBLIOGRAPHY

Broder, Patricia Janis. *Bronzes of the American West*. New York: Harry N. Abrams, Inc., 1974.

Craven, Wayne. *Sculpture in America*. New York: Thomas Y. Crowell, 1968.

Davies, A. Mervyn. *Solon H. Borglum: A Man Who Stands Alone*. Chester, CT: Pequot Press, 1974.

Exhibition Catalogues, Cowboy Artists of America. Oklahoma City, National Cowboy Hall of Fame, 1968–1972; Phoenix, Phoenix Art Museum, 1973–1979.

Exhibition Catalogues, National Academy of Western Art. Oklahoma City, National Cowboy Hall of Fame, 1973–1979.

Hassrich, Peter. *Frederic Remington: Paintings, Drawings, and Sculpture in the Amon Carter Museum and the Sid W. Richardson Foundation Collections*. New York: Harry N. Abrams, Inc., 1973.

Hedgpeth, Don. *From Broncs to Bronzes: The Life and Work of Grant Speed*. Flagstaff, AZ: Northland Press, 1979.

Jackson, Harry. *Lost Wax Bronze Casting*. Flagstaff, AZ: Northland Press, 1972.

Barrel Racer. *Don Polland. 1978. Height 3½ inches. (Photo courtesy Trailside Galleries, Jackson, Wyoming, and Scottsdale, Arizona)*

McCracken, Harold. *The Charles M. Russell Book.* Garden City, NY: Doubleday and Co., 1957.

McCracken, Harold. *Frederic Remington: Artist of the Old West.* Philadelphia: J. B. Lippincott Co., 1947.

Proctor, Hester Elizabeth (ed.). *Alexander Phimister Proctor, Sculptor in Buckskin: An Autobiography.* Norman, OK: University of Oklahoma Press, 1974.

Renner, Frederic G. *Charles M. Russell: Paintings, Drawings, and Sculpture in the Amon G. Carter Collection.* New York: Harry N. Abrams, Inc., 1973.

Schnell, Fred. *The Suicide Circuit.* Chicago: Rand McNally and Company, 1971.

Scriver, Robert. *An Honest Try.* Kansas City: Lowell Press, 1975.

Chapter 19 ❧ Modern Handmade Knives

SID LATHAM

With the renaissance in blade making now taking place in our country, craftsmen are turning out knives that have not been equaled at any time in history. Today's masters of the bench-made knife are using steels that were unknown to their predecessors a decade ago. These blades are the result of metallurgical research and experimentation, much of it by the craftsmen themselves. Progress has accelerated to the point where improvements evolve in months rather than years. Just six years ago, there were fewer than a dozen full-time knifemakers in the country; now there are more than 200.

The turning point in the history of knifemaking began in 1969 when men like Bob Loveless, Dan Dennehy, Lloyd Hale, Rod Chappel, Ted Dowell, Bill Moran, and a small group of other fine craftsmen suddenly received recognition by the sporting press. Their names became household words, at least among sportsmen, and orders suddenly began to fill their mailboxes. The knives were excellent, many crafted of steels that held an edge better than any knife used before, and the workmanship was superb. What had started as an adjunct to the sporting scene soon became a province of the collector as well.

The skill of modern cutlers in bringing together raw materials into a thing of beauty enters into the realm of art. Rod "Caribou" Chappel says, "When a man buys a handmade knife he is also buying something of the immortality of the maker." That there are degrees of immortality, or skill, enters the picture. But, in essence, any man working as an artist, regardless of the medium, is creating his vision of beauty.

Naturally, the collector frequently becomes confused by the plethora of knives offered; where to begin, or what to collect, can often become overwhelming problems. Some people collect everything in sight, while others, perhaps more selective, gain some experience before defining their interest. There are, for example, fighting knives, boot knives, Bowies, Arkansas Toothpicks, hunters, skinners, caping knives, fishing knives, replicas of ancient weapons, folders, knives for skin divers — and George Herron even makes a knife for shucking oysters. So it's easily seen there are enough sizes, shapes, and categories for the most ardent collector. Some specialize in the knives of one maker, but with the variation of style, model, blade length, handle material, and examples of

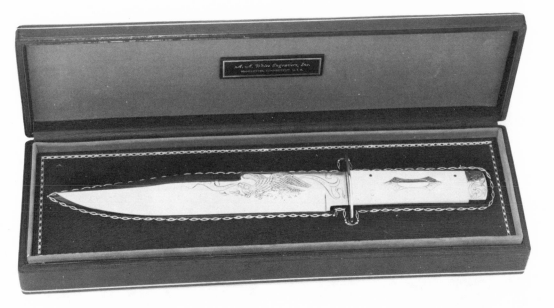

*A finely engraved Bowie by A. A. White. This is typical of an expensive collec-
tor's knife. It is 14K gold-mounted with ivory grips and is beautifully engraved.
The value is about $1,250.*

all those extras for dressing up a knife, it might take a lifetime to gather from a
prolific maker like Bo Randall, Jr.

What should the collector seek in a knife? Superb craftsmanship should be
the one prime requisite for the acquisition of any benchmade knife. If it's from
one of the better-known current makers, fine, but the work of many old-timers,
some of whom have passed on in recent years, shouldn't be ignored. Unfortunately, many of these oldsters didn't have the skills or tools of today's craftsmen, but their work is a valuable addition to any collection.

In spite of Bo Randall's popularity—and he is often regarded as the dean of
modern American knifemakers—the father of the custom knife was Bill Scagel,
who passed away at the age of 90, some 15 years ago. Scagel began making
knives in the mid-1920s and had some pretty revolutionary ideas even in those
days. Scagel believed that the Bowie style, a large cumbersome knife used by
sportsmen of the era, was impractical, and he was right. Scagel came up with
the idea of special knives for special needs: skinning, dressing game, and
filleting fish. He developed many excellent blades that were practically exten-
sions of the user's fingers. They were graceful, small, and light and were so
popular that sportsmen practically beat a path to his cabin in the Michigan
woods. While many regard Bill Scagel as the greatest knifemaker who ever lived,
it might be more truthful to record that he was probably the best craftsman of

A selection of knife types from master craftsman Lloyd Hale. The large Bowie is engraved by Henry Frank with fancy filework on the guard by Hale. The double-edged dagger at right has an ivory grip with buffalo-horn scabbard finished with sterling silver. The hunting knife (left of the Bowie) has an ivory handle,

and both boot knives are also finished with ivory. The value of these superb specimens is around $2,000.

his time. Scagel was an eccentric; he was a recluse who made his own tools, sanding discs, buffing wheels, and the other implements of the craft. He lived with a couple of dogs for company and ran all his tools off an old gas engine. Scagel knives were not only excellent for their time, but are a scarce item today. Collectors have recently paid as high as $400 for a knife that originally sold for between $20 and $50. Although Scagel lived a long life, and made knives for almost 40 years, few of his knives remain today. Bo Randall has a good collection, and a Southern collector has another dozen, but what happened to the vast output is indeed a mystery to collectors. A genuine Scagel is easily identifiable by looking at the blade. A small, curved dagger was his hallmark, stamped on the blade. Frequently he would add his name on the ricasso, but some well-known collectors have his knives and the name isn't always present. The handles are another clue, since most were made of leather washers topped off with a piece of horn or crown stag. Even in those early days Scagel had an eye for the unusual and would occasionally finish off a knife with an anaconda rib or hippo tooth for the handle.

The late Harry Morseth was another pioneer who belongs in the early group of American knifemakers. Although his work was probably finer than that of any of his contemporaries, his knives never reached the values of the old Scagels. The Morseth knives were originally made in Washington state. In those days they sold for around $35 and were bargains. Unfortunately, Morseth tried to maintain that price, even with constantly rising costs, and the company slowly moved toward financial disaster.

His grandson, Steve Morseth, took over, and while he proved to be an excellent craftsman, he wasn't able to salvage the company. A. G. Russell, a knife entrepreneur from Springdale, Arkansas, came along and purchased the failing outfit, moved it to Springdale, and set about to revive the famed Morseth name. The original knives were crafted of an unusual steel, and they are made the same way today. It had a Rockwell rating of 63–64 and was a high-carbon Norwegian product laminated between two pieces of ductile iron. Russell explains how to tell an original Morseth. "Hold the knife in the right hand and the name will appear on the right side of the blade. Brusletto, the name of the steel, will be seen on the left side of the blade. Those knives with the name on the right only were made by Steve Morseth, and the later models, made in Arkansas, have the name on the left." The present production has maintained modest prices, around $50 to $65, with Harry Morseth's early models bringing about $100 to $125 in the collectors' market.

The remaining member of the trio, Rudy Ruana of Bonner, Montana, is still pounding steel at the age of 70 and turning out honest knives for the prices he charges. While Ruana's knives never reached the perfection of some other early makers, there is no denying his are among the biggest bargains around and belong in any collection of early modern knives. Ruana forges his knives (he is a fine blacksmith) and practically fills an order by return mail. Even with today's rising prices he still charges between $15 and $20 for a hunting knife and around $70 for a Bowie. Ruana gives excellent value.

Among the modern makers, many are excellent craftsmen and there is a long wait for their knives: seven years for a fine Damascus blade from Bill Moran, and a couple of years for an intricately engraved folder from Henry Frank. Incidentally, while a fine folder from Frank might set you back over $400, with full engraving and ivory covers (sides), the cost could jump to $750 as soon as you took possession. So it's easy to see, fine quality will boost the value of a knife.

The collector should keep an eye out for the maker's marks on the blade. When Bill Moran began making knives he lived in Lime Kiln, Maryland, and when he moved to Frederick, in the same state, he refused to change his mark so the value wouldn't increase — but it did anyway. On the other hand, Bob Loveless' original shop in Lawndale, California, saw the production of many fine knives and were so marked. With the acquisition of a new partner, Loveless moved to nearby Riverside and the mark was changed to read Loveless & Johnson. With young Steve Johnson's injury in an accident a few years ago, Bob was left without a partner and soon changed the mark to read "R. W. Loveless, Riverside, Calif.," with a small nude etched under his name. Each change, and each mark, affects the value of a knife, and the Loveless & Johnson models will probably be the highest risers in value because of their limited production. Even early knives from good makers grow in value. When Bob Loveless first got into the business he sold knives to New York's Abercrombie & Fitch under the Delaware Maid mark. Although these first efforts were crude compared with today's perfection, they have taken a considerable jump in value. One knife dealer recently offered a couple for around $450, which is probably a 900 percent increase.

There is little doubt that fine knives will grow in value, but for the newcomer, it's safer and more fun to collect for the pleasure knives will bring. Even a noted collector like Phil Lobred of Anchorage, Alaska — certainly out of the mainstream of collecting — has his frustrations. For the past four years Phil has journeyed to Kansas City for the Knifemakers' Guild show, feeling it's one of the few ways he can add knives to his collection. "I want absolute perfection," Phil says, "and I hate waiting years for a knife." His lament is shared by many collectors who become frustrated trying to obtain knives through the mail from the makers. Visiting these knife shows is a good idea, since many new craftsmen display their wares for the first time. A few years ago, Corbet Sigman traveled to Kansas City from Red House, West Virginia (he has since moved to Liberty, West Virginia) and displayed some of the most beautiful knives any newcomer has ever shown. A former chemical technician, Sigman had quickly learned the skills of knifemaking, and the grind of the blade, bevels, and polish were superb. At that 1972 show, he had knives that could have been purchased for about $75. Now, with the public's acceptance of his work, his prices have almost doubled. Many collectors who were fortunate (or wise) enough to get an early Sigman knife have frequently been offered double or triple the purchase price.

The same thing happened with a couple of other fairly new makers. Billy Mace Imel and Buster Warenski both shot to the top after their first knife show. Imel, a tool and die maker from Indiana, sold everything he displayed, and even though many thought his prices were high, that didn't deter the public.

Buster Warenski, a quiet cowpoke from Richfield, Utah, is already famed for the spectacular quality of his work. His forte is making replicas of old Bowies, push daggers, and reproductions of early work. His sterling-silver sheaths and carved ivory grips, many inlaid with silver and gold thread and fancy escutcheons, aren't cheap—$500 to $1,000 or more—but they will enhance the collection of any serious, and wealthy, collector.

At the 1974 Knifemakers' Guild show, held in Kansas City, one investor was buying fine knives with an eye toward the future. Admitting he knew little about knives (his expertise was in porcelain and antique paperweights), he still felt he couldn't make a mistake with knives from the better makers. Whose knives did he select? Imel, Moran, Warenski, Frank, Hale, and Sigman. In spite of his being a novice, the connoisseur's eye had taken him to the top group of craftsmen.

But there are also top knifemakers who with great talent haven't yet received their share of fame—men like Don Zaccagnino, John Smith, and Dan Dennehy. Dennehy provides a good example with a recently completed Bowie. The ivory handle is inlaid with turquoise, the blade fully etched by Shaw-Leibowitz, and the guard and pommel engraved by Angel Garcia Santa Ana of Yuma, Arizona. The knife is now owned by Craig Fox Huber, a former lawman, who paid a handsome price for the privilege of adding it to his fine collection.

Artful decoration by fine engravers like Ralph Alpen, Winston Churchill, Lynton McKenzie, Alvin White, and Walter Kolouch will add value to any knife. But the novice collector should beware of poor engraving, even on expensive knives. It won't enhance the value and may even reduce it.

Acid etching is one of the more popular techniques used on blades because it may be done before or after heat treatment, and the hardness of the steel doesn't affect the work done. Sherrill Shaw and Leonard Leibowitz are two skilled artists who have brought this ancient skill to a high degree of perfection. They have developed a way of brazing gold, silver, or copper onto the blade to get striking new effects. A new method of miniature paintings on ivory handles, fully protected by space-age epoxy and lacquers, makes an unusual and highly decorative display piece. The Shaw-Leibowitz work is in great demand by knife-makers, and the knife owner may add scenes of historical significance or have a favorite picture reproduced in the most minute detail.

On the opposite side of the coin, however, are the exceptionally high prices recently asked for some ornately decorated knives. Even a $500 job done by a top artist shouldn't command $300 when it's executed on a $75 knife. There are many who feel such ridiculous prices will drive enthusiasts away. Even knowledgeable collectors are frequently shocked at the asking price of a knife, particularly from unskilled makers. But value has a way of seeking its own level and the less talented eager beavers soon fall along the wayside.

From left to right: Bill Moran's handsome Damascus dagger, selling for $125 per inch; fighting knife from Rod "Caribou" Chappel with acid-etched blade by Shaw-Leibowitz; Ted Dowell Bowie with engraving by Henry Frank; and a small boot knife by Buster Warenski with carved ivory grip and sterling silver sheath inlaid with ivory rose. These knives are fine examples of the knifemaker's art brought to a high degree of perfection. These four would cost better than $5,000.

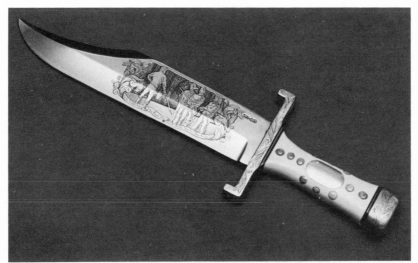

Dan Dennehy's famous Bowie with blade etched by Shaw-Leibowitz, guard and butt engraved by Angel Garcia Santa Ana, and ivory handle inlaid with turquoise by Dennehy. The knife is now owned by Craig Fox Huber and is not for sale. The value is estimated to be near $1,500.

Apart from those unusual or finely decorated knives, there are some blades that aren't available at any price—at least during the lifetime of the present owner. One such knife is the large brass-backed Bowie that Bob Loveless made for himself back in 1957. It has almost a half pound of engraved sterling silver on the hilt and pommel. Bob intended to keep the knife, but weakened in 1959 and sold it for $450. Since that time, it has been resold many times at ever higher prices and the present owner, who paid $1,100 and requests anonymity, has refused offers of $2,500. What makes it so valuable? Any Loveless knife will fetch a high price, but one marked "R. W. Loveless—his knife" is bound to command a high figure. It is also believed to be the first Loveless knife to incorporate a sub-hilt as part of its design.

As we said earlier, fine craftsmanship is one criterion for judging a knife. Another is unusual design. A few years ago, Ted Dowell conceived the idea of a knife with an integral hilt, and it was a lovely piece of work. The natural progression, of course, was a later model with integral hilt and butt cap. This knife is one of Dowell's most popular and expensive models. It will cost $250 to add one to your collection. Both hilt and pommel are machined from a 2½-pound block of steel. When the knife is completed, it weighs about six ounces. Since Dowell can produce only about ten a month and the work is pretty intricate, it can be easily understood why the wait is long and the price high.

Bargains are rare, and how to judge a knife is just as important as what to buy. There are some guidelines, and these include a thorough inspection of the knife. Turn it over and see if bevels meet on both sides of the blade. Is the solder work clean, without pinholes or excess material? Does the blade have an evenly ground edge, and is the polish excellent, without grind marks showing? All these are important points when judging any knife. In spite of poor work, a rare knife — a Scagel, for example — should be regarded as a find, and the flaws should be balanced against the collector's desire to add the knife to his collection.

Just being around knives (and knifemakers and collectors) will give anyone an opportunity to absorb knowledge, and there will come an instinct for quality work. Reading about knives will give an excellent education about the varied aspects of steels, handle materials, and the makers themselves.

Knife collecting is still in its infancy, so — in addition to the fun of owning fine blades — there's the hope that if the collector buys wisely and well, his collection will grow tremendously in value.

A new collector's item that has proved popular is the folding knife. Folders, or pocketknives if you prefer, have turned many makers exclusively to this new field. Jess Horn, when his replica of the Remington Bullet knife became popular, gave up sheath knives to concentrate on the more intricately crafted folder. Some of Horn's recent innovations are knives designed by Bob Loveless and crafted by Horn. Another superb craftsman is Ron Lake. While Lake makes fine sheath knives, the folder he introduced at the Houston show in 1971 won him the greatest praise. The innovation was a lock-release tab that extended the length of the top and didn't interfere with the smoothly flowing lines of the knife. Also innovative were the inlet sides of brass, inlaid with exotic woods or ivory. The early models could have been purchased for only $75. Now the price has jumped to $500.

Probably the most prized folders of all are those of Henry Frank, a native of Germany, who came to America in 1951 after a four-year apprenticeship as a firearms engraver. Henry began making knives in 1965 and has become the acknowledged leader in his specialty of making and engraving fine folders. Henry Frank does everything, even the heat-treating of the blades, and his knives are truly works of art. His skill with the engraver's tool enables him to do the most minute designs with animal heads and scroll work. Even the nail nick is delicately done. There are seven knives offered, even a tiny two-bladed pen knife with liners of solid gold, mother-of-pearl covers, and gold rivets. The price of this beauty is $750, and it will probably never be used even to trim a quill pen. Fine folders from a master like Henry Frank will undoubtedly be a smart investment for the future, and the owner will never tire of admiring it in the meanwhile.

Frequently an expert (and that means anyone who has written more than

Matched pair of Bowie and fighting knives with integral guards created by Ted Dowell. The engraving is by Henry Frank and grips are of coco bolo. The pair is valued at $2,500.

one article on knives) is asked to name the best knifemakers. Making "best" lists is akin to parachuting *sans* chute and is just as dangerous. But since the newcomer does require some guidance, here is a short list of those makers highly regarded by their peers. In no particular order it would include Buster Warenski, Lloyd Hale, Ted Dowell, Billy Mace Imel, Bill Moran, Don Zaccagnino, Bob Loveless, Rod Chappel, Jess Horn, Ron Lake, Henry Frank, Bob Hayes—and perhaps some unknown maker who may appear by the time this is published.

Remember, if you order a knife from any of these men, or from one of the dozens of other fine makers, don't hold your breath until it's delivered. All have a waiting list of from a couple of months to a few years. However, for the avid can't-wait collector, many knife shops have been opening around the country in the past few years. Knife World in Englewood, Colorado, the Knife Shop at El Paso's International Airport, and the Ramrod Knife & Gun Shop in New Castle, Indiana, are a few of the stores where custom knives are sold along with knife books, sharpening tools, and related items. You may not find exactly what you want, but most shops have at least a hundred knives on show, many from top makers, and the privilege of walking out the door with the knife of your choice should be worth the premium paid.

Once you've gathered a collection (meaning anywhere from a few to a few hundred), consideration should be given to the care of knives. Steel rusts and ivory and buffalo horn are famous for their propensity to crack. A true collector generally won't use a prized knife even to cut a piece of string. There are exceptions. Alaska's Phil Lobred even takes his best blades on hunting trips, but he has buffing wheels in his garage – and he knows how to use them – and keeps his knives in top shape. Andy Russell, the Arkansas knife expert, says the safest method is to coat the blades with oil, wrap them in waxed paper, and store them in a safe place. While the advice is sound, it defeats the purpose of the typical collector: to keep his treasures on display where they may be viewed and enjoyed.

Some collectors mount knives on fancy walnut display boards and hang them on the wall. Others use a glass-topped coffee table with a box inset and place knives inside as part of the room decor. A small amount of silica-gel will help absorb moisture. The greatest danger is storing knives in their leather sheaths. The fumes of tanning acids will eventually ruin any piece of steel. The leather will also collect moisture, and it's just as dangerous as storing a fine gun in a scabbard.

Ivory and horn are fragile materials, prone to tiny hairlines and cracks. While they are beautiful to behold, most knifemakers will warn their customers when these materials are ordered.

The question is always asked, why would anyone want hundreds of knives? The answer is, of course, that beautifully crafted knives are as much works of art as any painting or statuary. They are practical and beautiful, and were one of man's first tools and weapons.

The variations of blade shape, form, and design are practically unlimited. Rare and exotic materials are being introduced that make many knives even more desirable – and expensive. D'Alton Holder, an Arizona craftsman, uses a combination of Baltic amber and elephant ivory for handles. Other makers work in fossil ivory and Alaskan jade and even inlay gold nuggets. Naturally such hard-to-get materials will boost the price – sometimes by hundreds of dollars – but for the ardent collector who seeks the unusual, price seems to be no object.

When her husband began collecting in 1968, Rita Winters thought he was mad when he paid $45 for a Randall knife. But after George gathered about ten knives, Rita began to pay attention, and confesses that she began to notice the design and character of each individual piece. She became a collector herself.

"Workmanship is the most important factor for us," Rita says, "and there are a few knives in our collection I frown on because of sloppy work. If a knifemaker doesn't care enough to clean up the little places, he doesn't get my approval." Even George and Rita Winters concede there are almost too many knifemakers and feel it's impossible to get a knife from each. They have hit on a happy solution and now collect only from those who are members of the Knifemakers' Guild. Admitting it may seem snobbish, they have good reasons. Knives are becoming more expensive (they spend about $2,000 a year on their hobby), so

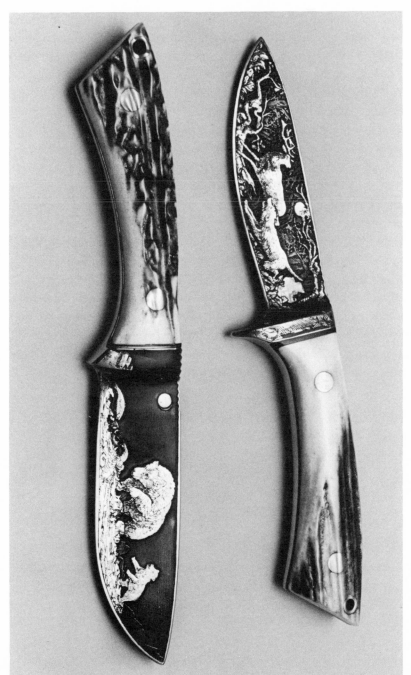

Two hunting knives by Billy Mace Imel with stag grips and etching by Shaw-Leibowitz. The etching is done in three tones and uses gold, silver, and copper. The knife at right, for example, has golden bears, silver moon, and a copper salmon. These are full-tang knives and are the work of a superb craftsman. The value is about $800 each.

they've had to limit themselves. Rita also feels those knifemakers serving a year's probation to enter the Guild put their work and reputations on the line. What direction are these two collectors moving in today? "We both feel the future of knife collecting is toward the more artistic knife. A hunter might acquire several knives in his search for the right blade, but the real collector will be more interested in artistry than utility."

What about faking, or reproductions of the modern maker? Although many old knives—Bowies, Case and Remington Bullets—have been faked, it isn't much of a problem in the custom field. If an unknown has the ability to produce a Loveless or Dowell, then he deserves the price paid. Making a fine knife demands too many different skills and too much time for anyone to indulge in forgery; it isn't worth the worry.

Aside from the potential growth in value, the fun of collecting shouldn't be forgotten. Visiting knife shows, talking to fellow collectors, buying and swapping are all part of that fun. There are also unexpected and exciting thrills. They tell the story of a collector who saw a John Owens knife and had to have it. He kept bidding higher and higher and finally offered a Henry Bowie in trade. The fact that both men knew knives, and the Bowie was perhaps worth ten times as much as the Owens knife, made no difference. One man saw a knife he wanted and was willing to give a lot for it.

REPRESENTATIVE PRICES OF HANDMADE KNIVES

Knives from the more famous makers, although priced high, still run a range of prices enabling most collectors to accommodate their own wallets. Nickel or sterling silver and exotic horns add to the cost.

Rod Chappel. Knives begin around $100 and move upwards for fancy daggers and Bowies. Expect to pay about $300 or $400 for the finer work.

Ted Dowell. You can purchase a Dowell knife in the neighborhood of $100 and go upwards to $250 for the integral hilt-butt knife.

Henry Frank. Around $175 to upwards of $475 for the most intricate engraving plus ivory or horn sides.

Lloyd Hale. Hale practically makes knives by cost. Send $200 and you'll get $200 worth of work. Hale doesn't limit the amount of work done, so the sky's the limit. It all depends on what you want to pay.

R. W. Loveless. Loveless is the king, and his knives start at $500 for a hunter. Tapered tangs, superb craftsmanship, and beautiful lines. His highly prized boot knives begin at $750, ivory will add another $200 or more.

William Moran, Jr. Moran's knives have always been classic to the collector. His famed Damascus knives start at $250 *per inch.* Fancy grips of rare material, plus gold or silver wire inlaid, will require you to check your bank account. If you order, there should be a 15-year wait.

Many lesser-known but equally superb craftsmen are doing fine work at prices considerably less than the most famous makers. Many of these pieces could well be the sought-after collections of tomorrow.

Dan Dennehy. Famed for his fighting knives during the Vietnam conflict. His lowest knives run about $100, and they run comfortably upwards of $400 or more.

D'Holder. Knives begin at $100 and go to $250 for a Bowie. Exotic material, amber, ivory, scrimshaw, and turquoise are his forte. Priced according to material.

Four folding knives by master knifemaker Henry Frank. These knives are made and engraved by Frank and all have ivory covers (sides). The small penknife at the bottom has gold bolsters and gold pins. With full engraving, plus ivory as shown, the penknife would be the most expensive, about $500 because of the amount of gold used. The others vary, but will run about $700 to $1,550 each.

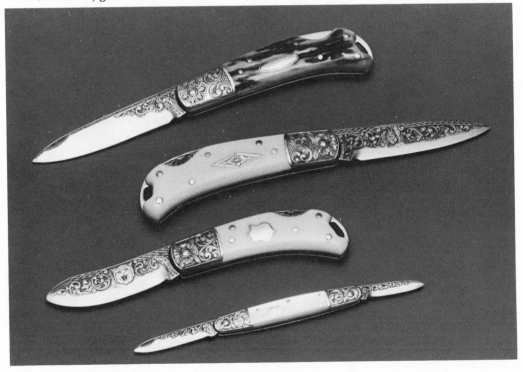

John Owens, Jr. Fine, well-made sporting knives begin at $50 and Owens rarely goes higher than $100.

John T. Smith. Another fine maker. His knives begin at $75 and run to $200 for a large Bowie. Fine, clean work with superb bevel lines and excellent polish.

Horace Wiggins. A fairly new maker from Louisiana. Wiggins does simply beautiful work. He is the only maker I know to use abalone shells, sea shells, and a glass-resin impregnated cactus for the handles (at extra cost). His prices are not high. Prices start at $70 to $100.

ADDRESSES OF KNIFEMAKERS MENTIONED

Rod Chappel
Davis Custom Knives
North 1405 Ash
Spokane, WA 92201

Dan Dennehy
Box 2F
Del Norte, CO 81132

Ted Dowell
139 St. Helens Place
Bend, OR 97701

H. H. Frank
1 Mountain Meadow Road
Whitefish, MT 59937

Lloyd Hale
609 Henrietta St.
Springdale, AR 72764

Bob Hayes
Box 141
Rail Road Flat, CA 95248

D'Holder
6808 N. 30th Drive
Phoenix, AZ 85017

Jess Horn
Box 1274
Redding, CA 96001

Billy Mace Imel
1616 Bundy Ave.
New Castle, IN 47362

Ron Lake
38 Illini Drive
Taylorville, IL 62568

R. W. Loveless
Box 7836, Arlington Sta.
Riverside, CA 92503

William Moran, Jr.
Route 5
Frederick, MD 21701

Morseth Knives
1705 Highway 71 N.
Springdale, AR 72764

John Owens, Jr.
8755 S.W. 96th St.
Miami, FL 33156

Randall Made Knives
Box 1988
Orlando, FL 32802

R. H. Ruana
Box 527
Bonner, MT 59823

Cobert Sigman
Liberty, WV 25124

John T. Smith
6048 Cedar Crest Drive
Southhaven, MS 38671

Buster Warenski
Box 214
Richfield, UT 84701

H. L. Wiggins
203 Herndon St.
Mansfield, LA 71052

Don Zaccagnino
Box Zack
Pahokee, FL 33476

KNIFE ETCHERS AND ENGRAVERS

Winston C. Churchill
Twenty Mile Stream Road
Proctorsville, VT 05153

Walter Kolouch
110 High St.
New Rochelle, NY 10801

Lynton McKenzie
6940 N. Alveron
Tucson, AZ 85718

Shaw-Leibowitz
Route 1, Box 421
New Cumberland, WV 26047

A. A. White Engravers
Box 68
Manchester, CT 06040

SELECTED BIBLIOGRAPHY

The American Blade. 112 Lee Parkway Drive, Stonewall Building, Chattanooga, TN 37421.

Bates, John and Schippers, James. *The Custom Knife*. Memphis: Custom Knife Press, 1974.

Guns & Ammo Guidebook to Knives & Edged Weapons. Los Angeles: Peterson Publishing Co., 1974.

Hughes, B. R. *The Gun Digest Book of Knives*. Northfield, IL: Digest Books, 1973.

The Knife Digest. A. G. Russel, 1705 Highway 71 North, Springdale, AR 72764.

Latham, Sid. *Knifecraft*. Harrisburg, PA: Stackpole, 1981.

Latham, Sid. *Knives & Knifemakers*. Tulsa, OK: Winchester Press, 1973.

Warner, Ken, ed. *Knives 81*. Northfield, IL: DBI Books, 1981.

Chapter 20 ❧ Antique Knives

HAROLD L. PETERSON

Almost from the beginning, men have used knives for sport as well as for work and welfare. Sports such as hunting, fishing, sailing, camping, and riding have required a knife as a necessary tool and companion. If one includes whittling and carving as a "sport," the knife is absolutely essential, as it is for knife-throwing. For most of history, however, the problem has been to distinguish the sporting knife from the weapon or the general-purpose knife. For at least three thousand years there was really no differentiation. A good knife was a good knife, useful for any purpose its owner wished. Thus the collector has a wide-open field. He can collect almost any knife and classify it as at least a part-time sporting knife.

If one goes back to the earliest of the metal knives, one can take as an example a beautiful knife from Mycenae with gold decorations depicting a lion hunt. In the Aachen Cathedral is a scramasax — the utility knife of the northern Europeans — that is known as "Charlemagne's hunting knife." It has a clipped point and is surprisingly similar to the Bowie knife of the nineteenth century. Hunting pictures, from the fifteenth century and later, show hunters with just such large knives.

TYPES OF SPORTING KNIVES

Perhaps the first specialized hunting knives appeared in the hunting trousses that were especially popular in the sixteenth century. These usually consisted of a series of knives and other tools, ranging from large cleavers to small eating knives plus bone saws and other tools for skinning and jointing game. Even royal hunters were supposed to take part in these activities, and there is a woodcut of Queen Elizabeth I of England being handed a knife by her huntsman so that she can take at least the first steps in dressing a stag. In Scotland, there was a special series of knives known as gralloch knives for hunting. They looked much like the Scottish dirk but usually had a staghorn handle, and these, with the trousse sets, are among the first precisely identifiable

German knife of the early seventeenth century.

sporting knives, dating mainly from the late eighteenth and early nineteenth centuries.

In America, hunters of the eighteenth century carried a knife that looked much like a butcher's knife. Then, in the 1830s, came the famous Bowie knives. Again, these were all-purpose knives, useful for fighting as well as camping, digging for water, and dressing game. Some are etched with inscriptions such as "For Stags and Buffaloes" and many show hunting dogs in their decoration. After the Civil War, the Bowie shape continued in a reduced size and acquired the designation "hunting knife" so that it was essentially a sporting type. Shortly after the beginning of the twentieth century, there appeared the smaller sheath knives, such as the Marble, with leather grips, base-metal pommel, and 4- or 5-inch blades. They became popular with both hunters and Boy Scouts and are now eminently collectible as sporting knives.

Still, these were multi-purpose knives. The trend toward real specialization began perhaps shortly after World War I, with the work of the fabulous William Scagel. Scagel designed and handmade a whole host of knives intended for specific hunting and fishing uses. Not only were they well shaped for their purposes, they were also beautifully made, and any knife found today that bears his distinctive mark of a curved dagger is a collector's treasure indeed. It was Scagel who inspired W. D. "Bo" Randall of Orlando, Florida, to start making specialized knives. Randall has carried the work of his predecessor still further with efficiently designed knives for almost every sporting purpose, including variations for type of animal, for skinning, scaling fish, and so forth.

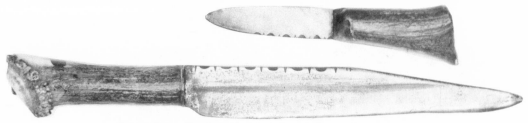

Scottish gralloch knives of the eighteenth century.

Since then, there have been a host of other knives, by skilled craftsmen, that are covered in the chapter on modern makers.

In his search for sporting knives, the collector should be certain not to overlook pocketknives. Many early hunters of the eighteenth century used jackknives—and actually a skilled hunter can dress a deer with a very small knife. As early as 1816, the *Explanation or Key to the Various Manufactories of Sheffield* by Joseph Smith illustrated four knives that it identified specifically as "Sportsmen Knives." All had two blades and a corkscrew, but some had a stone hook for removing stones from a horse's hoof, an awl, a saw blade, a fleam for bleeding, and tweezers. They were, in fact, much like the modern utility or Boy Scout knives, carried by many sportsmen.

Water sports also provide a number of specialized pocketknife forms, with fish scalers, marlinspikes for sailors, and the like.

The variety is almost endless, and so the collector of sporting knives has a wide open field. He can include almost anything that appeals to him.

STARTING A COLLECTION

The beginning collector has no real problem in starting his knife collection. For the early types, he usually must go to established dealers in arms, or the major auction galleries of New York and London. There are also clubs and dealers who specialize in knives. So many knives have been made in the last century, however, that there is still the chance to pick up specimens at low prices. Winchester and Remington pocketknives, as well as Bowies and ancient types, command prices in the hundreds of dollars from a knowledgeable source. Late-nineteenth-century hunting knives, pocket utility knives, and Marble sheath knives are well within a moderate budget. And it is surprising how many of these (and some rarer types) turn up in average antique shops, flea markets, and antique shows at prices ranging from $5 to $5,000. They are definitely still

An early Bowie knife with etched blade.

Hunting knife made in the mid-eighteenth century by Will & Finck of San Francisco.

available. All the collector has to do is know what he seeks and keep his eyes open. When it comes to selling a collection, however, it is usually best to seek out a leading dealer specialist. These men have a ready clientele, know what they can get for a given price, and can therefore afford to pay a better price than the nonspecialist. In obtaining an appraisal, the same rule applies. It is the specialist dealer who can best gauge value and whose word will hold most weight. Most of these dealers belong to the American Society of Appraisers or one of the other professional appraising organizations that set standards for competence, fees, and conduct.

As with all other types of collecting, the value of sporting knives is bound to go up. There are a finite number of specimens and an expanding market of collectors. Thus the law of supply and demand is in full play. The last 25 years have seen the price of many knives increase as much as 1,000 percent, and there is no indication that this trend will cease.

DISPLAYING AND PROTECTING YOUR COLLECTION

Once a collection has been started, there is always the question of how to display and protect it. This depends in large part on the size of the collection and the space available. Some collectors install glass cases or mount large specimens on the wall. For more compact storage, however, a great majority keep the bulk of their collections in felt-lined drawers. Some cases of drawers can be purchased ready-made, or they can be made to order, usually for less than $100. There are, however, certain precautions that must be taken to protect

Part of the Scagel collection in the Randall Knife Museum. These specialized knives are certainly antiques, but they represent the beginning of the modern era in sporting knives.

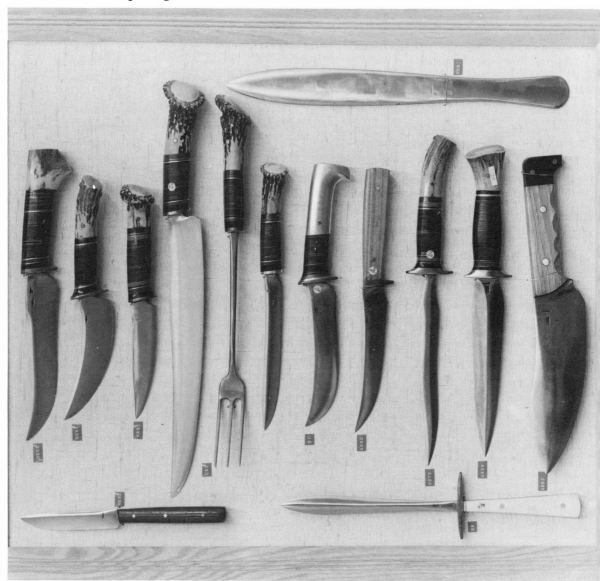

the knives whether on the wall or in a case of drawers. The iron and steel elements should be covered with a rust preventative. Some collectors prefer a silicon. I like a hard paste wax that does not have to be renewed. From personal experience, I know that a good acid-free paste wax applied and allowed to stand 20 minutes before buffing, followed by a second coat to eliminate skips, will prevent rust for a minimum of 20 years—the longest period I have tested—unless the blades are handled by careless visitors with sweaty hands. It is usually best to take sheath knives out of their scabbards. Some of these leather scabbards have been tanned with acid, and this is always hard on the steel. Even acid-free leather has a tendency to collect and hold moisture in humid climates and this also can be harmful.

There are also other corrosive elements that should be avoided. If you paint the inside of the drawers in which you store knives, use an oil-base or alkyd-base paint. Some of the acrylics will tarnish brass and silver rapidly in a confined atmosphere, as will some pigments, such as yellow chromate. Knives with celluloid, or some of the early plastic, handles should also be separated from the rest of the collection and possibly stored in reasonably airtight containers. These early plastics often release corrosive gases as they decompose.

The need for security, of course, varies with the value of the collection and the area of the country. In high-crime areas, good deadbolt locks on windows and doors, plus an alarm system, are always advisable for a valuable collection, and publicity should be avoided. Newspaper stories are flattering to the ego, but they are also an invitation to theft. Insurance agents now even advise that specimens illustrated in books should be credited simply as from a "private collection" without giving a name. It is a sad commentary on the times, but these precautions are all becoming more and more necessary. And so is insurance. For the collector, a fine-arts floater policy is usually the best. Each piece is listed and appraised, with the insurance company agreeing to the values. Such policies, which offer protection against theft and fire, are relatively inexpensive and provide much comfort and peace of mind. Normally they do not protect against damage from rust or from use. They are strictly for the collector, not for the active sportsman, and virtually all of the major insurance companies offer them.

SELECTED BIBLIOGRAPHY

During the last 25 years, many books have been published that offer guidance to the collector of sporting knives. Reprints of old Sears Roebuck, Montgomery Ward, Remington, and other catalogs illustrate what was available in the past.

The *American Blade* is a current journal on edged weapons of all sorts, and the *Knife Digest* is an annual on the subject. A few books are listed below.

Abels, Robert. *Classic Bowie Knives*. New York: Robert Abels, 1967.

Blackmore, Howard L. *Hunting Weapons*. New York: Walker, 1971.

Hardin, Albert N., Jr., and Heddin, Robert W. *Light but Efficient: A Study of the M1880 Hunting and M1890 Intrenching Knives and Scabbards*. Pennsauken, NJ: 1973.

Himsworth, J. B. *The Story of Cutlery*. London: Benn, 1953.

Peterson, Harold L. *American Knives*. New York: Scribner, 1958. Paperback edition, 1975.

Peterson, Harold L. *Daggers and Fighting Knives of the Western World*. New York: Bonanza Books, 1970.

Peterson, Harold L. *A History of Knives*. New York: Scribner, 1966. For young readers.

Chapter 21 ❧ Split-Cane Rods

LEN CODELLA with Ernest Schwiebert

In attempting to treat the subject of collecting split-cane fly rods, I have qualified my approach and emphasized those rodmakers whose work is most highly regarded. Integrity of workmanship, rod design, pride of craft, quality of component materials—these are but some of the factors that set off the group of skilled artisans discussed in this chapter. These qualities are not limited to the craftsmen of old, but apply equally to some of the contemporary builders.

I have chosen not to treat the split-bamboo rods of makers such as Shakespeare, South Bend, Montague, Dunton, Bristol, Landman, Devine, and Horrocks Ibbotson. Although these makers did build an occasional fine fly rod, the bulk of their work falls into the class of production rods. The techniques of mass production do not lend themselves to building quality equipment, and for the serious collector these rods are not as strong a consideration. It must be pointed out, however, that these rods are a part of the overall history of split-bamboo rods and do offer the collector an opportunity to assemble an interesting yet relatively inexpensive rod collection.[1]

All that is needed to get started in collecting rods is interest. From there, your pocketbook and degree of interest will determine the direction your collecting will take. There are as many different approaches to collecting as there are rods to collect. For instance, some people collect only production rods because of their relatively low cost and easy availability. These rods can be fun to collect. Another type of collector seeks at least one rod of every maker to fill out his collection. Another might concentrate on a single maker and attempt to build an extensive collection of that maker's rods. It is a democratic process and you are left to your own devices as to how to proceed.

WHY COLLECT?

In a word—appreciation. Bamboo rods are much like antique furniture or fine guns. In addition to pride of ownership and the possession of an exceptional rod, one can admire and appreciate the quality of workmanship and materials in the rod, the attention to detail, the taper designs employed to make the rod a fine fishing tool, or perhaps the special cosmetic treatments given each rod as a signature of its maker. There is another kind of appreciation associated with collecting bamboo rods—the inherent appreciation of dollar value. Many of these rods are irreplaceable, and as the demand for them grows, as it has over the past ten years, we find their cash value growing in even greater proportion.

Many bamboo rods are simply an excellent investment. Inflation has caused the cost of many products to double in price over the last ten years. During this same period we have watched the market value of classic rods increase by five to as much as ten times their cost of a decade ago, with no indications that this trend will lessen.

Finally, over and above the investment value, there is a certain reward for the fisherman in the use of truly first-rate tackle. While it is impossible to measure satisfaction in terms of dollars, it is indeed a pleasant side benefit available to the collector of fine fishing rods.

WHERE TO FIND RODS

Finding rods is probably half the fun of collecting. Local garage or tag sales, rummage sales, country auctions, antique shops, country sport shops, and your local sport shop are just some of the places to look for rods. The most reliable sources have proved to be reputable dealers in antique and classic fly tackle. Some rod manufacturers like Thomas & Thomas and Leonard actually publish periodic listings of used equipment for the collector and fisherman.

Len Codella of Thomas & Thomas Rodmakers, Turners Falls, Massachusetts, and Martin Keane of Bridgewater, Connecticut, were two of the first national dealers in classic tackle, and both are well known for reputable dealings. Rod and tackle lists are available from both for the asking.

Another reputable source for classic tackle is Allan J. Liu of the American Sporting Collector in New York. He, too, makes available a rod and tackle list.

On occasion rods turn up through ads in local newspapers, through friends and acquaintances, and at fishing clubs. Sometimes they become available under the most unlikely circumstances. Just recently, I acquired the remaining inventory of bamboo rods from a long-established local sport shop. These were a good number of Shakespeare production rods made in the early 1950s that had been put aside when glass "took over," and they had remained on the back shelves for more than 25 years, waiting for someone to seek them out. All were brand new, had been stored well, and were in prime condition. Finding them was a real treat. In short, if you are looking for them, you will find them.

Selling or trading rods can be done through some of the same sources as are used to acquire them. Most dealers are interested in acquiring quality rods for resale and will buy them outright, or they may be willing to sell your rods on a consignment basis, charging a nominal percentage of the sales price for this service. When dealing with another collector, you may find a reluctance on his part to pay the current market value for your rod, as all of us have a tendency to buy at bargain prices whenever possible. Often it is better to sell through a dealer because he usually has a market for what you are selling and, if he is honest, will work your deal out based on proper market prices so that you may actually realize more for your equipment than you would have on your own. There are no hard and fast rules for buying or selling used equipment, but in general it pays to know with whom you are doing business.

Consignment sales through dealers, if you are not in a rush for cash, are always a good bet, since you will realize a greater return on your equipment than by selling to the dealer outright. From his standpoint, he will be willing to accept a smaller profit on such sales since he is not required to invest his money in the rod. You get paid when the rod is sold.

The past five years have witnessed an unprecedented growth in rod and tackle collecting activity. This increased interest in a fascinating hobby has generated a rash of "dealers" in classic tackle whose credentials can be questioned. While it appears that most of these people, albeit inexperienced, are honest, it is abundantly clear that some are not. We must again caution you to be convinced of the honesty and integrity of those with whom you choose to do business. Be aware that misrepresentation of rods (their condition, parentage, originality, and the like) is indeed a current fact of life. Counterfeit rods do exist and have been sold at handsome prices to the unsuspecting. Refunds for misrepresented or bogus rods have taken months to be paid or have not been paid at all. This has also occurred with payments of proceeds due rod owners as a result of consignment sales. Some of these abuses have occurred in private deals as well. It is important that the collector be aware that they do occur, to avoid the unpleasant (and sometimes costly) experience of falling victim to them.

On the bright side, the incidence rate of these abuses is relatively low in proportion to the actual rod-collecting activity in this country. Nevertheless, some measure of caution is appropriate on your part. Know with whom you are dealing.

PROTECTING YOUR COLLECTION

As your collection grows, you will be faced with the question of insurance against fire, theft, and the like. It is wise to speak with your insurance agent about a rider on your present policies to cover the value of your collection. The cost of such insurance is quite nominal in comparison to insuring coin or gun collections. A professional appraisal of your collection will be necessary for insurance purposes. Such appraisals should be performed periodically, since your collection will grow and the items in it will appreciate in value. Collection appraisals should be performed by recognized authorities on classic rods and submitted to you in writing. Such documentation, which should be kept in a safe place, is relatively inexpensive and can save you hundreds or even thousands of dollars in the event of loss.

Cane fly rods should be kept in an area where they will not be subject to extremes in temperature or to excessive moisture. A cool, dry place is best. Unless you are planning to display the rods, they should be kept in their cloth bags and aluminum tubes for best protection. The rods in their cases should not be stored horizontally, such as on the top of a closet, as gravitational force can cause them to take a permanent set. The best method I've found for storage is in an absolutely vertical position. In just a few hours, the home handyman can construct a simple storage rack of pine shelving with 2¼-inch holes bored through and spaced as desired. This permits the rod cases to be inserted vertically, and new holes can be added as the collection grows.

The best protection for the rods themselves is paste wax. Your rods should be waxed periodically, using a high-grade paste wax. It is important that there be no abrasives or solvents in the wax; I have found the Butcher brand of furniture wax to be one of the best. Waxing of both impregnated and varnished rods periodically is suggested, as this will not only enhance the appearance of the rods, but help to keep the finish from drying and checking in storage.

If you desire to display the rods out of their cases, this is best done in a display cabinet such as is used for gun display. If it has locking doors, so much the better, to avoid damage from careless handling. Again the rods should be set up in a vertical position to avoid the possibility of sets or warping of the sections.

VALUES

Probably the most significant factor in determining the worth of any cane fly rod is its condition. Rods that are in mint (almost-new) condition are the most desirable and command the highest prices on the classic rod market. For example, there can be as much as $500 difference in the price of two identical-model Payne fly rods, if one is in almost-new condition and the other is in excellent average condition. These mint rods are unbelievably scarce; most rods encountered will have been fished and will show varying degrees of wear. This wear factor, along with a number of other criteria, is what determines any cane rod's value. Rods that have tips missing, joints broken short, joints repaired, joints replaced by other than the original maker, checking varnish, chips or digs into the finish or, worse, into the cane itself, scoring or scratching of the metal parts, guides broken or missing, loose ferrules, and so forth, are not as desirable, and in some cases may be of no value whatever, depending on their degree of disrepair.

Among collectors, a cane rod that is completely original, with all original wood, wraps, fittings, and finish, is eagerly sought after. Rods that have been altered can sometimes be valueless. Restoration and repair work that does not cosmetically change the appearance of the original rod and that has been done by a recognized rodmaker is quite acceptable. After all, it is unreasonable to expect a fine fly rod not to be used for its intended purpose, and of course, through fishing, guides do wear out and varnish and metalwork do get scratched.

If care is taken to preserve the integrity of the original rod, such refinish work should not alter a quality rod's value in any way. In fact, if the quality of workmanship of the shop doing this work is high enough, this may in some cases add to the value of the rod rather than detract from it.

As interest in fly-fishing has grown, the demand by collectors and fishermen for quality fly rods has increased. As a result, availability of top-quality sticks has dwindled, driving rod prices steadily upward. While no one can predict future values, it seems likely that prices will continue to appreciate. If past increases are any indication of future value, it is interesting to note that in 1971, a sound, used Payne fly rod sold for about $225. That same rod now brings up to $1,000 on today's rod market. There is no question that quality fly rods are a sound investment, in addition to being fun to fish with.

The most significant factor controlling the value of bamboo rods is their desirability as fishing instruments. In rod collecting today, there are very few purist collectors — that is, people who will simply acquire a rod to add to their collection and then never use that rod as a fishing tool. This phenomenon is more common to those who collect fishing reels, but almost nonexistent in the rod-collecting fraternity. Most rod collectors are fishermen (which is what may have piqued their interest in collecting rods in the first place), and as a result, they place nearly as much emphasis (and sometimes even more emphasis) on the fishability of a given rod as on its condition.

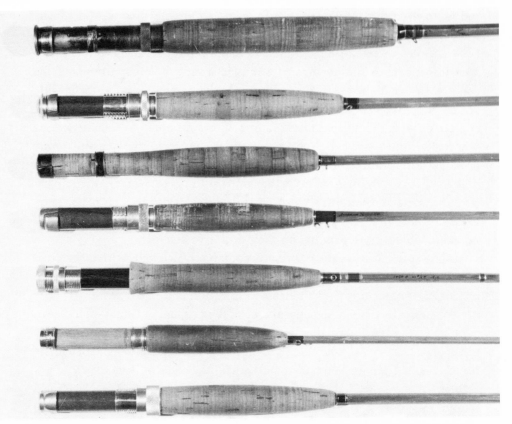

Handle styles. Top to bottom: Heddon salmon rod with blue metal seat and plug for extension; Payne down-locking reel seat with filler; Payne all-cork handle with blue ring and cap; Dickerson down-locking reel seat with wood filler; Howells up-locking reel seat with zebrawood filler; Leonard polished metal ring and cap over wood, and Gillum down-locker with wood filler. (Photo courtesy Matthew Vinciguerra)

Since rod use is such an important factor to most collectors, it is not uncommon to see the light-actioned trout rods of a quality maker selling for sometimes more than twice the price of a heavier-actioned bass or salmon rod from the same maker. For example a 7-foot through an 8½-foot Jim Payne rod in superb condition, made for a #4, #5, or #6 weight line size, would command $900 to $1,100 in today's market, while an 8½-foot or longer Jim Payne, for #7 through #10 weight lines in exactly the same condition, will sell for perhaps $400 to $600. Same maker, same quality, same cosmetics — but less demand for the heavier rods.

This desirability factor, which has always been part of the scheme of things, is even more dramatic today as graphite rods, with their very light weight, and excellent power-to-weight ratios in the heavier rods, continue to eclipse the demand for the long, heavier line-weight bamboo rods. While graphite has not affected the demand for trout-model bamboo rods at all, it has overshadowed to a great extent what small demand there might have been for heavy cane rods.

Surprisingly, for the collector, this may bode well! Consider these facts: (1) The interest in bamboo rods has increased immeasurably in recent years in spite of the new wonder material, graphite. (2) Currently, contemporary bamboo-rod makers are spending only a small fraction of their rod-building time making larger cane rods. (3) The heavy cane rods that were made by earlier makers are now a glut on the market in the face of today's graphite-rod competition, and their current market prices reflect this fact. How can this be good for today's rod collector? Consider further: (1) The rods of earlier makers are no longer made. Their numbers are fixed and their supply is not inexhaustible. (2) There are very few contemporary, long bamboo rods coming out of the quality rod shops to add to this supply. (3) The interest in collecting bamboo rods continues to increase, creating what might be a true "sleeper" situation in long cane rods.

Until and unless something comes along to change things, the long cane rods should prove to be an excellent investment. They are now readily available, and they are now market-priced far below their true value. At some point in the future, the available market supplies of these rods will be as exhausted as the supply of quality trout models has already become. As this occurs, you can expect a rapid increase in the market value of the long cane rods as a result of the supply-demand effect. This has already occurred with trout rods and must occur with the heavier rods as well, although more time may have to pass than was necessary for the trout rods.

In any case, it is a safe bet that today's near-giveaway prices on long cane rods will prove to be a boon tomorrow to the collector interested enough to capitalize on it. It might be interesting to begin acquiring a collection of finely made rods of 9, 9½, and 10 feet in length, and watch these rods appreciate in value.

THE GREAT AMERICAN MAKERS

Although the history of fly-fishing records that Solon Phillippe, Ebeneezer Greene, Charles Murphy, and Hiram Lewis Leonard were this country's pioneers in split-cane rod construction, it is clearly Hiram Leonard who can be considered the father of the modern fly rod. This is demonstrated both in the remarkable skill and technical knowledge his work displayed and in the truly great rodmakers he trained in his shop in Bangor, Maine: men like the Hawes brothers, Edward Payne, Fred Thomas, Fred Devine, Eustis Edwards, Thomas Chubb, and George Varney.

Hiram Lewis Leonard moved his rod plant to Central Valley in 1881 to be nearer to the New York and Philadelphia rod markets and to the controlling interest of the Mills family in New York. By that time, he had already developed and patented the modern split-shoulder type of suction ferrule that featured serrations on the bamboo edges and employed a waterproofing disc, silver-soldered in the ferrules to cap the cane and protect it from mold and deterioration.

By 1893 the famed Catskill Series of trout rods had evolved, firmly establishing the basic character of the modern Leonard rod. Skeletal-type reel seats with hardwood fillers, separate German silver butt caps and slide bands, cigar-shaped grips, and full-reel seats of ornamentally machined German silver tubing were characteristic of the early Leonard rods, and have carried down to the more modern Leonards.

The Catskill Fairy was already on the scene in a 7½-foot rod of three-piece design weighing about two ounces. Catskill rods were made in lengths from 7½ to 10 feet in three-piece design with light trout actions.

Under Reuben Leonard, the major transition from the earlier Leonard rod to the more modern version took place. Reuben Leonard pioneered and developed the entire Tournament Series of rods. Initially, these Tournament rods were built as 9-footers weighing between 5¼ and 6 ounces. Later the series included 8- to 10½-foot rods, all of three-piece design and ranging in weight from 3¼ to 7½ ounces.

Some of the best-loved Leonard fly rods are classics that were developed under the direction of Reuben Leonard, a noted champion caster. The most popular of these was the Model 50 DF, first introduced in 1915. The rod is an 8-footer of three-piece design weighing about four ounces. Many of these rods were fitted with the now classic, and very graceful, reverse-cigar grips that tapered directly to the hooded nickel-silver butt cap with a sliding ring on the continuous cork handle.

The Leonard shop produced many truly fine classic rods from 1915 to the disastrous fire in the mid-1960s. During the period from pre-World War II to his retirement in 1965, George Reynolds was instrumental in refining and further honing the already sophisticated Leonard tapers into such classics as the Model 38 ACM (a delicate 7-foot, two-piece rod of 2¼ ounces), the 36L at 6 feet and 1 ounce, the modern 38H at 7 feet and 2¾ ounces, and the 37 ACM at 6 feet and 1½ ounces for #3 line. The 50 DF was well established and was joined by the famous Hunt Pattern, an 8-foot, three-piece counterpart of the 50 DF. The Hunt Pattern was designed by the late Richard Hunt, author of the classic *Salmon in Low Water*. His specifications included a slightly faster action, and weight of 4⅝ ounces, and the rod was fitted with oxidized fittings and ferrules against a brown-toned cane, much darker than the traditional Leonard straw color. The wraps were dark brown to offset the medium-brown cane color.

Before the fire, Leonard also made a series of three-piece rods with particularly delicate actions suited to traditional wet-fly work. These ranged from the Model 35 at 7 feet and 2¾ ounces to the Model 46 at 9½ feet and 5½ ounces.

Some of the Leonard rods of two-piece design that became classics after midcentury included the very popular Model 65 at 7½ feet and 3½ ounces, the 8-foot Model 66, and the powerful 67H at 9 feet and 6 ounces. Most of these rods were fitted with the standard screw-lock seat and are cherished by their owners as fine fishing tools.

You might add to these some of the special tapers designed over the years— like the Knight 99, a powerful 9¾-foot rod for #9 line at 7¼ ounces, designed by the late John Alden Knight for bass bugging; the Model 38½, a 7½-foot, three-piece rod at 3⅝ ounces, considered by some owners to be one of Leonard's best; and the countless special-built and custom rods made for exacting customers. The array of fine fishing tools to come out of the Leonard shop is mighty impressive.

For the serious rod collector or collector-fisherman, this is a blessing, since the large number of Leonard rods built over a 60-year period puts most of the better models out of the "rare" category and into the realm of reality in market value. The current price level on today's market for used Leonard rods ranges from $200 to $400, with an occasional model worth up to $450 for such reasons as relative scarcity, fishing worthiness, exceptional condition, or a combination of these factors.

It is important to note that Leonard was one of the few shops to manufacture some fine one-piece rods over the years. Other builders made an occasional one-piece 6-foot rod, but not like the Leonard rods of 7, 8, and 8½ feet. These rods are rare and range in market value to $750 for a mint-condition specimen.

Many Leonard rod collectors define their interest in these rods by breaking the history of Leonard into four distinct periods. The first interval is from the earliest days to the pre-World War I period, which represents the oldest of the

Leonard rods. Most of these are classed as antique rods and exhibit the earmarks of the development of the Leonard rod through the work of men like Hiram Leonard, Ed Payne, Fred Thomas, and Eustis Edwards.

The period from 1915 through 1965, beginning with the developmental work of Reuben Leonard and culminating with the work of George Reynolds, produced the Tournament Leonard Tapers and many of the now classic Leonard actions, and brought the Leonard product to the modern rod level. Rods of this period are often called "Pre-Fire Leonards" and are among the most eagerly sought of the Leonard rods. For many knowledgeable collectors, this period is considered the Golden Era at the Leonard factory. To aid the collector in identifying rods of this period, it is important to note that none of these rods carries a factory serial number. The rods of this period often command the highest used-rod prices, ranging in value to $500 on the market.

After the disastrous fire in 1965, which completely consumed the Leonard shop and destroyed many of the original templates used to cut the Leonard rod tapers, the chore of rebuilding and regenerating was given to Hap Mills and Ted Simroe. These two men produced some exceptionally fine cane rods, utilizing both old and newly developed rod tapers created by master rod builder Simroe. These rods are characterized by the traditional red wraps, butternut reel seats, and straw-colored cane. They are always factory-serial numbered, and many of these rods are highly prized by their owners. They range in value to $400 on today's market.

In 1978, the Leonard shop was purchased by the Johnson Wax Company. Current rod production is under the management of Thomas Maxwell. Recently produced rods have sold for $250 to $375 on the used rod market.

Some men have spent a lifetime collecting only Leonard rods. I know of one such collection that numbers in excess of 60 rods and represents one of the finest samplings in the country of over 50 years of the Leonard tradition. While most collectors turn their efforts into acquiring representative samplings of each of the great rodmakers, it is a very easy matter to become enamored of the rods of one maker and concentrate most of one's efforts on collecting his rods.

Edward Payne and his legacy are a curious note in the history of the split-bamboo rod. Payne's beginning, as only the ferrule machinist in the original Leonard shop in Bangor, points up the remarkable realization that it was his E. F. Payne Rod Company that ultimately equaled and, according to many disciples, surpassed the work of his original master. There are many who believe that the Payne fly-fishing rods are the ultimate in the rodbuilder's art.

The rods designed and built by Edward Payne at the turn of the century were little different from the rods his son was making 60 years later. There were some minor cosmetic differences, but there were surprisingly few changes in the appearance of the Payne rod in the 80-year history of the company. When Edward Payne died during World War I, his interest in the company passed to his son, James Payne, who had worked in the shop since boyhood.

The design and workmanship of these rods were so good that the demand for them was never equaled by the supply of finished rods. In fact, when Jim Payne passed away in 1970 there was a run on the remaining Payne rods in stock at Abercrombie & Fitch, which drove their prices up so dramatically that two weeks after Jim's death, the last rod sold for almost $200 higher than the going market price of $225.

Edward Payne built rods of three-piece design in a limited choice of models, ranging from an 8-footer at 3¼ ounces for #4 line to a 10-footer at 6 ounces for #9 line. The series included another 8-footer for #5 line at 3¾ ounces and a light 8½-footer at 4¼ ounces for #6 silk. There were two 9-foot rods — a lightweight 4¼-ounce stick for #6 line and a 4¾-ounce rod for #7 line. Two 9½-foot rods weighing 5¼ and 5¾ ounces, taking #7 and #8 lines, rounded out the selection. Ed Payne worked with equal relish on rods constructed of either straw-colored cane with natural-finish German-silver ferrules and fittings or the darker brown-toned cane with oxidized ferrules and fittings.

In the early 1930s, Jim Payne dropped the lighter-colored rods in favor of the brown-toned sticks, which have become the Payne hallmark. Jim also added smaller rods and offered two 7-footers at 2⅞ and 3⅛ ounces in three-piece design, and a pair of 7½-foot rods at 3 and 3¼ ounces. The 10-foot rod had disappeared and was succeeded by a series of rods of two-piece design. These included the rare 6-foot wand of 1½ ounces, a 7-footer of 2¼ ounces, a 7½-footer at 2⅝ ounces, and an 8-footer of 3⅞ ounces. This two-piece line was topped off by an 8½-footer of 4¼ ounces and a 9-footer at 5¼ ounces. By 1939, Payne had stopped building three-piece rods under 7½ feet and was concentrating on rods of two-piece design. The famous Payne screw-locking seat, and the four Parabolic designs, had now been introduced. There were now 15 three-piece models from 7½ to 9½ feet. The two-piece line had expanded to include a 6-foot rod of 1⅝ ounces, a 7-foot taper of 2¾ ounces, two 7½-foot designs of 3 and 3¼ ounces, three 8-footers ranging from 3½ to 4⅛ ounces, an 8½-foot design that evolved from the butt and tip sections of a 12-foot two-handed Payne salmon rod owned by A. E. Hendrickson, and finally a 9-footer at 5½ ounces.

The Parabolic Payne rods evolved from designs developed in France by Charles Ritz, but it was actually John Alden Knight who worked with Jim Payne to develop the American versions.

These rods were of two-piece design and were fitted with graceful full-cork reel seats to reduce weight. The smallest of the four rods was 7 feet 1 inch in

Left: Gillum stamp on aluminum band. Right: Payne pocket cap with marking. Note machining on cap. (Photos courtesy Matthew Vinciguerra)

length, weighed 2⅞ ounces, and handled a #3 or #4 silk with equal ease. The 7½-footer weighed 3⅜ ounces and used a #5 line. The 7¾-foot taper was built in two models at 3¾ and 4⅛ ounces, which handled #5 and #6 weight lines, respectively.

The final Payne catalog, itself a collector's item, lists 14 fly rods of three-piece design from 7½ to 9½ feet and 14 tapers of two-piece design from 6 to 9 feet. It shows a 6½-foot rod at 2¼ ounces not found in earlier catalogs, and reduces the Parabolics to only two models at 7 feet 1 inch and 7¾ feet. There are seven dry-fly salmon rods with detachable extension butt. Five of these rods are of three-piece design from 9 to 10½ feet and 6⅝ to 9 ounces, and two are two-piece designs at 9 feet and 6 ounces and 9½ feet and 7 ounces. Also listed are four three-piece dry-fly salmon rods with a permanent 2-inch extension butt giving the rods odd finished lengths. There is a 9-foot-2-inch rod at 7⅛ ounces; a 9-foot-5-inch stick at 7½ ounces; a 9-foot-8-inch and a 10-foot-2-inch rod at 7⅝ and 9¼ ounces, respectively. Payne salmon rods, those from 9½ to 10½ feet, were made with double-built butt sections for increased strength. The series of two-handed salmon rods listed are of three-piece design, and ranged from 10½ to 14 feet in length and from 10½ to 20¼ ounces in weight. These rods were double-built in both the butt and midsections and demonstrated unbelievable power. The catalog shows three bonefish rods with special noncorrosive guides and fittings, as well as rods for spinning and bait casting, and four special fly rods. These last four were a 9-foot bass bug rod at 6½ ounces, two streamer rods at 8½ and 9 feet and 5⅝ and 6 ounces, and a Canadian canoe rod at 8½ feet and 5 ounces.

No one knows for certain the total number of rods produced in the Payne shop over the 80-year history of the company, but the rods have proved to be relatively scarce in comparison with rods of other makers. I am not certain whether this is because a low number of rods were produced, or because they are such fine fishing tools that their owners are always reluctant to sell or trade them. Whatever the reason, the rods are not always easy to come by and they range to $1,500 on the collector's market for mint, never-fished specimens. Used rods in excellent or better condition range from $400 to $1,200, depending on their length, with the shorter rods, 8 feet and under, being the most desirable and therefore higher priced.

There are countless anecdotes about Payne, many touching on his search for perfection or his stubborn honesty and integrity. Even without these reminders of his uncompromising craftsmanship, his rods tell it all.

Eustis Edwards began his rodbuilding career at the Leonard plant in Bangor. He was a cane workman of great skill and performed the bamboo functions in his brief partnership with Fred Thomas and Ed Payne, which produced the Kosmic rod, a rare antique rod of considerable value. Although Eustis Edwards built rods under his own name for a number of years, it was his sons, William and Eugene, who truly blossomed as rodmakers.

Many early Edwards rods were made in volume lots for large companies or sporting-goods stores, like Von Lengerke & Detmoldt, Abercrombie & Fitch, and Abbey & Imbrie. Later in his career, he did produce some superb modern fly rods that exerted considerable influence. He made a run of 7½-foot rods for the Winchester Repeating Arms Co., which were marketed as the Winchester rod, and which created quite a stir on the Catskill rivers because of their exceptional actions—the popularity of 7½-footers on American rivers has been largely attributed to Eustis Edwards.

His best rods were a dark, deeply colored bamboo with purple wraps, tipped in yellow, and were built with a smooth medium action that worked almost to the grip.

I own an 8-foot, three-piece rod that began life as a Eustis Edwards made of Calcutta cane. Over the years, the mid and tips were replaced as a result of breakage, but always with care to protect the integrity of the original action. After a recent refinish session at Thomas & Thomas, the only part of the rod that remains original is the Edwards Calcutta butt—the mid and tips are of Tonkin cane by Edwards, Heddon, and Thomas & Thomas. The grip and reel seat are Thomas & Thomas, as are the ferrules, but the rod retains its original, full working action and is one of my favorite fishing rods.

It was Billy Edwards who broke the mold and developed a unique line of four-strip rods with accompanying special ferrules, grip checks, and reel seat fittings, and his tapers were superb. These rods were built in both two-piece and three-piece designs ranging from 6 to 9½ feet. In two-piece, he produced the 6-foot rod for #3 line at 1¾ ounces, a 6½-footer for #3 line at 2⅛ ounces, a 7-foot rod for #4 line at 2⅝ ounces, the 7½-foot design for #4 line at 3⅛ ounces, a 7½-foot rod for #5 at 3⅝ ounces, an 8-footer for #5 line at 4⅛ ounces, and a powerful, faster action 8-foot taper for #6 line at 4⅝ ounces. The three-piece rods included an 8½-foot rod for #4 line at 4⅛ ounces, and a 9-footer at 5¼ ounces and a 9½-footer at 5¾ ounces, both for #7 line. The biggest one he offered was a 9½-foot rod at a full 7 ounces for a #9 line.

Gene Edwards stayed with the standard six-strip rod construction and can be credited with the Special and Deluxe models. These were top-quality sticks that displayed the family resemblance to the work of Edward Payne, Eustis Edwards' colleague. The Edwards Rod Company produced less expensive models such as the Mt. Carmel and the Bristol. These too were well-constructed rods but were usually fitted with less ornate and less costly fittings.

Bill Edwards' quads range to $450 on the current market, with most selling between $250 and $350. The six-sided Deluxe and Special rods are comparably priced, while the originally less expensive rods, such as the Bristol and Mt. Carmel, bring $175 to $275, depending on size and condition.

Fred Thomas was the only one of the original group of Leonard to return to Bangor. He started making rods under his name and was unquestionably one of the best who ever split cane.

His rods retained a strong resemblance to the Leonards and were similarly softer action rods. He worked both in the straw-color cane with bright fittings and in the browntone color of rich chocolate with oxidized fittings. The Thomas grip check and check windings are unique in that the nickel-silver check ring also incorporates the fly-keeper ring. The check windings above the grip were a signature of delicate brown winds in a grouping series of three, seven, three. He used similar wraps at the top guide, which also had a unique German-silver reinforcing tongue under the silk.

His rods fully equaled the work of Hiram and Reuben Leonard and are prized by their owners. Although many of the Maine customers demanded rods to handle huge streamers and heavy tippets, Thomas and his son, Leon, built some of the finest light-action rods that money can buy.

His top-of-the-line rods were the Special and Special Browntone. The second-quality line was the Dirigo, and his least expensive model was the Bangor. The Special and Browntone rods are exquisite, with few rivals. These rods carried the best fittings and employed hardwood spacer reel seats of slide-band and screwlock design. Some of these rods were mounted with all-cork seats reminiscent of the Leonard 50 DF. The Dirigo and Bangor rods were not produced in the browntone color and employed less ornate and expensive fittings.

The Thomas shop produced three-piece rods from 7½ feet long to a 15-foot, two-handed salmon rod. The two-piece designs were 7 to 8½ feet long. The 8½-foot, three-piece rod at 5¼ ounces is one of the finest tapers in its length. There was also an 8-foot, three-piece at 4⅛ ounces, which fishes a #5 line to perfection. One of the two best 7-foot Thomas rods I've ever seen was a two-piece Special with intermediate winds at 2⅝ ounces for a #4 line. This was a very early Thomas and is now in the collection of a doctor in Houston, Texas. The other was an exquisite two-piece Browntone Special for a #3 line at 2½ ounces, now owned by actor William Conrad.

Fred Thomas and his son Leon built rods under the Thomas hallmark for over 40 years, but after Fred died, the company foundered and passed into receivership. Its equipment and designs were subsequently divided between Walt Carpenter and Sam Carlson, who currently own the rights to the Thomas tapers and name.

The Thomas Bangor and Dirigo rods currently range to $300 on today's market, with most selling between $175 and $250. The Special rods range to $450, with most in the $300 to $375 range. The Browntone Specials command a bit higher price, ranging to $500, with most in the $350 and $450 bracket, depending on length and condition.

Thomas & Thomas, not to be confused with the F. E. Thomas Rod Co., is a contemporary rod shop located in Turners Falls, Massachusetts. The company is co-owned by Tom Dorsey and Len Codella.

From its beginning, Tom Dorsey has directed the rod-building work at T&T. In the past decade, the rods designed and built by Dorsey under the T&T marque have proved to have had the most significant impact on the bamboo rod world since Payne, Edwards, and Thomas left the Leonard Rod Company to set out on their own nearly 90 years ago. Tom Dorsey's work is compared today with that done by rodmaking's finest builders of decades past. To be recognized in just one short decade as a maker of contemporary classics that are worthy of comparison with the best work of a bygone era is fitting testimony to the genius and creativity of the very small group of craftsmen at the T&T shop.

Through Dorsey's efforts, Thomas & Thomas has pioneered quality standards, construction techniques, and cosmetic appointments that are now being copied by a number of other contemporary makers. This is reminiscent of the traditions and standards set by that earlier pioneer, Jim Payne, whose work is still emulated by contemporary builders more than 12 years after his death. It is interesting to note that Dorsey, who is totally self-taught, has been called the modern-day Payne. The Thomas & Thomas rod lends credibility to that belief.

Thomas & Thomas was the first company to use modern thermosetting adhesives in rod construction. It is the first and only company to build both varnished *and* impregnated rods to the same exacting quality standards. The Thomas & Thomas morticed, walnut reel seats, special grip designs, and uniquely distinctive hardware are now world famous, and were the first of their type ever used on high-grade rods. The translucent look of the T&T wraps has been brought to a "state of the art" level at Thomas & Thomas and is now copied by many builders.

In short, the impact of T&T's rod work in taper designs, construction, and cosmetics has changed the quality standards by which today's rod makers are guided, and have set a merry pace for all to follow.

The Thomas & Thomas cane, a large store of 40-year-old bamboo, was purchased from Sewell N. Dunton in the early 1970s, along with rodmaking equipment, by Dorsey and then co-owner, Thomas Maxwell. The name of the firm derives from the first names of these two men. Maxwell left the firm in its earlier years and has recently joined the Leonard Rod Company as a rodmaker.

The handcrafted rods of Thomas & Thomas are offered in two ranges. The Classic Series defines eight models ranging in length from 6½ feet to 8½ feet, with line weights from #3 to #7. The Classic rods are made with either a varnished finish or an impregnated finish as desired, and offer a host of reel seat and grip options available to suit the buyer's taste. Sophisticated compound tapers and 40-year-old cane combine to produce a lively, medium-fast rod action, which is the measure of any high-quality rod built today.

The Individualist Series of rods includes five trout model categories—the Caenis Series for #3 line; the Midge Series for #4 line; the Hendrickson Series for #5 line; the Montana Series for #6, #7, and #8 lines; and the Paradigm Series, built on special parabolic tapers, for #4, #5, and #6 lines. Rod lengths range from 6 feet to 9 feet and are available in two- or three-piece design. There are over 40 Individualist Trout models from which to select. The Individualist Salmon Series offers rods of two- and three-piece design from 8 feet to 10 feet for line weights from #6 through #10.

The Sans Pareil Series of rods is a category reserved for T&T's finest custom-made rods. This series offers one-piece rods from 6 feet to 10 feet, in line sizes from #3 to #10, as well as two- or three-piece rods in the same lengths and line weights. Sans Pareil actions are always unique, as are many of the custom cosmetic options available to the buyer. All T&T Individualist rods are available in either a varnished or impregnated finish.

The list of back orders at T&T is fairly extensive, and the current wait for a new rod from this firm is 14 to 18 months.

On the used rod market, the T&T rod retains much of its new price level, with the Classic Series ranging to $425. Rods in the Trout and Salmon Individualist Series range between $550 and $650, while Sans Pareil rods generally resell for $600 to $800, depending on the model.

Lyle Dickerson was born and raised in Bellaire, Michigan. During his high-school years he built a few bait rods from such materials as ironwood and white cedar. He completed his degree from Hillsdale College on the eve of World War I, and both his fishing and rodmaking were interrupted by service with the fledgling Air Corps in France.

Upon his return to Detroit, he found work in truck and real-estate sales. He fished streams like the Mantisee, Au Sable, and Pere Marquette. The Great Depression forced him into handcrafting furniture, where he associated with highly skilled artisans with fierce pride in their work. This contact developed in him a passion for quality that undoubtedly carried over to, and influenced, his later work.

When he finally decided to build bamboo rods, he found no help either from books or from the craftsmen at Heddon, since their shop was closed to outsiders and the secrets of split-bamboo craftsmanship were closely guarded. He managed to purchase a few culms of cane from Heddon and by dismantling unserviceable rods was able to unravel some of the mysteries of the art. Dickerson then borrowed some fine split-cane rods and calibrated them, attempting to duplicate their tapers with homemade planing blocks and tools. Subsequent fishing on his home rivers resulted in extensive modifications of

Dickerson signed and numbered his rods just forward of the hook keeper. "R.B." on a Dickerson means it was sold by Ray Bergman, who was a sales agent for Dickerson. (Photo courtesy Matthew Vinciguerra)

his designs and ultimately led to the unique performance associated with his rods.

Dickerson's move back to Detroit initiated his professional rodmaking career in the early 1930s. Although the quality of his work rapidly became known on Michigan's rivers, there were few buyers of rods even at the modest price of $35 because few anglers could afford that price.

It was the late Ray Bergman who really launched Dickerson and his reputation for quality. On a fishing trip to Michigan, Bergman met Dickerson in Detroit. Bergman's favorite rod was a steep-taper tournament-type 7½-foot Leonard, which Dickerson calibrated and then offered to match action for action. Bergman was immensely pleased with the new Dickerson and recounted that pleasure in print, giving Dickerson his first taste of national recognition.

I recently acquired a 7½-foot three-piece Dickerson built on the Bergman tapers. The rod is initialed R.B. after the model number above the grip and is in near-mint condition. It weighs 3¾ ounces and handles a #5 line with flawless precision. The rod's action is moderately fast, working fully toward the grip. It is the epitome of the classic dry fly rod, and the craftsmanship is exquisite. The rod displays a medium-brown color, is wrapped with chocolate winds tipped black, and is fitted with precision oxidized ferrules and a walnut-filled reverse-screw lock seat. Dickerson used extremely large culms of thick-walled cane and transmitted the density of the cane through his steep tapers into remarkably fast actions.

The Dickerson line included seven three-piece rods: a 7½-footer at 3¾ ounces, an 8-foot design at 4¼ ounces, an 8½-foot rod of 4¾ ounces, a pair of 9-footers at 5½ and 6 ounces, and two 9½ footers at 6 and 6½ ounces. Two-piece Dickersons included a 7½-footer at 3½ ounces, two 8-foot rods at 4 and 4¼ ounces, an 8½-footer at 4½ ounces, and a 9-foot design at 5½ ounces.

I recently acquired one of Ray Bergman's personal Dickersons that had been custom-built for him. It is a 10-foot, detachable-butt, salmon rod at 6¼ ounces for a #7 line. It is fast and powerful, but extremely light in the hand, and a valuable collector's rod.

Dickerson's rods are rare and on a par in both performance and craftsmanship with any of the finest. In the supply-demand rod market, it is amazing that his rods do not command a higher price, since his total lifetime production was only slightly more than 2,000 rods. In comparison with other rodmakers, Dickerson was not as well known and I am certain that this has had much to do with the relatively low prices for his rods. This has already begun to change as more people have become aware of his work. The prices paid just recently for Dickerson rods are considerably higher than those paid as little as two years ago. The rods range currently to $800, with most bringing $500 to $600. A rod of special significance, such as the Bergman rod mentioned earlier, would command perhaps $100 over top price. The scarcity of Dickerson's rods makes them an excellent investment if you are fortunate enough to find one.

The R. L. Winston Rod Company was formed in 1927 by Robert Winther and Lewis Stoner. The name was a contraction of their initials and last names. Although Winther liquidated his interest in 1933, Stoner decided to leave the company name unchanged. W. W. Loskot became a partner at the Winston shop the following year and continued for nearly 20 years until leaving in 1953. Douglas Merrick had come into the Winston Shop in 1945 to buy a new rod and never left. In 1953 Loskot sold his interest to Merrick, and the unique collaboration between Stoner and Merrick was probably the Golden Age at Winston.

Stoner died suddenly in 1957, and Gary Howells, who had been Stoner's protégé for almost 10 years, came to work in the shop full-time shortly thereafter. Howells and Merrick made fine fly rods together until the early 1970s, when Gary decided to build his own rods. Merrick recently sold his controlling interest in the Winston shop to Sidney Eliason and Thomas Morgan. Tom Morgan has continued the Winston tradition, producing fine bamboo rods with a quality of workmanship that remains unchanged.

The quality of the Winston product is a reflection of the genius of Stoner, and the patents for the fluted hollow-built construction he made famous. Even the ferrules on the Winston rods are uniquely Stoner, being made from an alloy of silicone, copper, and aluminum called *duronze*. They are lighter and stronger than steel, corrosion-resistant, and more costly than nickel-silver. Winston ferrules are cut from bar-stock duronze and individually centered, bored, drilled, reamed, and hand-lapped for a perfect fit. They are tapered to ricepaper thinness at the transition point to the cane, and the cane itself is turned to match the exact internal dimension of the ferrules. They are then driven home over a coat of cement and pinned for permanent security.

The Winston reel seats are unique, too. The fillers are turned from a costly high-strength Bakelite, which is almost totally free of expansion and corrosion. The fittings are jewel-polished aluminum. The smaller Winston rods are fitted with a slotted cork filler, and the grips are the traditional half-Wells style.

The most popular Winston rods in the East are the Leetle Feller Series. The tapers, which are designed for relatively short, delicate casts where accuracy is critical, carry #3 and #4 lines. There are four rods for #3 line: a 5½-footer at 1¾ ounces, a 6-footer at 2 ounces, a 6½-footer at 2⅛ ounces, and a delightful 7-footer at 2½ ounces. The 7-footer at 2⅝ ounces and 7½-footer at 3⅛ ounces, both for a DT4 line, round out the series.

The Light Trout Series handle #4 and #5 lines. These rods, too, are delicate but demonstrate more muscle than the Leetle Fellers. There is a 5½-footer at 2 ounces and a 6-footer at 2¼ ounces, both for DT4 lines. The #5 rods include the 6-footer at 2½ ounces, two 6½-footers at 2½ and 2¾ ounces, two 7-foot rods at 2⅞ and 3 ounces, and a pair of 7½-foot tapers of 3¼ and 3½ ounces.

The Standard Trout rods include an 8-foot design for a #4 line at 3⅝ ounces, and two 8-footers at 3¾ and 4 ounces, and an 8½-foot rod at 4⅛ ounces, all for a DT5 line. There are two 8½-foot rods at 4¼ and 4½ ounces for #6 lines, and an 8½-foot stick of 4¾ ounces for a #7 line. The two 8¾-foot rods are 4⅝ and 4¾ ounces and take #7 and #8 lines. Classed as steelhead rods, the three 9-foot Winstons of 5, 5¼, and 5½ ounces take #8 and #9 lines. These rods are magnificent performers on our Western steelhead rivers as well as on salmon rivers all over the world.

Winston rods are of two-piece design and range to a high of $375 on the used-rod market for two-tip specimens. The one-tip rods range to $250. Condition is the determining factor, and average or better rods sell for $175 to $300 used, with the higher price for rods in mint condition.

Some collectors believe that rods built by Stoner in the 1930s and early 1940s are worth a bit more in price than current rods, but I think that a good Winston is a good Winston and the nostalgia bug should not be taken too seriously.

Edwin C. Powell built his first cane rod in California about 1912. By 1922, his shop in Marysville was famous. The rods he constructed prior to 1933 were all of six-strip solid construction. That year he was granted his patent for semi-hollow construction, which launched his construction technique in a new direction. Even before embarking on a full-scale program of semi-hollow construction, the technique Powell used in building standard six-strip rods was rather unusual. Showing signs of Hardy influence, Powell would mill the inner pith from the inside of the rough-cut cane strips until there remained about ⅛ inch of dense outer power fibers. To this inner face he would glue a strip of Port Orford cedar and, when the laminated strip was cured, would complete the final milling cuts on a machine that he also designed and built. It was quite remarkable work and employed the interesting concept of replacing quite useless pith material with a stronger, although not heavier, material. Powell developed the semi-hollow concept to further reduce the weight of the finished rod. This was accomplished by scalloping 6-inch hollows out of the cedar, thus leaving small solid sections for gluing strength. The result was an extremely lightweight rod of significant power with yet a delicate action for its length. Indeed many of the vintage Powell hollow-built steelhead rods are

eagerly sought by knowledgeable fishermen-collectors for their fine performance on big waters.

Powell rods were glued with animal glues, which made them a bit fragile,
and the finely done, intermediate winding, spaced about two inches apart, was
more than ornamentation. His rods were wrapped in either brown or antique
gold, and the signature wrap above the grip—which also held the fly keeper—
was all black on his solid built rods or black edged in white on his semi-hollow
designs. He used a reverse-screw lock seat of jewel-polished aluminum with
a distinctive Bakelite filler, again a result of Hardy's influence. His grips were
of full-Wells design and never varied for 30-odd years.

Most vintage three-piece Powell rods are solid-built, while his two-piece
sticks are for the most part semi-hollow. Powell worked mainly in longer
rods suited to the northern California rivers. His 9½-foot steelhead models
weighed 5½ to 6 ounces; the 9-foot rods, 4¾ to 5½ ounces; the 8½-foot trout
rods, 4½ to 5 ounces. He built a few 8-footers at 4 to 4½ ounces and even fewer
7½-footers at 3½ ounces. These last designs are very rare.

Powell rods in mint condition range to $500 on the classic rod market,
with most rods in average condition selling in the $250 to $400 range. The rare
7½-footer would command about $750 in mint condition and about $400 to
$500 in average shape.

With Tonkin cane again available, Edwin's son Walton Powell is again
building the Powell rod, using his father's patents and tapers. He began as an
apprentice in the Marysville shop in 1922 at age seven and, discounting one
or two departures from rodbuilding over the years, has almost a half-century
of rodbuilding experience.

Gary Howells left after 22 years in the Winston shop in 1970 to build rods
under his own signature. He "wanted to build rods with the lightness and power
of a Winston or Powell—yet with the elegance and grace of a Payne." He has
certainly reached his objective. While the Winston influence shows in his
work, he has made subtle modifications in the tapers, which are uniquely
his. The tempering process he uses produces a richly toned brown cane color,
and his butts are hollow-built, giving lightness to his rods. Howell machines
his own ferrules from solid bar stock duronze and hand laps each for final fit.

In all, Howells builds 40 standard rod tapers, ranging from 6 feet to 9 feet 3
inches and works in two-piece designs only. Gary Howells is a master craftsman who insists on performing every operation himself and is capable of producing about 100 rods a year. As his circle of devotees continues to grow, so
does the wait for one of his rods, but it is well worth it.

His rods are priced new in the $450 to $500 range depending on size, style,
and so forth. They are, without question, modern classics.

Paul Young was a paradox among rodbuilders. Born in 1890 in Arkansas, his background included accomplishments as a commercial fisherman, a taxidermist, tackle salesman, fly-tier, tackle-store owner and finally master rodbuilder. He possessed an intuitive knowledge of actions and rod tapers and began his rodbuilding career by modifying the wet-fly actions then in fashion. By 1927, his first experimental compound tapers had appeared, which 12 years later were labeled "parabolics" when John Alden Knight wrote about these unique actions. Paradoxically, we see Paul Young, with beginnings as a set-line catfisherman on the Mississippi, becoming the self-taught Stradivari of the semi-parabolic taper—a remarkable accomplishment considering the rodbuilding vacuum, (with the exception of Lyle Dickerson) in the Midwest.

Young's first rods were the Special Series, which included a 7½-foot taper at 3⅜ ounces, two 8-footers at 4 and 4½ ounces, an 8½-footer at 4¾ ounces, and a 9-foot Special 17 at 5¼ ounces, all of two-piece design. There was also the Special 18, a three-piece rod of 6½ ounces for a #9 line.

Young was an innovator—a creator. He cared little for how his rods looked and was constantly experimenting with new techniques, glues, and finishes. His early rods were worked in natural-color cane, and some show experiments with dark synthetic glues and resins. It was not until near midcentury that Paul more or less standardized the appearance of his rods, using a flame-tempering technique to achieve a darkened, half-carbonized finish. Even then, he never stopped trying new things and sought to reduce the power-to-weight ratios in his rods. He went as far as developing black, anodized aluminum ferrules, which proved surprisingly good, and employing a unique method of laminating and waterproofing the rod joints.

By midcentury, the now famous Midge rod—a 6¼-foot rod for a #4 line at 1¾ ounces—was on the market. This rod is one of the most sought-after of the Youngs, running second only to the 7½-foot Perfectionist. The Midge has the capability of protecting 5X and 6X tippets and yet delivering the fly at 50 feet with precision.

The Driggs River Special at 2⅞ ounces is a 7-foot 2-inch taper for #5 line with a fast, powerful action.

The Perfectionist is *the* Young rod and the most difficult to obtain of all the Youngs. It is a 7½-foot rod for a #4 line at 2⅝ ounces. It has the ability to cast 80 feet of line *and* protect 7X tippets—indeed a rare combination in any rod.

The Martha Marie was designed and named for Paul's wife, who maintains a cottage on, and still fishes, the Au Sable in Michigan. It is a strong 7½-foot dry-fly rod at 3 ounces, designed for use on larger rivers. It handles a #6 line.

The Parabolic 15 is an 8-foot rod made with separate dry-fly and distance tips. The rod weighs 3¾ ounces with the dry-fly top and handles a #6 line. With the distance tips, it weighs 4 ounces and takes a #7 line and larger flies.

There was also the K. T. Keller version of the Para 15 with a slow-action butt and a bit more delicacy.

The Parabolic 17 is an 8½-footer at 5⅞ ounces for hair bugs and poppers. The Bobby Doerr was a 9-foot 6-ounce rod for #9 line. The Parabolic 18 at 6½ ounces and 9 feet carries a #9 line, and the Para 19 at 6½ ounces and 9 feet takes a #10. The Powerhouse rounds out the line at 9½ feet for a #11 line.

During his career Young also made a number of special rods and experimental tapers such as the Parabolic 16 — a lovely 8½-footer for #7 line.

Of most interest to the collector is a series of six rods Paul built in 1958, two years before his death. He called them the Princess model, at 7 feet and 2¾ ounces for a #4 line. These six experimental rods were fitted with a skeletal seat and were wrapped in black silk. They are an example of the restless nature of their maker. During the same production run, Young built one 7½-foot Princess for his personal use. It was assembled with a light and heavy top characteristic of the Para 15 rods. Fitted with the light top, it does well with 8X tippets and tiny flies. The heavier tip will deliver a streamer with authority at 80 feet. This very special rod is now in the collection of Ernest Schwiebert and is one of his most cherished fly rods.

Young's son Jack has been carrying on the family business since his father's death in 1960 and continues to manufacture the most popular of the Young rod models with the same eye for quality and workmanship demonstrated by his father.

Although new Young rods are available today at about $500, the rods built by Paul can and do command higher prices in mint condition. The Midge through the Para 15 models range to $900 among collectors, with rods that are in average condition selling at $350 to $600.

The larger models range to $400 in mint condition and about $50 less in average shape.

A mint condition rod from current production is worth about $400 and will sell for about $325 in average or better condition.

The total lifetime production of rods by Paul Young is relatively small, and this makes the more popular models extremely difficult to acquire.

Because of their rarity, the unique Princess rods are worth about $1,000 in any reasonable condition and perhaps as much as double that figure in mint condition.

Harold Steele Gillum began his rodmaking career as an apprentice in the Payne rod shop, having earlier learned how to build split-bamboo rods through his friendship with Eustis Edwards. Gillum's rods bear a strong resemblance to the designs of Jim Payne. His rods have characteristically fast tapers and are basically fast-action fly rods influenced by Edward R. Hewitt's early theories concerning rod actions. Gillum was a moody individual, and his character had a cantankerous side, often triggering quarrels with everyone, even his friends and customers. He was a friend and almost partner of George Halstead, another craftsman of split cane. Gillum's and Halstead's careers were curiously intertwined over the years and business often brought the two together. Their partnership started and failed over ferrules. Halstead had been a machinist at the Leonard shop, where he made reel seats and ferrules. The partnership centered on Halstead making the metal fittings while Gillum made the rod sections. All was go until Halstead was late in delivering the promised metalwork, and the icing on the cake for Gillum was that when they finally arrived they were not even completed. The welts, water stops, plugs, and nickel-silver tubing for the male and female ferrules were all shipped loose and mixed up in the box. Gillum was furious and ended the partnership on the spot.

"Pinky" Gillum never quite standardized his tapers or fittings, building with whatever suited his mood at the moment. His early rods were fitted with ferrules by George Halstead, and after Halstead's death he used the Super-Z ferrule and even some Payne ferrules, finally turning to making his own later on. His cane color varied from medium to dark brown, and after a bad experience with hide-glue adhesives, he turned to using a black epoxy adhesive suggested by Everett Garrison. As on the Garrison rods, the black glue lines are prominent on Gillum's later work.

Gillum's total lifetime rod production never exceeded 2,000 rods, making any Gillum a scarce collector's rod. He worked mostly in two-piece design and rods from 7½ to 8½ feet surface occasionally. One of the nicest Gillums I've had in hand was a two-piece 8¼-foot rod at 4¼ ounces for a DT5 line. This rod was fast in action but extraordinarily sensitive, as fine a fishing tool as I've ever seen. Gillum also made a few three-piece rods in the 8-foot length with most in lengths from 8½ to 9½ feet. Short Gillum rods in lengths to 7 feet are exceedingly rare. I have seen rods at 6 feet, 6¾ feet, and 7 feet, but only a very, very few.

Gillum rods currently range to a high of $2,000 for the shorter lengths in mint condition. Rods that are in average condition range from $850 to $1,500 on today's market.

George Halstead had a relatively short rodbuilding career. He lived at Brewster, New York, and built a few rods of surprisingly good parabolic action with his own ferrules and fittings. The bamboo workmanship was good; however, Halstead failed to assemble some of his rods with first-rate adhesives. Many of his rods separated along their glue facets, and very few survive today.

Halstead died at a relatively young age, and his skills as a rodbuilder never reached their full potential.

Obviously Halstead's rods are very rare, since few were built and not many have lasted over the years. These rods can be reglued, if they delaminate, and can be restored by competent rod shops, but be prepared — this sort of rebuilding work is very costly, sometimes running to $400 to $500 for extensive reconstruction. Halstead rods that undergo such treatment, provided it is professionally done to only the highest standards, should carry a market value equivalent to any original condition rod, as such work removes all doubt concerning the rod's integrity. Halstead's rods range in price to $1,500 for a mint-condition specimen, with rods in average condition ranging from $900 to $1,200.

Everett Garrison was born in Yonkers, New York, in 1893. In 1922, he met Dr. George Parker Holden, the famous amateur rodmaker and author of *Idyll of the Split Bamboo*. It was through Holden's influence that Garrison began his long rodbuilding career and launched the most disciplined, painstaking approach to rodmaking in the history of split bamboo. Garrison's background and education in engineering led to his scientific approach to the development of his now famous rod tapers. He also developed his own tools, precision planing forms, and other equipment. His forms used differential setscrews to control the tapers; one full turn opens or closes the forms .008 inch for absolute control.

Garrison built almost every part of each rod himself, including his fittings, rod cases, and even the poplin bags to hold the finished rod safe in the case. His attention to detail even carries over to the assembly of the planed sections.

Garrison signature with typical Garrison wrapping on top of handle instead of winding check. (Photo courtesy Matthew Vinciguerra)

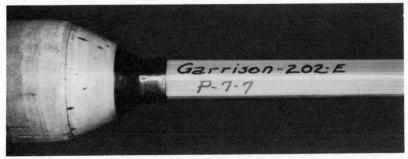

Two tips from the same rod show that the same nodes in each section were adjacent splines in the original culm, a Garrison technique to make both rod tips as identical as possible. His node placement ensures that each node is isolated, with no other nodes in the same area on the rod section. His guides are wound in opposite directions to equalize the twisting forces in the section. The finished Garrison rod has a scarlet tipping on one of the tips, green on the other, to mark it so that the angler can alternate his tips from trip to trip.

Typical Garrisons include a 7-footer at 2¾ ounces for #4 line, a 7¼-footer at 3¼ ounces for #4 line, a 7½- and 7¾-footer at 3½ and 3¾ ounces for #5 line, and an 8-footer at 4 ounces, the last an exceptional all-around rod that helped Garrison make his reputation during the 1930s.

Everett Garrison was a genius at building split-cane rods, and his insistence on building every part himself allowed a lifetime production of only 900 or so rods. His rods were always prized as collector-fishing rods, and since his death in 1975, their price on the collector's market has continued to climb.

Currently Garrison rods are bringing $1,500 to $2,000 for rods in average condition. I know of one mint-condition rod selling recently for $2,500, probably some kind of record price for a single cane rod, but a fitting tribute to one of the art's better builders.

Goodwin Granger developed his talents in isolation in Denver, where he began making fine handcrafted cane rods after World War I. The Leonard influence is unmistakable in his very first rods. These were of three-piece design, done in straw-color cane with red silk winds and the unmistakable swelled butt. His early handles were copies of the Leonard cigar shape, with a nickel-silver reel seat with fixed reel hood and a sliding band. The quality of workmanship in these few early Grangers is on a par with the work of the master he copied, and they are highly prized by collectors.

Early on, Granger changed the cosmetic appearance to the more familiar browntoned cane, fitted with a full-Wells-style handle with different colored wraps for each of the grades or models he made.

The Granger Champion was one of his first, with red wraps tipped in black, and was built in lengths from 8 to 9½ feet at weights of 4¼, 4¾, 5½, and 6½ ounces. Of the same design and length was the Goodwin model, with jasper winds tipped in yellow. The Special had yellow silk winds and introduced the unique German-silver reverse-screwlock seat, which remained a standard of the Granger line. The Special model was the first built in the 7½-foot length at 3¾ ounces, and later the Aristocrat model brought in the 7-foot two-piece at 3½ ounces. Early Aristocrat models were wrapped in tan silk, tipped dark brown. Later rods in this model were simply wrapped in a medium-brown color, but the rod tapers were redesigned and the 7-foot model was changed to a delightful 2¾ ounces for a #4 line.

The Granger Deluxe was a top-of-the-line rod featuring jasper winds, tipped yellow, and included the full series of designs from 7 feet to 9½ feet.

The Deluxe Registered rods were Goodwin Granger's best and were built only to order. I recently saw one of the Registered models with two different sets of two tips. This 8½-foot classic used a #6 line with the lighter tips and a #7 with the heavier set, and showed absolutely no difference in action or casting cycle when switching from one to the other.

The Granger feel is a smooth, full-working medium-fast action that seems to change very little from model to model.

The Goodwin Granger Company was acquired by Wright & McGill after World War II. The rods built under their ownership are among the finest factory-production rods ever built. At midcentury, their shop foreman was Bill Phillipson, who would later build fine fly rods under his own name.

The six models in production then were the Victory, with orange/black variegated winds, tipped in black; the Special, with lime-green wraps; the Aristocrat, with tan-tipped chocolate wraps; the Favorite, with jasper winds, tipped pale yellow; the Deluxe with black/silver variegated winds, tipped yellow; and the Premier model, with intricate yellow wrappings.

A small number of Granger Deluxe rods were built after Wright & McGill had abandoned cane for fiberglass. These rods were of two-piece design, at 7 and 7½ feet and 3 and 3¼ ounces, and used a reverse slide-band seat over a cork filler. The three-piece 8-, 8½-, and 9-footers weighed 3¾, 4½, and 5½ ounces and were fitted with walnut seats with the fixed-butt-cap slide-band arrangement. The handles on these rods were the elliptical full-Wells type, later the trademark of Phillipson, and were wrapped with deep scarlet winds. In spite of their Granger markings, they are unmistakably early Phillipson products.

The Goodwin Granger rods are rarer than the Wright & McGill Grangers and are considered by many nostalgia bugs to be the better rods. They range from $100 to $350 on the used-rod market. The Wright & McGill Grangers range from $100 to $275 currently.

Bill Phillipson rods included the Peerless series made with walnut screw-locking seats. There was a 7½-foot 4-ounce rod, an 8-foot design at 4 ounces, the 8½-footer at 5¼ ounces, and the 9-foot rod at a full 6 ounces. Later, these rods were made with full metal reel seats. The Peerless Specials paralleled these rods and were made to accommodate a full line size heavier in each corresponding design.

The Phillipson Pacemakers were moderately priced rods from 7½ feet and 4 ounces, to 9 feet and 6 ounces, and were fitted with anodized aluminum seats. The rods were wrapped with lime green winds, tipped yellow.

Some of Phillipson's finest work came through the Paramount 51 series, which were made with both walnut and metal reel seats. The tapers were more delicate with the 7½-footer at 3½ ounces, the 8-foot rod at 4 ounces, the 8½-footer at 4¾ ounces, and the 9-foot rod at 5½ ounces. These rods were wrapped with jasper winds, tipped with yellow and black.

The Preferred rods were of two-piece design, made in 7- and 7½-foot lengths at 3¼ ounces and 3¾ ounces. Both rods handled a DT4 line.

Current market value of a sound, used Phillipson runs from $100 to $225.

James Heddon & Sons in Dowagiac, Michigan, produced over the years some of the finest production-made fly rods this country has seen. Their only rival in terms of quality and workmanship were the factory rods of the Goodwin Granger Company.

There were a number of models produced in a surprising range of prices. The Model 10 was the least expensive, with oxidized ferrules, scarlet wraps, and a cork-filled reel seat. Of this model, made in a number of lengths and weights, the 7½-footer at 3½ ounces was the most popular size. As with all Heddon rods, the cane was a rich brown color, and the rod displayed the customary swelled-butt construction, perhaps a throwback to the influence of earlier rodbuilders like Leonard and Murphy.

The Heddon Folsom model was a well-done two-piece rod in 7- through 8-foot lengths. It was fitted with oxidized ferrules and a walnut-filled screwlock seat. Wrapped in chocolate brown, tipped yellow, it looks very similar to the Payne rod. The 7½-foot model weighs 3⅛ ounces, with a medium action, and takes a #4 line.

The Model 17, Black Beauty, was the most popular of all the Heddon rods, since it was a moderately priced rod of superb quality. Offered in lengths from 7½ to 9 feet, this three-piece design was wrapped originally in black silk with a Bakelite screwlock seat, oxidized ferrules, and a half-Wells cork grip. Later the black wraps were tipped in orange, which changed the rod's appearance somewhat. The 8-footer in this model weighs 4 ounces and takes a light DT4 line.

There were several other factory models, culminating in the Model 35 Deluxe and the Model 50 Deluxe-President. These two rods were built in lengths from 8 to 9 feet, ranging from 3½ to 5½ ounces. They were fitted with black ferrules, a graceful half-Wells grip, and screwlock seat with burled walnut filler and were wrapped with brown winds, tipped black. They represent some of the finest factory rods ever made.

One of the finest casting Heddons I've ever seen was a Drueding Special—an 8½ footer at 4⅝ ounces for a #5 line. It was built to tapers designed by Harold Drueding, one of the guiding lights in the rod shop at Dowagiac, and is a superb fly rod.

From the skilled hands of Sam Anson, master rodbuilder at Heddon, came a very few Model 100 rods. These were called the "Rod of Rods" and were hand-worked throughout. They were fitted with gold-lacquered seats with walnut fillers, black precision ferrules, and gold-toned guides and tip-tops. They were the best Heddon had to offer. They sold in the late 1940s for almost four times the price of the Black Beauty at $35 and were made only to special order. They are rare and are exquisite casting instruments.

A mint-condition Heddon of moderate quality is worth about $250 on today's market, with rods in average condition selling for $125 to $175. The Deluxe and Deluxe-President in mint condition sell for up to $400, with most ranging to $300. The Model 100 ranges from $350 to $500 depending on condition.

The South Bend Bait Company acquired the Cross Rod Company after World War I and for over a decade produced some excellent production rods.

The Cross rods were both single- and double-built in construction; most were double-built. The Cross action was a smooth semi-parabolic, working well down into the grip. The cane color was honey, and the winds were a medium tan. The reel seats were full German-silver and engraved with a Cross medallion. They were built from 7 to 9 feet in length, and the 8½-foot, three-piece model at 5¼ ounces took a surprisingly light #5 line. The famous 7-foot Cross Sylph was a two-piece rod of medium-fast action, weighing 3 ounces—a surprisingly light rod, considering its double-built construction.

The most unusual Cross rod I've ever seen was a one-piece 9-footer for a #7 line at 5¼ ounces. It was a rod of unbelievable power with its double-built construction and had the capability of extending a cast beyond the backing knot.

Wes Jordan, Orvis's master rodmaker, was a Cross protégé until Cross died in the 1930s.

After World War II, South Bend continued to make production rods under its own name and also for Shakespeare.

Cross rods on the current market will bring about $175 in mint condition, with rods in average condition ranging between $100 and $125.

Wes Jordan has been synonymous with Orvis bamboo work for almost 33 years. Jordan was born in 1894 and joined the Cross Rod Company in 1919, forging a considerable reputation as a rodmaker. When Cross died and South Bend absorbed the Cross Company, Jordan went along to supervise the work.

In 1940, he joined the Orvis Company to supervise rodbuilding, where he remained until his retirement several years ago. In 1941, Wes Jordan designed the screw-locking reel seat with its rich walnut filler, which has distinguished the Orvis rods ever since. He and D. C. Corkran, then owner of Orvis, pioneered the techniques of impregnating the bamboo fibers with a resin compound to provide almost maintenance-free blanks. Jordan developed the entire Battenkill series of rods, as well as most of Orvis's present battery of rods, including the Midge, Flea, and Nymph rods. The Orvis Deluxe and Superfine rods were built under Jordan's influence, and the Wes Jordan series of Battenkill rods are tapers personally preferred by this master craftsman.

In addition to the Battenkill-grade rods, Orvis also manufactures a less-expensive line called the Madison. Most of these rods are built with one tip section instead of the customary two tips, and are advertised as Battenkill-quality rods except for their coloration.

Used Battenkill rods sell for $175 to $250 on the current market, and used Madisons range to $125.

Chapter 22 ❧ Antique Reels

MARY KEFOVER KELLY

There seems little doubt that the Chinese were fishing with reels long ago, possibly as early as 300 to 400 A.D. As seen in a surviving painting, they were continuing to use them in the sixteenth century. Did the reel, therefore, come to the western world from China? The answer remains a mystery, with investigations by modern western historians dead-ended in the seventeenth century.

For western historians, the reel, down through its history variously labeled a wheel, barrel-winder, pirn, and/or winch, had its beginnings in England sometime during the early-to-mid-1600s. The first written references to it, which were British, are by Barker who, in *The Art of Angling* (1651), noted that the reel was used in pike fishing, and by Izaak Walton who, in *The Compleat Angler* (1653), reported that in northern England some anglers, when salmon fishing, used reels. Walton also wrote he had never seen one.

The original barrel-winders were conceived as a storage unit, a place to hold the line that was not in use in the water—a very helpful device in fighting big fish. As far as western culture is concerned, casting from a reel, today called plug or bait casting, is an idea only about 150 years old.

When angling without a reel, the fisher tied the line (which measured half the length of the rod if, on a calm day, he was dabbing a fly) to the rod, drawing it out through a loop at the tip end. If he planned on working the fly, real or artificial, at a spot that required a cast of six feet of line, and if he had seven feet tied to the rod, he wrapped the extra foot either around the rod or his wrist. To adjust for a longer or shorter toss, he simply increased or decreased the number of wraps. Thus the mechanics of rigging the rod and casting were, if primitive, at least simple. Not having a barrel-winder posed no problem.

As seen in early illustrations described by John Waller Hills in *A History of Fly Fishing for Trout*, published in 1921, the first winders were single-action, without click or drag. They were used for pike and salmon, the reel not being used with smaller types of fish such as trout until roughly the second half of the eighteenth century—well over 100 years after it was first mentioned in western literature.

Why trout fishers shunned the reel for so long is conjecture. In part it was probably a result of the winder's original purpose as an aid in overpowering

H. L. Leonard 1877 patent fly reel. Raised pillars and end rings are bronze, side plates are nickel silver.

large fish, which meant it would seem unfair and unsporting to use it for smaller game. Tradition, habit, and the reluctance to change old ways all doubtlessly accounted for some rejection. An additional reason was that fishing with a reel was not itself without complications.

Naturally, mechanical failures occurred. Yet there was a period soon after the advent of the multiplying reel when it was overwhelmingly preferred for every kind of fishing, threatening to make the single-action winder obsolete. Even at this time, a reel's malfunctioning was not a big issue. Rather the basic headaches were how to secure the reel firmly to the rod and where on the rod to place it: above the hand or below; on top of the rod or under the rod. Satisfactorily solving these problems, which at times tried the patience of the most gentle anglers, took over two centuries.

An early semisuccessful answer to placement was the use of a universal reel base, called a hoop and screw. It was similar to the modern-day hose clamp, a ring with a thumb screw. A reel with this base could be positioned at any spot on the rod the angler chose. Reels with hoop and screw bases were still being built in the 1880s.

The rarity of old reels with perfect, unfiled bases attests to the troubles of easily and firmly securing reel to rod. One facet of this problem was the total lack of standardization. In other words, the reels made at one shop, subject to the normal irregularities of handcrafting, were built with bases measuring, as an example, 2½ inches long by ⅝ inch wide by 1/16 inch thick. At another shop, the bases were 2 inches by ½ inch by 3/32 inch. The rodmakers, on the other hand, built their reel seats to an altogether different set of measurements. The chaotic result was that rods and reels were not interchangeable at the angler's will. Instead, one first had to use a file to reduce the size of the reel base or, conversely, shim the reel seat.

In America during the 1830s, there was an unsuccessful attempt made to standardize seats and bases. Not until the 1920–1930 era, when large companies and twentieth-century mass-production methods dominated the tackle industry, was the problem mostly eliminated.

The simple single-action barrel-winder became a multiplier, that is, the spool making more revolutions per turn than the handle, with the addition of a pinion and spur wheel. It is difficult to date exactly when this multiplying achievement occurred. However, in 1770 one British tacklemaker, Onesimus Ustonson, advertised multiplying reels for sale, and by the 1780s English angling authorities were preferentially recommending multipliers, the authorities at this time being almost unanimously in favor of reels for every type of angling — from fly-fishing for trout to trolling for pike.

Unfortunately, the eighteenth-century angling authors neglected to mention what the multiplying ratio was: 2:1, 4:1, and so forth. Thus Alfred Ronalds in his impressive work *The Fly Fishers Entomology* (London, 1836) made the first reference I have found on ratios. Writing that the first desideratum of a reel was "a capability of winding up the line rapidly," Ronalds noted that five multipliers were available but that the most commonly used reel, and what he recommended, was the four multiplier made of brass.

An occasional reel is found with a stop/lock. This is an addition to the reel that is hard to place in time. The references to it with which I am familiar all date to the early 1800s. In them, the stop/lock, which is not described, is not endorsed, being considered old-fashioned and "passé." Apparently, however, the idea was not willing to die, and I have seen reels dating to the 1875–1885 era that are equipped with locks. There are two types. The type on single-action reels consists of an additional cross pillar between the side plates. This pillar is longer than the reel is wide, and to lock the reel, one slides it from left, the back side of the reel, to right, the handle side, at which point the portion of

*Edward vom Hofe trout reel, S style counterbalanced handle. This rare trout
model has an adjustable drag.*

the pillar extending beyond the reel slips into a hole in the reel's handle, rendering the handle immobile and thereby locking the spool in place.

The lock mechanism appearing on multipliers, which is mounted inside the reel, consists of two parts. The first is a long flat spring that is attached at one end to the disc plate. A post is attached to the spring at its underside at about its midsection. The post fits into a hole in the disc. The second part is the activating pin, or stud—one end protruding outside the reel, the other end sliding in and out under the free end of the spring. To engage the lock, the stud is swung out from under the spring. The spring then lies flat against the disc plate. This lowers the post, and because it is long enough to pass through the hole in the plate, it enters a hole drilled through the side of the spool. The spool is thus frozen. The post-to-spool lock is built on the same principle as the multiplying drag except that for a drag the post is shortened so that it bears only on the spool and does not enter a hole in it. We will discuss drags later.

The idea for the stop/lock originated about the time of the reel's western beginnings. The purpose for holding the spool fast was to obtain absolute control over the amount of line let out. This would have been a matter of prime importance for the old anglers who were extremely, almost superstitiously, precise and methodical. For example, when fishing on the bottom, or "ground fishing" as they called it, they overlooked no detail. Before beginning, they took a string with a lead weight on one end and a float on the other and plumbed the water to determine the exact depth. They then fished with just that length of line needed to reach the bottom. No more, no less.

Fitting the reel with a click mechanism, a "check" as the English called it, occurred during the first quarter of the nineteenth century. The earliest record of it that I have found, dating to the late 1830s, was written by Theophilys South, a pseudonym of Edward Chitty. Chitty, a London barrister by profession, wrote *The Fly Fishers Text-Book*. In the spring of 1839, excerpts from this book (which was not published until 1841) were reprinted from a British magazine in the *Spirit of the Times*, a weekly magazine that was then America's foremost sporting publication. Chitty's position on reels reflected the start of the trend away from the omnipotence of the multiplier. He felt one should use both kinds, recommending the single action for salmon and the multiplier for trout. However, he asserted that whichever one a person chose, "both kinds of reels should have a check or click machinery, which prevents slight catches from pulling the line off."

Chitty did not describe the click mechanism, but on reels from the early-to-middle nineteenth century that I have seen, the click was the same as that used 100 years later: a pawl-to-rachet or -pinion, the pawl being set in a large circular spring if the click was to be adjustable. Otherwise the pawl was fixed to a smaller spring.

Following are some interesting comments about the origins of some of the other ideas applied to the reel. In 1839, in the *Text-Book*, Chitty suggested covering the spool's axle with cork to increase its diameter. Ronalds, in 1836 in the *Entomology*, made note of a type of automatic reel: "A reel has been invented lately containing a spiral spring which acts, in the manner of a spring in a window blind, upon the axis to wind up the line." Based on the Appendix in Jesse's *Walton's Compleat Angler* (1856), this reel, called the Chesterman's Self-winding reel, was at that time still being marketed.

In dealing with the period up to the 1830s, I have made no mention of American-made reels, American technology, or American literature. This is not an oversight. It was not until the 1830s that the United States could boast of having any of these things. Few persons during America's early years ever had time for sport angling. The colonists and settlers who did have the time brought English tackle, as well as British methods and literature, with them when they came to this country. Later, if these people ever needed to replace anything or acquire something new, they preferred that it be from England, and there was a flourishing tackle-import business. Thus there was no demand for American-made fishing tackle or American literature about it.

During this time, if a reel or rod ever needed repair, and importation was not

Julius vom Hofe trout reel, star type steel spring below grease cap. Adjust drag by placing pressure against cap, which has a pin that bears against spool.

feasible, the angler took the reel or rod to the local watchmaker, gunmaker, or blacksmith, who would make the repair or, using the old reel as a model, duplicate it. Thus when American artisans finally began manufacturing reels on a professional/wholesale level, they did not start at the beginning, but instead copied the English design and technology, thereby beginning at the point at which the British had advanced the reel.

America's entry into reelmaking was on two fronts: in the North with a 2:1, occasionally 3:1, ratio multiplier that is sometimes called the New York reel; and in the South with a 4:1 ratio known as the Kentucky reel.

Little has ever been written about the New York reel so that historians and reel collectors are often unaware of its significance. Aside from being used for trout fly fishing, reflecting the ever-present British influence, it was used in the coastal areas in both freshwater and saltwater for striped bass. Starting in the early-to-mid-1800s, the surf anglers began to cast directly from it, using their thumbs to control the spool. An early report of this type of casting appeared in the Supplement to the second edition of the *American Angler's Book* by Thaddeus Norris (1865). Later, in *Forest and Stream* and *American Angler* magazines, it was called "Cuttyhunk," named for one of the famous striper-fishing clubs.

It has been written that the American method of casting from the reel originated in the southern United States with black-bass angling. Not to detract from the South, and there may very well have been a simultaneous development of methods, but the evidence nevertheless supports the idea that casting from the reel began with, and spread from, the striper fishers along the upper East Coast.

The Kentucky reel developed in the area around Frankfort, Kentucky. The standard reference work in every reel collector's library, the revised second edition of *The Book of the Black Bass* by Dr. James A. Henshall, published in 1904 and reprinted often, contains a lengthy discourse on the history of the Kentucky, with the claim that the multiplying reel was an American invention, rooted in the South.

It is certainly unfortunate that Dr. Henshall did not have rapid transportation or communication, with the result that reference material, old books, and periodicals may not have been readily available to him, although he claimed they were. What Dr. Henshall often wrote, therefore, concerning the history of fishing, and especially British tackle and methods, is frequently quite misleading and inaccurate.* Thus, rather than what Henshall claimed, the Kentucky reel began just as the New York multiplier did — a duplication of a British reel.

Soon after the reel industry was established in America, a number of improvements were made to the reel. Among these was the use of the balanced handle. John C. Conroy, who must be considered America's first full-time professional tacklemaker, opened his shop in New York City in 1830 and in 1838 was advertising his multiplying reels with balanced cranks in the *Spirit of the*

---

*As an example, his description of the Nottingham winch is incorrect. This reel, generally made of wood, a fact that Henshall stated correctly, was made in two pieces, a frame and a spool — the spool, as in many modern fly reels, riding in the frame on a fixed center post. It was very frictionless and free-running, and to control it while casting and playing a fish, the angler used the index finger of his free hand. The Nottingham reel was not a primitive single-unit circle with "a deep groove in its peripheral border for the line," as Henshall claimed. When casting with a Nottingham winch, the angler pulled off from the reel the amount of line he needed for the throw, letting it fall to the ground in coils. He then made his toss, easing the line out through his hand as necessary, using his index finger against the reel's spool to prevent the weight and momentum of the bait from drawing off additional line. Henshall, in the 1881 first edition of *The Book of the Black Bass*, stated that the Nottingham style of casting was not using a reel. This error was corrected in the 1904 edition.

Actually, the doctor was not familiar with much, if any, angling literature/history. From the 1780s forward, the English angling pundits, without exception, at least mentioned the multiplying reel, the earlier authors preferentially praising it. Once American anglers began to write, Porter, Brown, Roosevelt, Norris, and Scott also discussed it. Yet Henshall stated that in no book that he read could he find mention of the multipliers.

A "Smith Age" Kentucky reel dating about 1845, turned out by J. F. & B. F. Meek of Frankfort, Kentucky. Meek later moved to Louisville, where he established a factory and made the famous Bluegrass reels, the finest casting reels that have ever been built. A closeup of the markings on the 1845 Meek shows that even the screw heads are number-matched with their corresponding slots. These early Kentuckys are considered museum-quality.

Times. William T. Porter, editor of the *Spirit*, and a devotee of Conroy's, implied in 1843 that the idea originated with Conroy. There is no proof of this, but the Conroy ads are the first reference to balance cranks that I have seen. The principle behind the balanced handle was to maintain the spool's momentum, thereby gaining casting distance. It also resulted in more evenly distributed wear on the ends of the spool shaft.

It is difficult to pinpoint when drags were first used on reels and to determine whether the idea originated with Yankee ingenuity or British (although the odds favor the British), or if the honor should be shared. It was around the mid-1800s that the word "drag" began to appear in both American and English angling literature. Unfortunately, however, in each case the meaning is vague, and one is never quite sure if the author is using "drag" as a synonym for the old familiar pawl-to-rachet click or if he means a different mechanism, a spring with post-to-spool.

The similarity of the mechanisms for the drag and for the multiplying stop raises the intriguing question of which came first. Did the drag system happen accidentally as an outgrowth of the multiplying lock? Or was the drag invented first and its mechanism then applied to stopping the spool? It will take much more information than is currently at hand before these questions can be answered.

One certainty, however, is that reels with drags were being built in America by the late 1840s to early 1850s by makers such as J. F. and B. F. Meek, John C. Conroy, and probably others whose names are currently lost to history. Henshall stated that George Snyder of Paris, Kentucky, used them early in the 1800s. In *The Book of the Black Bass* (1904), he illustrated a George Snyder reel with a drag inscribed with the date February 1, 1821. According to the records of the Bourbon County Historical Society in Paris, Kentucky, George Snyder died in 1813. It seems safest not to use Henshall as a reference.

The first U.S. patents issued for reels were to John A. Bailey in 1856 and to Edward Dayton in 1857. Both patents were for free spool devices, that is, mechanisms by which the spool was freed from the crank shaft, and both were assigned to John Warrin of the J. and T. Warrin Co., New York City, which was the predecessor of Andrew Clerk and Co./Abbey and Imbrie, and which at the time was a wholesale tackle import house. In 1857, in the *Spirit*, the Warrin company advertised for sale reels based on these patents. John Conroy is believed to have been the maker.

In the first edition of the *American Angler's Book* (1864), Thad Norris noted that jeweled bearings were on some American-built multipliers. Norris did not identify the maker(s) of these.

The most easily recognized change in reels during the nineteenth century was in materials. At the start, reels were brass, quickly followed by German-silver for better quality reels, while the British always had a love affair with bronze. Aluminum was tried for a short while in the late 1850s and early 1860s, but the metal proved too soft and easily corroded and was abandoned. The alloy, improved, reappeared in the twentieth century. In the 1870s, hard rubber was introduced, and fast on its heels came nickel-plating. Both materials proved practical, with the result that by the end of the century a brass reel was rare except under plating and German-silver only appeared on the more expensive reels. Wood has always been used for one type of reel or another.

While the U.S. had an international reputation as the world's premier maker of multiplying reels, by 1860, the country seems to have lagged behind in the manufacture of single-action reels. This may have been because the majority of American anglers preferred the multiplier. However, once there was a clamoring for the single action, American innovation came to the fore.

One of the early practical patents, still utilized today, was issued in 1874 to C. F. Orvis. Orvis's idea, which he applied to the simple, narrow, spooled reel, which even then the British were calling "contracted," consisted of perforating a reel's side plates as well as those of the spool. This allowed for air circulation, hence, line drying; but, more significantly, it lightened the reel without structurally weakening it.

The perforated concept, for which there does not appear to be an earlier historical reference, was copied in one way or another by others. In the mid-1880s, A. F. Meisselbach and Brother of Newark, then a fledgling company, issued the Expert series of single-action reels, which was soon followed by the Allright and Featherlight. The British firm of Hardy Brothers came out in the 1890s with the Perfect. Later in the twentieth century, Pflueger introduced the Progress.

According to a receipted bill on file at the Museum of American Fly Fishing in Manchester, Vermont, Orvis, who was a manufacturer of rods, had the first dozen of his Patent 1874 reels built by the Manhattan Brass Co., New York.

Another widely copied patent that provided maximum line capacity for minimum weight was the profoundly simple idea of offsetting the cross bars. This raised-pillar approach was the brainchild of Francais J. Philbrook, although the English were probably toying with a similar thought in the 1850s. Philbrook, a reelmaker who lived in Bangor, Maine, received the patent, 191,813, June 12, 1877. He assigned it to H. L. Leonard, a rodmaker from the same town. It is believed that Philbrook, in partnership with Edward Payne (the rodmaker) manufactured the reel and Leonard marketed it. Later Leonard joined the New York City wholesale-retail-import tackle house of William Mills and Son. In 1884 Philbrook and Payne dissolved their partnership, although Philbrook is believed to have continued making reels until his death in 1888. The manufacture of this reel under the Leonard-Mills name finally moved to New York City and the shop of Julius vom Hofe.

Aside from the offset cross bars, Philbrook's patent specified that the sides of his reel be "struck up" and for a pawl-to-rachet arrangement that was especially adopted to the recess of the back side plate. The side plates were also recessed into the frame, resulting in a protective rim. The many details covered by the patent may explain why numerous other makers were able to use the raised pillar idea with apparent impunity from patent infringement.

Among the companies manufacturing such reels in either or both multiplier and single action were: Julius vom Hofe, Hendryx, Meisselbach, Conroy, and the Carlton Manufacturing Co. of Rochester, New York, who built the Lightweight, a reel very similar to the Featherlight.

There were never at one time many reelmaking shops/factories in the U.S. For example, based on national advertising and information culled from old tackle catalogs, in 1915, three years before Heddon introduced a reel, there were possibly as few as 18 companies engaged in the business: J. A. Coxe, San Francisco, California; Enterprise Mfg. Co., Akron, Ohio; Ft. Wayne Bait and Reel

Co., Ft. Wayne, Indiana; Geo. W. Gayle and Son, Frankfort, Kentucky; Andrew B. Hendryx Co., New Haven, Connecticut; Horrock-Ibbotson, Utica, New York; E. Holzman, New York City; Martin Automatic Fishing Reel Co., Mohawk, New York; A. F. Meisselbach and Bro., Newark, New Jersey; B. F. Meek and Sons, Louisville, Kentucky; B. C. Milam and Son, Frankfort, Kentucky; Montague City Rod and Reel Co., Brooklyn, New York; Rockford Reel Co., Chicago, Illinois; Wm. Shakespeare, Jr., Co., Kalamazoo, Michigan; South Bend Tackle Co., South Bend, Indiana; Talbot Reel and Mfg. Co., Kansas City, Missouri; Edward vom Hofe, New York City; and Julius vom Hofe, Brooklyn, New York.

"Trade reels" is a broad term covering private labels, house names, and the like. It means that a company whose principal occupation is volume-retailing and/or wholesaling does not want to be involved in manufacturing but, for various reasons, wants a product line to bear its name. The wholesale firm, therefore, seeks a maker to build the reels—sometimes to its specifications— or selects from the maker's standard model line. The finished reels are then stamped with the name, or private label, of the retailer/wholesaler. There are instances, too, when a manufacturer has used a name other than its own. For example, the Enterprise Mfg. Co. marketed their products under such names as Pflueger, 4-Brothers, Portage, and Bull-Dog. For a year in the 1920s, Winchester Repeating Arms Co. labeled their reels with the Barney and Berry brand.

Trade reels, marked and unmarked, can be frustrating as the collector attempts to identify the maker. However, they become a very rewarding and fascinating part of reel collecting when one realizes that without them possibly as much as 80 percent of our American angling heritage would be lost. We would have no record of names like Andrew Clerk and Co., Abbey and Imbrie, and the Philadelphia house of Edward K. Tryon and its Pennell label. Conroy reels of the twentieth century would be unknown, since Conroy ceased manufacturing late in the 1890s. Names like William Mills and Son, and Kosmic would disappear.

DEALERS WHO SPECIALIZE IN HANDLING ANTIQUE REELS

Heritage Rod and Reel
P.O. Box 1183
Tryon, NC 28782

American Sporting Collector
Arden Drive
Amawalk, NY 10501

Martin Keane's Classic Rods
Mine Hill Road
Bridgewater, CT 06752

Thomas & Thomas
22 Third St.
Turners Falls, MA 01376

REPRESENTATIVE VALUES OF ANTIQUE REELS

Maker and description	Current value
Abbey and Imbrie	
Abbey model hard rubber fly reel	$225–300
Abbey model 4-multi raised pillar	150–200
Imbrie model 2-multi	225–300
Salmo fly reel	40–50
4-multi hinged take-apart	40–50
Barney and Berry, Inc., any type	100 and up
Andrew Clerk and Co., any type	500 and up
Conroy	
early 3½" diameter German-silver striper	750–800
early 3½" diameter brass striper	700–800
early 2" diameter single action	700–800
early 2¼" diameter 2-multi brass	250–300
J. A. Coxe, every type	100 and up
4-Brothers 2-multi	40–50
Heddon	
3–35	150–200
Chief Dowagiac	75–100
Imperial 125A fly reel	40–55
Pal p 41	25–30
Winona	25–30
Hendryx, any type	35 and up
Horrock-Ibbotson	5 and up
Kosmic, any type	200 and up
Leonard nickel-silver 1877 trout reel	800 and up
Leonard-Mills hard rubber and aluminum raised-pillar trout reel	400 and up
Martin Automatic early type	50 and up
J. F. and B. F. Meek	750–800
B. F. Meek and Sons, Louisville, Kentucky	300 and up
B. F. Meek and Sons/Horton Mfg. Co.	150 and up
A. F. Meisselbach and Bros.	
Tripart and Takapart	40–50
Good Luck wood	40–50
Featherlight #250	75–100
Featherlight #270	75–100
Expert	50 and up

Maker and model	Current value
C. F. Orvis 1874 patent fly reel with wood box	500 and up
Pennell, early J. vom Hofe maker, every type	50 and up
Pflueger	
first model Medalist	75–90
Bull-Dog Supreme	100–125
Bull-Dog Redifor	100–125
Progress	50–60
Hawkeye	100–125
Portage, any type	45–55
Shakespeare	
first model Level Wind	125–175
Tournament	75–100
1922 Model Professional wide spool take-apart	100–125
Russell fly reel Model HE	40–55
South Bend	
Model 1115 fly reel	40–55
Model 1200	75–100
Talbot, any type	150 and up
Edward vom Hofe	
#423 salmon reel	200–250
single-action, trout-size reels	150 and up
Julius vom Hofe, any type	150 and up
Winchester Repeating Arms Co., any type	40 and up

Chapter 23 ❧ *Hardy Reels*

JACK DUGREW

For over 90 years, the fly reels created by the Hardy Brothers of Alnwick, England, have enjoyed great popularity and a large following among fishermen. Throughout this period, Hardy reels have been manufactured in a great diversity of models, diameters, widths, finishes, and fittings. Over 30 distinct models of fly reels have come to us from these craftsmen.

In addition to the standard Hardy models, it must be remembered that Hardy was a custom shop where a fisherman could have a reel built especially for him. Hardy reels, such as the Barton and the Bouglé, were developed on request from prominent anglers of the day.

The strong point of the Hardy reel is its durability, as evidenced by the fact that there are many Hardy reels in use today that have been passed down from great-grandfather to grandfather to father to son. These third- and fourth-generation Hardy reels are still giving their owners honorable and faithful use today. The durability, craftsmanship, and diversity of models in the Hardy line have made the Hardy reel a natural for the collector.

STARTING A COLLECTION

The Hardy reel has been available throughout this country for many decades, and it is still possible to acquire some of the earlier, more popular models at reasonable, or on occasion, bargain prices. The Hardy Perfects, St. Georges, Uniquas, and Lightweights fit into this category. Just last year, while vacationing in upstate New York, I was able to pick up a nice Perfect and two Uniqua reels for less than $50 at a country auction. On another occasion, a second-hand shop in western Maine was the source of a 3⅜-inch St. George. At present, any one of these will easily bring $100 or more. In addition to auctions and second-hand shops, garage sales, church tag sales, pawn shops, antique shops, and other fishermen are good sources for finding Hardy reels.

There are also several dealers throughout the country who specialize in selling new and used tackle. The most notable are Allan Liu at the American Sporting Collector in Amawalk, New York; Martin Keane in Bridgewater, Connect-

An early 2½-inch Brass Perfect. Note Hardy trademark and drag adjustment guards. (Photo courtesy Jack Dugrew)

icut; the H. L. Leonard Rod Company in Central Valley, New York; and Thomas & Thomas in Turners Falls, Massachusetts. I have acquired such unusual reels as the Hardy Davy, a 3-inch Super Silex, and a wide-spool, early Perfect through these sources. Each of these dealers publishes used fishing-tackle lists, several times each year, containing many interesting items. On occasion, there are bargains to be found here, although prices are generally high. Orders for items on these lists are handled on a first come, first served basis, and the desirable items are the first sold. A quick telephone call to these dealers will ensure that a hold is placed on the item you want.

The present market values for Hardy reels are listed at the end of this chapter. More exacting figures depend on the condition of the reel. I am qualified to give appraisals on Hardy reels (send requests in care of the American Sporting Collector). In addition to appraising the reels, I can offer a fair price should you be interested in selling them.

Three-inch Hardy St. George. Blue finish that, with use, acquires a lovely patina. Note three screws holding on latch cover and brass foot. (Photo courtesy Jack Dugrew)

POPULAR MODELS

The most popular of the Hardy fly reels is the Perfect, first introduced in 1891. From its origins as a brass reel, the Hardy Perfect has undergone many changes. The earliest of the Perfects was available in a multitude of sizes, with the smallest at 2 ¼ inches and the largest at 6 inches in diameter. These early brass Perfects had ivory knobs and carried the Hardy trademark stamp — a hand holding a fly rod. Early reels with this stamp are most eagerly sought by collectors, with the smaller sizes being the most valuable.

At the turn of the century, the narrow-spool Perfect, forerunner of the modern Perfect, was introduced. In the following 40 years, the appearance of the Perfect remained essentially the same. There were, however, many changes in the click and drag mechanisms during this period. Perfects were available with agate stripping guides, with metal stripping guides, without stripping guides, with ivory knobs, with hard rubber knobs, in right-hand or left-hand retrieve, and in many other variations. Several collectors specialize in the collecting of Perfects alone.

St. Georges, 2⁹⁄₁₆ inches and 3 inches. Enameled finish and aluminum foot, two screws holding on latch cover. (Photo courtesy Jack Dugrew)

Of special interest to collectors are several unusual Perfects such as the Silent Perfect, the Wide Spool Perfect, and the Raised Pillar Perfect, called the "Bouglé." The Silent Perfect, upon first look, is identical to any of the other Perfects. However, on winding the knob, it is very different. There is no click mechanism, but there is an adjustable drag that applies tension to the spool through an adjustable felt pad. Silent Perfects are very rare.

The Hardy Bouglé, introduced during the mid-1900s, was never made in large quantities. It was catalogued in both a 3- and 3¼-inch diameter. As the Bouglé reel is the only raised pillar Hardy fly reel ever produced, it is a superb collectible. As with the standard Perfects, the Bouglés with the Hardy trademark stamp command the most interest and value.

During the late 1950s, the finish on the Hardy Perfects was changed. The previous rich blue finish, which took on a lovely patina with age, was changed to an enameled finish. Hardy Perfects with the earlier blue finish command higher prices on today's market. In addition, the hardware—reel feet, gearing, rivets, and so forth—was changed from brass to aluminum and stainless steel.

In 1967, Hardy discontinued the Perfect reel, much to the dismay of the angling fraternity. Until its reintroduction in 1976, the Hardy Perfect reel was in

Blue Hardy Perfect. Ball bearings and working mechanism finished as well as outside of reel. Brass foot. (Photo courtesy Jack Dugrew)

tremendous demand, and the prices of these classic reels escalated in value. At present, the new Hardy Perfects are available in diameters of 3⅛, 3⅜, and 3⅝ inches.

The second most popular of the Hardy fly reels is the St. George. Introduced shortly before World War I, the Hardy St. George is my personal favorite among all the diverse models. The St. George reel, Hardy Patent #24245, was made in several sizes and types—2⁹⁄₁₆ inches (the St. George Junior), 3 inches, 3⅜ inches, 3¾ inches, and a salmon reel of 4¼ inches. Of all the St. Georges I have owned and seen, all have ventilated spools and circular agate line guides. There were two unusual St. Georges manufactured during the 1920s and 1930s, the Silent St. George and the St. George Multiplier. Both are very rare reels. Both of these reels, as well as the 2⁹⁄₁₆-inch St. George Junior and the 3-inch size, command the highest prices. I think that the 3-inch reel is the epitome of what a trout reel should be. It is lightweight, extremely attractive and durable, and will hold a full DT-5 line with lots of backing. It effectively balances just right with most of my 7- and 7½-foot bamboo fly rods. As with the Perfects, the earlier St. Georges with the blue finish and three-spool latch mechanisms command the most interest and attention by collectors. It is most unfortunate that the smaller size St. George fly reels have been discontinued by Hardy. Only the 3¾-inch model is currently available.

Discontinued in 1958, the Uniqua is another of the more popular Hardy fly reels. The Uniqua, introduced by Hardy in the early 1900s, was the first of the lightweight Hardy reels. It was available in sizes ranging from 2⅝ inches to 4½ inches in diameter, with the smaller sizes commanding most collector interest. Early Uniquas sported ivory handles and a "unique" spool latch mechanism. It was only late in their production that the more modern drum latch mechanism, currently in use on the Lightweight series reels, was utilized.

The Uniqua had a solid spool, although I know of at least one Uniqua with a ventilated spool, a custom version, no doubt. Many of the larger reels had adjustable drag mechanisms, as did the previously discussed Perfects and St. Georges, although again, I have seen a few Uniquas in the salmon sizes lacking this feature. Never available in large numbers, the Uniqua is truly a "sleeper" in reel collecting.

An interesting variation of the Uniqua is the Hardy Sunbeam (not the current model having the same name). Never very popular, the Sunbeam was an open-spool, light fly reel, available in 3- and 3⅛-inch diameters with a brass wire line guide, an interesting reel to many collectors.

A Silent version of the Uniqua, called the Hardy U.S.A., was discontinued during the early years of World War II. The U.S.A. in my collection was obtained for a few dollars, several years ago, at a flea market on the New Jersey shore. I haven't seen another since.

One of the more unusual reels produced by Hardy was the Barton. Having a diameter of 3⅝ inches, the Barton, at first sight, particularly to a novice collector, appears very similar to the St. George. On closer look, there are several important differences. The most apparent difference is the offset brass reel foot on the Barton, designed so that when it is mounted on a fly rod, the reel itself will not extend beyond the butt cap of the rod. The second difference is a very large tapered handle that makes cranking the reel most comfortable. The stripping guide is the final difference. Instead of utilizing the circular line guide, as found on the St. George, the Barton has a rectangular metal stripping guide. Manufactured for only a few years, the Barton is one of the rarer Hardy fly reels, but a most innovative one!

Another unusual reel manufactured by Hardy is the 3-inch Super Silex. It is not a true fly reel, but a classic Hardy spinning reel. Although it has a silky smooth free spool feature, the Silex has an elaborate brake, activated by a lever with an ivory knob that activates a click mechanism. With the brake and click engaged, the reel is a superb fly reel. The drag is regulated by means of a brass knob on the reel rim. As the drag is adjusted, a gear inside the reel causes a brass indicator on the side of the reel to turn, indicating the adjustment setting

Three-inch Bouglé. A custom-ordered Hardy with Perfect insides, but with perforated spool and raised pillars for greater line capacity — ideas so sound that Hardy incorporated them into a production reel. (Photo courtesy Jack Dugrew)

on a small ivory panel. The removable "rim control" spool is attached to the reel by two latches, one on the spool itself and the other on the reel. The engineering, craftsmanship, and beauty of this reel are staggering.

A Hardy fly reel that I have not been able to acquire is the Cascapedia. Styled in the classic manner of the American Edward vom Hofe reels, the Cascapedia, a salmon reel, was available in sizes from 3⅛ to 3⅞ inches in diameter. The reel had an elaborate adjustable drag system, an S-shaped counterbalanced handle, and ebonite side plates.

The current Lightweight series of Hardy fly reels had their origins first with the Uniqua and later with the Lightweight (model) in the 1930s. Very similar to those produced today, the Lightweight had a solid, nonperforated spool and a nonadjustable drag. The reel in my collection has a black enameled finish with a bright aluminum spool. Prior to the present Lightweights, Hardy manufactured other Lightweight models throughout the years for relatively short periods. The Davy, the Gem, the St. Andrew, and the Hydra are some of the most notable.

The present series of Lightweight reels has undergone several changes in finish and fittings. Originally finished in all black, some of the Lightweight reels had a green enameled finish for a period, particularly the L.R.H. and the Princess. Changes in stripping guides were also noted, with the earlier reels having brass guides with the Hardy patent number stamped on them. The current reversible stripping guides are held to the frame with one screw, while the earlier ones had two screws.

An interesting variation on the Lightweight series reels was distributed by Abercrombie & Fitch. These reels are known as the "Silent Check" models. Silent Check Lightweights were offered in the Flyweight, Featherweight, L.R.H., and Princess sizes. All Silent Check Hardy Lightweight reels command premiums over the standard models because they have been discontinued. Current Lightweight Hardys consist of the following models: Flyweight, Featherweight, L.R.H., Princess, St. Aidan, St. George (3¾ inches), St. John (a super salmon reel), and Husky. Multipliers are available in the Featherweight, L.R.H., Princess, and Husky. Hardy is also making fly reels for several other companies, the most notable being the Scientific Anglers System series and the Orvis CFOs, both potential collector's items.

Hardy Silent Perfect, 3⅜ inches. Silents were also known as a poacher's reel since there were no telltale noises when playing a fish. Excellent workmanship. (Photo courtesy Jack Dugrew)

DISPLAYING YOUR COLLECTION

A reel collection can be displayed in a number of ways—shadow boxes, glass-covered coffee tables, or glass-covered bookcases are but a few. I know of a few collectors who display their reel collections by mounting their reels on reel seats attached to walnut mounting boards.

   The older Hardy fly reels make a very interesting collection and are a fine investment of both time and money. The collecting of fly reels, for me, has been an extension of my interest in fly fishing and fly tying and my enjoyment of the great outdoors. It can be yours too!

Hardy Barton. Note tapered handle and offset brass foot so that reel would ride higher on its seat. (Photo courtesy Jack Dugrew)

RELATIVE VALUES OF COLLECTIBLE HARDY REELS

Model	Description	Value
Brass Perfects	3⅛ inches or smaller	$500 and up
	3⅜ inches and up	up to $500
Perfects	Contracted	$300–400
	Special Perfect	$400–500
	Bouglé	$500 and up
	Silent	$400–500
	Mark I	$300–400
	Blue Mark II	$200–300
	Enameled	up to $250
Uniqua	up to 3 inches	$200–300
	3⅛ inches and larger	$100–200
St. George	3 inches and 2⁹/₁₆ (3 screw)	$300–500
	3 inches and 2⁹/₁₆ (2 screw)	$250–450
	larger sizes	$175–250
	Silent	$400 and up
	Multiplier	$400 and up
Sunbeam		$150–250
Barton		$400 and up
Cascapedia		$350 and up
Lightweight (solid spool)		$125–200
Hydra		$125–225
U.S.A.		$150–250
Field		$200 and up
Davy		$200 and up

SELECTED BIBLIOGRAPHY

Keene, J. Harrington. *Fishing Tackle*. New York and London: Ward, Lock & Co., 1886.

McClane, A. J. *McClane's New Standard Fishing Encyclopedia*. New York: Holt, Rinehart & Winston, 1974.

Melner, Samuel, and Kessler, Hermann. *Great Fishing Tackle Catalogues of the Golden Age*. New York: Crown, 1972.

Schwiebert, Ernest. *Trout*, Vol. 2. New York: E.P. Dutton, 1978.
Stockwell, Glenn. *Fly Reels of the House of Hardy*. London: Adam & Charles Black, 1978.

In addition to the above, the Hardy Brothers catalogs are invaluable reference material.

Chapter 24 ❧ Fishing Flies

THEODORE A. NIEMEYER

Unlike the fine collections of guns, books, rods, reels, and sporting art, the search for historic and important fishing flies has been undertaken by only a handful of collectors whose backgrounds are as diverse as anyone could imagine. They are not, as one might suspect, all fly-tiers bent on studying the styles, patterns, and techniques of others.

The finest and most extensive collections in existence today are those located in museums, private fishing clubs, and fly-tying authors' dens.

A substantial amount of material is available if one has the intensity and persistence to plan a simple approach to collecting and is willing to invest a small amount of money and a lot of time in achieving his goal.

Unless you are blessed with a substantial bank account, I would direct your search for old and historic flies to those of North American origin. That is not to say that the beautiful flies of Halford, Lunn, Baigent, Pryce-Tannant, and the like do not exist. They do exist; however, they are in the possession of collectors who guard them well, and it would take a lot of money to obtain them. For these and other reasons, I place particular attention on the North American market. The history and intrigue of fly patterns tied by Gordon, Hewitt, Cross, Martinez, and the like can be a challenge of sufficient proportions to test the most ambitious collectors.

Before you attempt to put together a collection, I suggest you consult some of the excellent reference books dealing with fly-tiers and their fly patterns. You will find that only a small number of good-quality color photographs are available in these books. To guide you in your search, it is best to study the fly-tiers' work firsthand. This means locating a collection and spending a substantial amount of time studying.

The collector has a great variety of types and styles of flies from which to choose. I suggest you start by concentrating your efforts on the types of flies you know best. The advantages of this approach are many. If you have a limited budget, collecting one or two styles of flies will keep your expenditure within its limits. Remember that the cost of framing and preserving your collection is considerable. Some may prefer the "scattershot" approach to collecting, but I would discourage that, since one ends up with little of value and a great quantity of garbage. If you concentrate on the very best work of a handful of tiers, a col-

Above: A finely tied Red Quill by Art Flick. (Photo courtesy Matthew Vinciguerra)

Below: Innovative pattern for Isonychia bicolor by Matthew Vinciguerra. (Photo courtesy Matthew Vinciguerra)

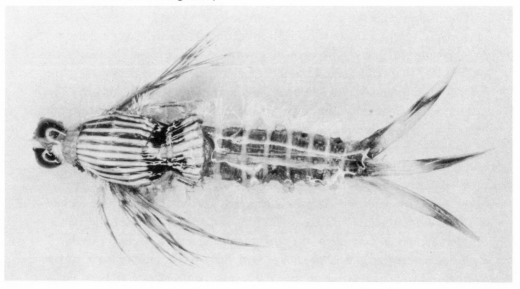

lection of considerably more substance and greater resale value will result. Many collections I know of contain only those flies available in quantity from retailers coast to coast. This approach is fine if your intent is to have a fine collection of "standard" flies to pass on to your son's son. It would be of little value for at least another 20 to 50 years. There are some exceptions, but it follows that most good contemporary fly-tiers will not be given proper credit for their abilities until their tying days are over. Fly-tiers are much like artists in this respect.

STYLES OF FLIES

In the early days of trout fishing and bass fishing on the North American continent, flies were generally European patterns purchased from the excellent tackle stores of London and the fly-tiers of Scotland and Ireland. That has changed dramatically, and today we find the North American fly-fisherman using patterns designed specifically for our waters by local tiers.

The following list of styles could well form the basis for a fine collection utilizing only one or two from the total.

Trout flies. These include traditional flies of European origin but tied for North American trout waters: hackled flies, representing aquatic insects during the (subaquatic) larval and pupal stages; winged wet flies, probably the most prevalent style of fly fished today; nymph flies, more popular today than ever before and the least known in number of patterns among trout flies; streamer flies, traditional, hackled, and hair-winged to represent the small fish that trout devour in great quantities; and dry flies, used and touted by the "purist."

Salmon flies. These include traditional flies, copied from the many pattern books of English, Scottish, and Irish authors, and hair-winged flies, conceded to be of North American origin and now a favorite style of many fly-fishermen.

Bass flies. These include traditional flies, usually a large solid-winged fly in vogue during the early 1900s, and deerhair flies, very popular among today's better bass fly-fishermen.

Saltwater flies. These include shad flies—few patterns exist since the number of fly-fishermen seeking the shad are small when compared with trout, bass, or salmon fly-fishermen—and other patterns for stripers, coho, tarpon, bonefish, and many other saltwater species. Such flies are limited in number but gaining in popularity each year.

CATEGORIES FOR COLLECTING

I tend to get better results in searching for flies by following various categories and placing relative values on each category. In that way, expenditures can be controlled much better. Here are those that I have attempted to follow.

Fly-tying authors, deceased. This can be subdivided into North American authors and foreign authors. Obviously the amateur category among deceased authors is a difficult one to fill. They tied primarily for themselves and a few friends, and there is little chance of locating more than a handful. The professional is another matter. Those who wrote books found considerable demand for their flies after publication and sold a great quantity as a result. Many old-timers still have good quantities of flies purchased from now-deceased pros.

Commercial fly-tiers, deceased. Most of our "standard" patterns, although developed by nonprofessional tiers, were best tied by early professionals. Since the use of flies for fishing in North America is relatively new when compared with Europe, this category is rather small. It is one of the most important categories nonetheless. Availability of these flies on the market is surprisingly good.

Fly-pattern originators. The most pleasing of all flies to obtain is a popular pattern tied by its originator. I can think of no greater success in collecting flies than to obtain a pattern directly from its originator along with a note signed by him or her. No question of authenticity here.

Contemporary fly-tying authors. Obtaining flies from the gentlemen in this category can be both easy and difficult. It depends of course on your approach and the attitude of the author. A sincere approach and good price are consistent with success.

Contemporary tiers. These can be either professional or amateur. It is relatively easy to obtain the work of the contemporary professional fly-tier. He is actively tying all year, and although he may only tie for a retail outlet, he will willingly advise you where his flies can be purchased.

The amateur in this category is another matter. Do not be discouraged, however, by the seeming unavailability of a certain tier's work. The amateur is very proud of his work, and my experience in collecting from these people indicates an eagerness on their part to display their talent. More often than not, they refuse to accept compensation. A trade is often the best offer you can make. Fly for fly, a book for a dozen flies, or a box of hooks, for example, are good trade bait.

The futures. I use the term *futures* for lack of a better term to describe the many excellent young (some not so young) tiers who are developing new patterns, sometimes crude but nevertheless effective. I willingly accept all such patterns offered to me as gifts or in exchange for my patterns. The fly-tier-collector has an advantage here. I learn a great deal as a tier and am also confident that some of what I receive will become important in the future.

STARTING YOUR COLLECTION

Whether you choose to start a small or a large collection, it is wise to set some expenditure limits in advance. Consider not only the cost of the flies you are seeking, but the additional expense of preserving and displaying them. Space must be set aside to accommodate large collections, and care must be taken to provide the best physical location in your home or club.

Upon choosing a style or category, next list the fly-tiers you feel best represent the tying skill you want displayed. Choose the patterns you want from each tier selected and locate a source for purchase. With your most persuasive approach in person or by letter, you have made a good start. Fly-tiers are notorious for seldom answering mail and are even slower in filling a request. As any good collector will tell you, persistence pays rich dividends.

I have found it advantageous to appear in person when seeking a purchase of important flies. The seller of flies generally wants to know that his item is being sold to someone who will assure him of its continued safekeeping and proper display. The intent of the purchaser is easily recognizable to the fly-tier. He is proud of his work and of necessity has come to judge the quality of the person seeking his flies.

MARKET VALUES

I was surprised recently when one of my contemporaries offered me a set of his flies at what I considered to be about four times the fair market value. When I paid the amount specified to avoid offending my friend, he told me, without being asked, that flies being sought by collectors are becoming quite scarce, and that if a collector wanted a tier's very best work, he had best be prepared to pay for it. I found this to be a bit coarse on the part of my friend, but it is true that tiers more and more are realizing that a new and distinct market of collectors is emerging. The old standard agreement that called for 50 cents or "a buck a fly" is a thing of the past.

Referring to the categories previously listed, I offer a broad-based price guide. There are exceptions to each category, and it is expected that all categories will increase from year to year.

Fly-tying authors, deceased. Complete set of flies by the author as described in the text: no limit. Individual flies by the author as described in the text: $5 to $200. Individual flies by the author not described in the text: $4 to $50.

Commercial fly-tiers, deceased. Individual flies originated and tied by the tier: $4 to $100. Standard individual flies tied by the tier: $2 to $50.

Fly-pattern originators. Individual flies tied by the originator: $4 to $100. Individual flies not originated by him but tied by him: $2 to $50.

Contemporary fly-tying authors. Individual flies tied by the author: $2 to $10.

Contemporary tiers. Individual flies: $1 to $4.

The future – no minimum.

FINDING FLIES

I have frequently been asked by persons observing my personal collection of flies and art, "Where do you find all this material to display?" The answer is not an easy one. I previously mentioned that if you are beginning a collection, seek the fly-tiers who will best represent the category of flies you have selected. Visit them in person if at all possible and don't forget to show a sincere interest in their total work. The slightest indication that the intent is to turn a quick profit from your collection and you will be sent home with an empty bag.

One factor continues to stand out when I am seeking flies of a particular tier: for every accomplished fly-tier there must be at least 100 fly-fishermen who do not tie their own flies. Flies tied by some of those aforementioned tiers have a habit of ending up in the fly boxes of the non-tier. The stuffed fly boxes of some of these fellows would astound you. Surprisingly, this tends to be my best source of valuable flies.

Be alert to any auction where fishing equipment is listed in estate contents. Some extremely valuable items have found their way into my collection as a result of auctions.

Contacting other collectors in person and suggesting an agreement to trade or purchase is becoming commonplace. None of the collectors I know today is actively engaged in selling valuable flies. I suppose this will change as the market value increases and the collecting activities of fly-fishermen and others also increases. For now, we must be content to seek our prizes from other sources. As more persons enter the field of fly collecting, undoubtedly there will emerge a broker of sorts.

A seldom-used approach is advertising in the various sporting magazines and club and organization publications. Dealing through the mails can be a risky business at best, and I strongly suggest a "no deal" basis if what you receive cannot be authenticated during an agreed-upon inspection period.

AUTHENTICATING AND APPRAISING FLIES

For many years now, we have been blessed with excellent books listing many of the fly patterns both old and new. How many of these books can you name that show the author's or originator's flies in quality color reproduction? Without top-quality photographs or authentic originals in his possession, the average collector cannot determine whether the purchase he is contemplating is an authentic one. The purchaser must then honor the statement of the seller as to its authenticity.

Losses from unauthentic purchases can be minimized by a thorough study of originals in another person's collection or by visits to museums to study collections held there. You will be in a position to determine authenticity "on sight" if some attention is paid to study.

There are many persons capable of verifying the authenticity of certain patterns tied by a limited number of selected fly-tiers. But there are only a handful capable of determining the authenticity of the work of more than three or four tiers.

Fly-tiers can be identified much the same as artists. There will always be a signature of sorts built into each fly, and this is the key to knowing the real thing. It is virtually impossible to duplicate another tier and dupe the well-trained collector or appraiser.

I suspect that almost every active fly-tier today has in his possession the beginnings of a small collection of important and historical flies. There is a natural inclination to simply trade flies with other fly-tiers, and I believe most of us accumulate many flies in this manner. We placed little value on them at first and were more interested in the technique of tying than starting any type of collection. But the value is there and should not be overlooked. If your collection of flies has now reached the point where you are interested in selling all or parts

An all-black streamer tied early in the fabled career of Mrs. Carrie Stevens. Its value is enhanced because it is attached to its original identifying card. (Photo courtesy Matthew Vinciguerra)

of it, I can only suggest that you solicit the appraisal of the handful of acknowledged experts in this field. Most of them are associated with museums, and they will surely charge a fee for their services.

As with any art form, the collector of old fishing flies wonders what value might be placed on his prized possession some years from now. I personally think such collections will increase in value and, if properly preserved and displayed, will bring a considerable return on one's investment.

I can assure anyone who is hesitant about starting a collection that he can escalate the value of his collection dramatically if he will cleverly, but in good taste, complement his flies with suitable art work. The art need not be expensive, but the viewer should be able to observe some correlation between the flies and the print.

PRESERVING YOUR COLLECTION

The most handsome fly displays I have seen were those framed with the artist's original paintings, complemented with flies created at his own tying vise. That is a very unusual combination, but nonetheless exists as a sample of what can be created. To be certain that these flies would not be lost to insects devouring them, or to the ravages of rust, causing the fly body to discolor and disintegrate, special precautions must be taken before sealing them permanently in glass frames.

Fishing flies are tied directly to some form of metal hook, probably made of steel or steel alloy with a protective coating. Given the proper combination of moisture and exposed metal surface, rust will appear and eventually harm your display. To avoid such problems, it is suggested that a light coat of machine oil be applied to all of the exposed hook surface, taking great care not to touch any parts of the materials bound to it. Some of the newer silicone sprays may be used, but caution must be taken not to spray this substance on any of the feathers, fur, or hair.

When mounting the fly, do not allow any materials such as metal mounts, wire, or moisture-bearing substances to rest against the hook.

Those materials containing natural animal oils seem to last indefinitely. Those materials that appear to be drying out and look brittle should not be steamed or brushed. The results could be devastating. In cases where you must repair, feathers can be salvaged by application of feather-glazing, purchased from fly-tying supply houses. Glazing in this manner tends to darken a dried-out feather, but this is better than losing a valuable fly.

Should you obtain flies that appear to have lost some of their material to the ravages of insects, it is suggested that you place them in a sealed glass jar containing a liberal quantity of paradychlorobenzene crystals for two weeks or more. This will kill any insect that may have infested the fly but may not destroy insect eggs. Remove the flies from the bottle and carefully brush all fur, feathers, and hair with a fine camel-hair brush, taking care to remove all loose material.

Everyone has heard of steaming flies to restore the original shape, but you can totally destroy flies with this method. Because steam is water, if you hold the fly in steam, you will saturate it. The shank of the hook, which is buried under body materials of fur, floss, or tinsel, will probably rust as a result of the steaming. A better method of restoring the appearance of your flies and minimizing rust is to apply a small quantity of hot air with a hand-held portable hair dryer.

DISPLAYING YOUR FLIES

All fishing flies have a good side and a bad side, and it is to your advantage to display only the good side. This may not always be possible because of the design of your frame and the layout of the flies. It may be necessary to sacrifice the good side in favor of maintaining a good color balance.

The materials used in most fishing flies will eventually become bleached if exposed to direct sunlight or bright lights. Avoid placing your collection where such damage might occur.

Discourage insects from ruining your collection by sealing each frame as airtight as possible. Check each frame periodically, and at the slightest indication of trouble, open the frame and correct the problem.

FLY-TIERS IMPORTANT TO THE COLLECTOR

The following list is by no means complete. However, it will provide a good start for anyone beginning a collection. The tiers are listed in alphabetical order.

John Atherton. Author of the classic book *The Fly and the Fish.*

John Aucon. A Canadian tier of superb Atlantic salmon flies.

Dan Bailey. Proprietor of one of the finest tackle stores in the world.

Ray Bergman. One of the all-time greats of Catskill fame and author of the great book *Trout.*

William Blades. Fly-tying author and superb innovator.

Edgar Burke, M.D. Author and superb tier.

William Charles. Trained in the "Bill Blades" school, and master of nymph patterns.

Herman Christian. Known primarily among eastern trout fishermen; schooled in the "Catskill" theory.

Rube Cross. "Eloquent dry flies" best describes this Catskill great.

Elsie Darbee. Flies tied with her "home-grown duns" are sought by all eastern trout fly-fishermen.

Harry Darbee. Superb fly-fisherman, fly-tier, conservationist, and a real gentleman.

Charles DeFeo. Dean of all salmon fly-tiers. No finer man ever set foot in the crystal waters of North America.

Cock robin by the dean of American salmon-fly tiers, Charles DeFeo. (Photo courtesy Matthew Vinciguerra)

James Deren. Owner of the Angler's Roost, where all the great North American tiers eventually pass through.

Walter Dette. Considered by many to be the finest tier of dry flies in North America.

Winnie Dette. Superb tier of those great Catskill patterns.

Wallace Doak. Supplier of fine Atlantic salmon patterns.

Art Flick. His book, *Streamside Guide*, tells it all. Demanding and particular in his tying.

Keith Fulsher. A unique talent as an innovator and a top-rated salmon tier.

Don Gapen. Father to the great "muddler."

Syd Glasso. An excellent West Coast tier.

Theodore Gordon. A fly by Mr. Gordon could "make" your collection. They won't come easily.

George Grant. Great, great innovator of western nymph patterns.

Elizabeth Greig. Her ability to tie the wet fly has gone unmatched, with the possible exception of one other tier.

This mottled stone fly creeper unmistakably shows the tying artistry of George Grant. (Photo courtesy Matthew Vinciguerra)

Ira Gruber. Self-styled tier of primarily Atlantic salmon patterns.

Don Harger. Tier of superb western fly patterns.

Edward Hewitt. Catskill fly-tier supreme.

Herb Howard. Close ties to Ray Bergman style are evident in his fine work.

Preston Jennings. Unique tying talent covered in his *A Book of Trout Flies.*

Walter Johnson. Superb tier of western steelhead patterns.

Poul Jorgensen. Author of two fine books, he is top-rated as an innovator specializing in salmon flies.

Lefty Kreh. You have to like this guy! His saltwater flies are super.

Charles Krom. Wet flies and nymphs tied by Krom are among the finest ever tied in North America.

Jim Leisenring. Copied, but never equaled, in his talent to tie hackled wet flies.

Edson Leonard. Author and good tier.

Chauncey Lively. Excellent tying talent—dry fly oriented.

Mary Marbury. Author and tier of many of the early North American patterns.

Vincent Marinaro. Selective fly-tier and author of *A Modern Dry Fly Code.*

Don Martinez. A leader in the development of western patterns.

Joe Messinger. Performed matchless work with spun deer hair.

John Mickievicz. Excellent nymph designer and tier.

Bill Nation. Originator of many splendid British Columbia patterns.

Ted Niemeyer. Nymph design–oriented tier.

Lew Oatman. The dean of hackle-wing streamer patterns.

Jim Pray. West Coast "great" and developer of many unique steelhead patterns.

Louis Rhead. A wonderful imagination and deft hands produced a multitude of unusual patterns.

Mike Roche. A proponent of the exact-imitation school.

Alex Rogan. Superb designer of the "old world" style.

Polly Rosborough. Great fisher, author, and super tier.

Richard Salmon. Author and expert on the Catskill fraternity of tiers.

Peter Schwab. Accomplished tier of western steelhead patterns.

Ernest Schwiebert. Superbly gifted tier and fly-fisherman.

Ed Sens. Creator of many excellent nymph patterns.

Helen Shaw. Extremely talented tier and author.

Ernie St. Clair. Uncanny ability to create exact copies of nymphs.

Roy Steenrod. Catskill tier supreme.

Carrie Stevens. Creator of many great streamer patterns for Maine waters.

William Sturgis. Author and talented tier.

Al Troth. Superb western nymph tier.

Ted Trueblood. Superior fly-fisherman and tier of superior fish-taking patterns.

Harry Van Luven. Designer of unique western steelhead patterns.

Matthew Vinciguerra. A student and photographer of entomology whose unique fly designs have influenced many eastern tiers.

Ralph Wahl. Another of the good West Coast steelhead tiers.

Leonard West. Author and pattern historian.

Charles Wetzel. Designer of many patterns and author of considerable fly-tying literature.

Dave Whitlock. Artist, author, and superb "big fly" designer.

Lee Wulff. Superb fly-fisherman, conservationist, and tier.

Yas Yamashita. Incredible, exact imitation work on nymphs.

Hook, ribbing, and wing are all that remain of this unique mayfly pattern attributed to Alex Rogan. (Photo courtesy Matthew Vinciguerra)

SELECTED BIBLIOGRAPHY

A study of the following books will enlighten the collector of fishing flies sufficiently to begin to recognize significant differences and unique traits of the
many tiers.

Bates, Joseph D., Jr. *Atlantic Salmon Flies and Fishing.* Harrisburg, PA:
    Stackpole Books, 1970.
Bates, Joseph D., Jr. *Streamer Fly Tying and Fishing.* Harrisburg, PA:
    Stackpole Books, 1966.
Blades, William F. *Fishing Flies and Fly Tying.* Harrisburg, PA: Stackpole
    and Heck, Inc., 1951.
Combs, Trey. *The Steelhead Trout.* Portland, OR: Northwest Salmon-Trout-
    Steelheader Co., 1971.
Flick, Art. *A Master Fly-Tying Guide.* New York: Crown Publishers, Inc.,
    1972.
Smedley, Harold Hinsdill. *Fly Patterns and Their Origins.* Muskegon, MI:
    Westshore Publications, 1943.

Chapter 25 ❧ Fishing Lures

SETH R. ROSENBAUM

It seems that an era is ending. The days of buying fishing tackle for the sole purpose of pleasurably catching fish are gone. At last, fishing tackle has joined other memorabilia and true antiques as items to be collected, as well as used. The first pieces of fish-catching equipment to become collectible were reels, especially precision-made casting reels. Next, fine bamboo rods were bought for display, rather than for fishing. Other traditional, old equipment, related to fly-fishing, followed. The latest type of fishing equipment to become collectible is lures.

What are lures? They are any nonedible (by fish) device, with hooks, that deceives fish. This deceitfulness causes the fish to take the lure in its mouth and become hooked. Lures, especially flies, go back to the 1600s, when Izaak Walton described an artificial caterpillar made of chenille. George Herter, president of the large Minnesota company that bears his name, produces a lure he attributes originally to Dame Juliana Berners. As the good Dame wrote her angling treatise while Columbus was mucking around Cuba (1496), this lure would certainly be the ancestor of all. This oldest type of lure, not a fly, was a metal fish. The metal was so shaped that water resistance made the lure move and flash in an eccentric fashion. These pieces of metal evolved into English Devons and eventually into the present-day spinners and spoons.

Nothing much happened in the next 300 years. Kings fell; governments were formed; wars started; forks were invented; but if you disdained live bait, you were limited to using flies, spoons, or spinners. In 1810 something new emerged. This was a fishlike device, consisting of a finned metal head and a painted body made of soft material, either silk, canvas, or porpoise hide. This device, called a False or Phantom Minnow, incorporated two new hook techniques—the barbed hook and the treble hook. As with many fish lures to follow, as many as six trebles, netting 18 hooks, were put on a 4-inch lure! No further major type of lure innovations appeared until 1890.

The lures described so far were developed for freshwater fishing. For collection purposes, note must be made of lures developed for sea fishing. The use of artificial saltwater lures goes back to the earliest Polynesians and to the Eskimo and American Indians. They all used lures made of bone and shell, usually as part of a fish hook of the same materials. These carried over to the 1800s, when

Tin Liz. Fred Arbogast. Also Maid, a Sunfish, and Pickeral Tin Liz.

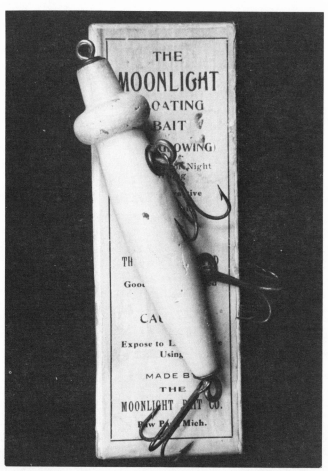

Moonlight Liminous. Original lure of the Moonlight Company. Directions say, "Expose to flashlight rays for a few minutes. Will glow all night."

Dowagiac. James Heddon. Named after Dowagiac, Michigan, where Heddon's factory was located.

Buel Spoon. J. T. Buel. Possibly the first spoon pattern Buel made.

American fishermen used similar lures, called jigs, to catch fish. These lures were trolled on tar lines from sailing ketches and heaved out and hauled in the surf, also without rod or reel. In 1911, N. A. Dickson invented a wooden jig for tuna trolling. A characteristic of all jigs of this era is the use of a black, hand-forged blacksmith's hook.

The first recorded lure, now defined as a plug, appeared in 1897. A plug, also called an artificial minnow, differs from other lures because it basically imitates a minnow and is usually made of wood. In the beginning, there were a few made of hollow aluminum, and by 1910, they were made to look like frogs, crawfish, and mice. But basically, a plug is still minnowlike in appearance. Granted, some look more like Salvador Dali's idea of a minnow, but they do have a recognizable head and body, and most have painted or glass eyes. In later years, rubber and plastic have been used in place of wood.

IDENTIFYING LURES

Plug collecting is still a new field. Prior to 1960, there were a few collectors, and these, mostly, were unknown to each other. From the 1960s, the number of collectors increased. As this increase occurred, a similar increase took place in the price of the lures collected. Even so, prices of lures can still be considered

Detroit Glass Minnow. Detroit Glass Minnow Company. Again, the directions are worth reading. They say, "Put minnow in tube. It will stay lively all day."

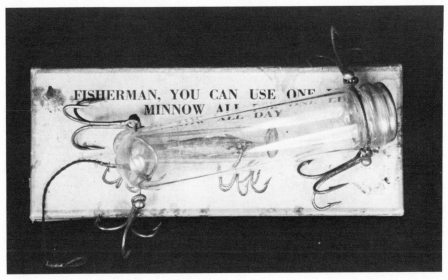

Tantilizer. Wm. Shakespeare Company. One of Shakespeare's specialties was metal fins.

reasonable. One reason for this is that many lures are bought from junk sources. The person who has plugs for sale will almost always be someone who doesn't know if the plug is new or old, rare or common, original or imitation. Therefore, the collector will have to look for certain identification on a plug.

The first and most helpful identifier is writing of some sort. This is present about a third of the time. Some manufacturers, such as Heddon, Creek Chub, and South Bend, have identification on 80 percent of their plugs. Others, mostly manufacturers of single plugs, do not. The two places to find writing are on the metal (engraved), usually the mouthpiece or spinner, or on the body (stenciled), usually the back. Also, if the plug is in the original box, the box will have identification on it. Most plugs made before 1950 were individually boxed. Some of these earlier boxes are also collectible, especially the metal and wooden ones.

In addition to the writing on a plug, other points of identification are helpful, but not infallible. Look for wood bodies and glass eyes. In later years, fewer and fewer plugs were made this expensive way. Look for patent dates on the metal; that plug can be no older than the date. Look at the hook hangers. Many plug manufacturers had their own specific style of hook hangers. Some always used grommets of a specific size. Heddon, in particular, changed its hook style many times (at least five) over its 75-year history. Like other companies, it also changed, in small detail, individual plugs. A similar example of this detail change is the Jitterbug, a popular surface lure, made by the Fred Arborgast Co.,

Chub Minnow. Creek Chub Bait Company. The first lure Creek Chub made. The more popular Creek Chub Pikie Minnow came 10 years later.

which, during World War II, could not get metal for the face lip. A colored plastic front plate clearly dates this lure. Luckily there have been recent printings of identification manuals for plugs (see Bibliography).

For collecting purposes, plugs are classified as being manufactured by a "major" or a "miscellaneous" company. The major companies are those that were in business for all, or a large part, of the best years of lure manufacturing (1900–1941) and, during this period, turned out a multitude of collectible items. The five companies in this category, in order of plug desirability, are James Heddon's Sons (still in business), William Shakespeare (still in business), Creek Chub Bait Company (no longer in business), Pflueger Enterprise Manufacturing (still in business), and South Bend Bait (no longer in business). The miscellaneous companies, while individually producing fewer lures (in some cases single lures), came out with many highly collectible items.

REFERENCE MATERIALS

There are three types of fishing catalogs. All can have excellent reference material and pictures. The oldest of these for plug information are from 1901, and those for spoons and spinners are from 1860 on. The first type is the manufacturer's catalog. This, of course, shows only the company's product, but shows the complete line available during the catalog year. These catalogs describe the lures as to size, color, and special characteristics. Some companies were mostly lure manufacturers. Others had all types of tackle, with plenty of lures

Paw Paw Underwater Minnow. Moonlight Bait Company. Made by Moonlight, not the Paw Paw Bait Company. Both were located in Paw Paw, Michigan.

included. All companies issued new catalogs every year. These catalogs always had the company's basic lures plus a few new ones. Tackle companies published a wholesale, as well as a retail, catalog. For lure-identification purposes, the only difference between these is that the wholesale catalog usually has additional descriptive detail.

Secondly, there is the sporting-goods catalog. These were published for mail-order businesses. They never covered just lures, like the manufacturers' catalogs; they advertised mixed fishing tackle, mixed sporting goods, or mixed everything. An example of the last group would be Sears Roebuck & Company catalog and Montgomery Ward's. The advantage of all these catalogs is that they carry lures of all major and popular companies at that time. From them, you can get a broad collection of plug pictures for each year. They do not always

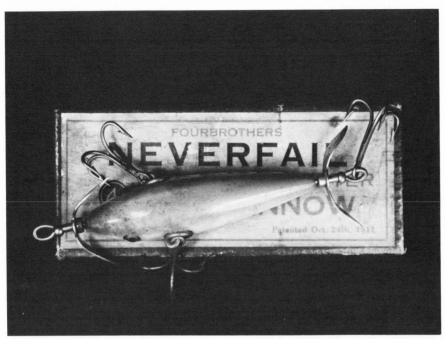

Neverfail Minnow. Pflueger Bait Company. Put out under the name Four Brothers Bait Company, which represented the four Pflueger Brothers.

Rainbow Ball Bait. Made by the Detroit Bait Company, later bought by Jamison.

give full information. In many cases, the plug is named but the lure maker's name is not given. Sometimes, large mail-order houses, for example, Abbey and Imbrie (New York City, 1860–1940), had companies such as Heddon put "Abbey and Imbrie" on a Heddon plug.

The third type of fishing catalog is the pocket catalog. These little gems were packed with the plug and contained many pictures. Many of the smaller plug makers only put out pocket catalogs. The same catalog was usually used year after year. Also, pocket catalogs, unlike larger catalogs, rarely had dates, so the year of manufacture cannot be determined from them.

Most readers are familiar with hunting and fishing magazines. They go back to the 1890s. Before that, they existed in tabloid form. Many libraries have excellent magazine collections, together with copying machines. A day spent riffling through a library's files will result in the start of an excellent reference file. Note that the page-numbering system used in early years was quite different from today's system. The early magazines started the year (January issue) with page 1. If there were 80 pages in January, the February issue started with page 81. That means that if you pick up a middle-of-the-year issue, it might start on page 416, or some other large number. A further point to remember when looking something up is that the advertising pages were in the beginning and end of the magazines. These were normally numbered with an "A" after the page number. A typical August 1915 issue of *Field & Stream* would start with page 1A to page 8A, start again with page 333 to page 440, and close with page 9A to page 38A. These magazines usually had advertisers' indexes (either in front or in back) that were broken down by type of advertiser. So you find the

Redfin Floating Bait. Made by Jim Donaly, 1912.

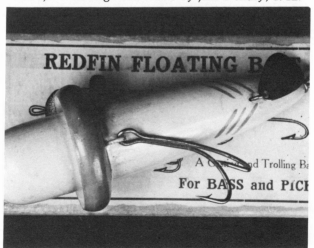

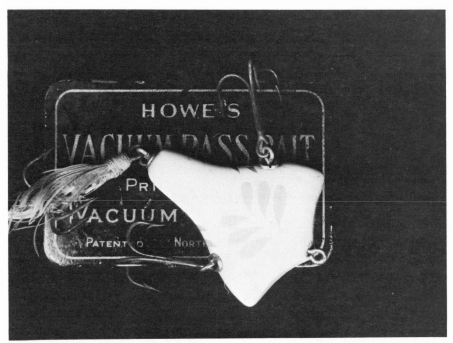

Vacuum Bait. Made by the Vacuum Bait Co., then Howe, then South Bend.

Chippewa Bait. Made in 1920 in Michigan by Frost.

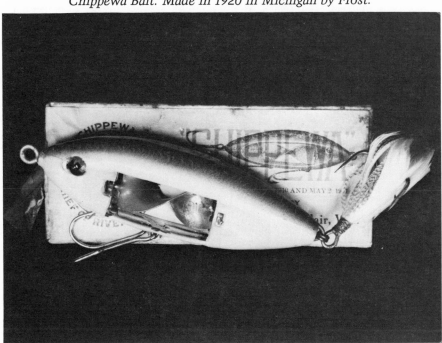

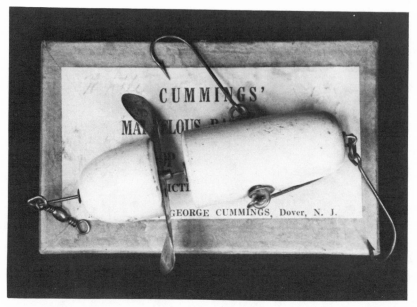

Cummings Bait. Many propeller-type baits like this were made from 1910–1925.

index, look under Fishing Tackle, and check out these ads for plug pictures.

A few fishing books published between 1900 and 1940 have plug pictures. Unfortunately, for many years, tradition, if not logic, frowned on using company or trade names. As a result, many authors drew a picture of a "typical" plug, which, of course, is useless to a collector.

STARTING A COLLECTION

The three "Fs" of plug collecting are: fathers, fishing-tackle stores, and flea markets. Start with your fishing relatives, the older the better. If your father, or your friend's father, or grandfather, fished (does anyone have a fishing mother?), see if you can locate a fishing cache. Fishermen rarely throw tackle out. Don't assume that a veteran trout or bait fisherman wouldn't have plugs. These are just the people who receive incongruous, nonusable gifts such as plugs, and store them away, unused, for years. It doesn't hurt to ask any boy you meet, with a tackle box, if he has any old plugs to sell. Fathers give them their old worn-out tackle to start them fishing. Some of this old stuff is highly collectible and can be had for small change. If you feel that this is taking advantage of small children, offer them a new plug for their old one.

Until 1950, you could walk into a tackle store and have hopes of turning up a

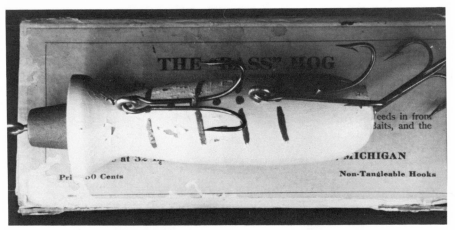

Bass Hog. A collared bait similar to the "Moonlight."

few plugs that were 20 or 30 years old. Many stores had trading boards where, for a quarter, you could take a plug you wanted from the board and leave your own. If a store didn't sell a plug, it stayed on the shelf for many dusty years. After the 1950s, with new merchandising methods and the advent of blister packages, goods no longer gathered dust. However, if you pass a tackle store that doesn't look too modern, go in.

Flea markets, tag or garage sales, and auctions are all a prime source of collectible fishing tackle. Unfortunately, you will have to spend lots of time to find a small amount of tackle. Of this, plugs will be the least. Dick Miller, a reel collector from Hudson, Massachusetts, attends flea markets carrying a tied bunch of very long fishing rods. He says this lets the dealers spot him as someone who wants fishing tackle, and if they have any tackle to sell, he gets called.

From 1900 to 1950, a new name-brand plug cost 75 cents to $1.25. Spinners and spoons cost less. Even today, with the exception of oversized muskellunge or saltwater plugs, the cost of a new plug rarely exceeds $2.50. This means that you can still find collectible plugs selling for a small amount of money. Undoubtedly, when plug collecting becomes more advanced, prices will increase.

CARE AND DISPLAY OF LURES

All wood and metal lures are very durable. Even plugs that have received heavy use for a long time maintain their good looks. The same cannot be said for plugs wholly or partially made of rubber or animal dressing (feathers and bucktail).

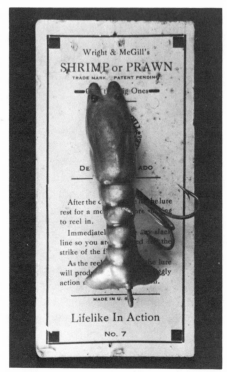

Shrimp. An early Wright and McGill.

Do-Gettum. Outing Mfg. A floater made of hollow brass.

Rubber wears worst of all. Many rubber lures, especially frogs, were made 50 years ago. Most will be in poor shape today. Creek Chub's Fintail Shiner was made with rubber fins. It rarely can be found with the fins still intact. Also, early attempts (1930) at painted plastic lures were unsuccessful. The paint never dried. Some of these, 40 years later, are still tacky. Heddon's first Spooks were this way. But with those exceptions, delicate handling is not needed with old lures.

Lures can be displayed in many ways. They look quite well in small shadow-boxes. Their small size lends them to mounting in older printers' type-slug boxes. If space is available, they can be hung on fish netting or hammock netting. For this last, bear in mind that plugs have hooks. Don't hang the net where people pass frequently.

Plug and lure collectors collect differently and classify differently. While most lure collectors specialize in plugs, others collect only spoons, or spinners, or saltwater lures, or only West Coast salmon plugs. Some plug collectors specialize in just one, or only a few, of the many lure manufacturers. As far as classifying, plug collectors are individualists. You can classify your collection according to color, size, or special characteristics, such as number of hooks, or whether jointed or not jointed. No matter how you arrange your collection, you will find it advantageous to keep a file index. Simply write the name of the plug and the name of the manufacturer on an index card. You can write a small story on the back of the card saying where and when you got it, how much it cost, and where to find an identification picture. You should have only one card for each plug name. When you get more than one of a plug, put all this information on the back of the card. If you collect on a broad spectrum, you will find that about a third of your plugs cannot be identified, or can be only partially identified. In these cases, an exchange of information with fellow collectors is most helpful. A lure collectors' club could formalize this exchange or serve as a valuable affiliation.

SOME PLUG MANUFACTURERS AND PLUGS 1900-1950

Company	Best-known plugs
Arbogast	Hawaiian Wiggler
	Jitterbug
	Tin Liz
Bunyan	Dodger

Company	Best-known plugs
Creek Chub	Darter
	Ding Bat
	Fintail Shiner
	Gar Minnow
	Injured Minnow
	Pikie
	Tiny Tim
	Wiggler
Decker	Decker Bait
Donnaly	Jersey Wow
Heddon	Crab Wiggler
	Crazy Crawler
	Dowagiac
	Flaptail
	Gamefisher
	Luny Frog
	River Runt
	Super Surface
	Tadpolly
	Vamp
	Zaragosa
Jamison-Shannon	Coaxer
	Wig L. Twin
Millsite	Beetle
	Paddle Plug
Moonlight	Moonlight Bait
P&K	Wirlaway
Paw Paw	Wata Frog
Pflueger Enterprise	Globe
	Mustang Minnow
	Neverfail
	Pal O'Mine
	Pop Rite
	Surprise
Rush	Tango

Company	Best-known plugs
Shakespeare	Dopey
	Glo Lite Pup
	Grumpy
	Kazoo
	Mouse
	Paddler
	Revolution
	Rhodes Frog
South Bend	Bass Oreno
	Dive Oreno
	Fish Obite
	Surf Oreno
	Vacuum Bait
True Temper	Crippled Shad
	Speed Shad
Wilson-Hasting	Wobbler

SELECTED BIBLIOGRAPHY: MAGAZINES

One of the best ways to track down a lure is through the outdoor magazines, using the advertisers' indexes as I have described. The most useful magazines for this purpose are the following:

Field & Stream

Forest and Stream

Fur, Fish and Game

Hardings

Hunting and Fishing

National Sportsman

Outers

Outing

Outdoor Life

Rod and Gun

Sports Afield

Sporting Goods Journal

SELECTED BIBLIOGRAPHY: ILLUSTRATED BOOKS AND CATALOGS

Bergman, Ray. *Fresh Water Bass*. New York: Knopf, 1942.

Bergman, Ray. *Just Fishing*. Philadelphia: Penn Publishing, 1932.

Boyle, Robert. *Bass*. New York: W. W. Norton, 1980.

Carroll, Dixie. *Fishing Tackle and Kits*. Cincinnati: Stewart & Kidd, 1919.

Fox, Charles K. *The Book of Lures*. Rockville Centre, NY: Fresher Press, 1975.

Harbin, Clyde. *Heddon Catalogs*. CAH Enterprises, 1977.

Kimball, Art and Kimball, Scott. *Collecting Old Fishing Tackle*. New York: Aardvark Publications, 1980.

Luckey, Carl F. *Old Fishing Lures and Tackle*. Decatur, IN: Americana Books, 1980.

Major, Harlan. *Salt Water Fishing Tackle*. New York: Funk & Wagnalls, 1955.

Melner, Sam, et al. *Great American Fishing Tackle Catalogs*. New York: Crown, 1972.

Outdoorsman's Handbook. Field & Stream Pub., 1910.

Outers Book. Out Pub., 1911.

Rhead, Louis. *Fisherman's Lures and Game-Fish Food*. New York: Scribner's, 1920.

Streater, R. L. *Streater's Reference Catalog of Old Fishing Lures*. Raines Press, 1978.

Chapter 26 ❧ Fish Decoys

ROBIN STARR

F ish decoys seem destined to become one of the last nationally recognized forms of American folk art to be discovered by collectors. Whereas other collectible items such as patchwork quilts, baskets, duck decoys, and weathervanes were made and used in every corner of the country, fish decoys have derived a large measure of anonymity from their very localized use. It was only on the large and frozen freshwater lakes of Minnesota, Wisconsin, Michigan, New York, and New England that hardy sportsmen could enjoy the sport of spearfishing through the ice. The only remaining bastion of spearfishing is Minnesota, where it is still legal to spear northern pike. In all other states, and for all other species of game fish, spearing is now illegal.

As the name implies, a fish decoy's purpose was to attract certain game fish to a point close enough to the surface to be within range of a deadly wrought-iron spear. This was done by cutting a hole in the ice, lowering the decoy on a line to the bottom, and slowly raising it to the surface in a circular motion. Covering the hole in the ice was a shanty, darkened for better vision into the murky depths. Stories are told of upwards of 10,000 shanties on one lake, stretching as far as the eye could see. The most prized targets for the spearfisherman were the pickerel, muskie, northern pike, and sturgeon, but many other species found their way via the spear to the frying pan.

Although decoys are found in numerous shapes and sizes, there are certain characteristics that are common to all authentic fish decoys. First, and most important, is that unlike most other forms of fish lures, a fish decoy has no hooks. Occasionally an illegal spearing decoy was used carrying one or more hooks, but this practice was frowned on by the law and by sportsmen. Second, to force the decoy to sink to the bottom, some sort of weight had to be attached. In the majority of cases, this was done by filling a cavity in the underside of the decoy with molten lead. Finally, all decoys have some number of fins attached to a wooden body. These were usually made of copper or tin and were designed for both realism and stabilization in the water.

Collecting fish decoys is naturally easier if you are fortunate enough to live near the areas where they were used. Here one can still chat with the old carvers, and occasionally locate an old spearfisherman, with a cigar box full of his hand-carved fish decoys tucked away in a dusty corner of the cellar. Getting him to

Part of the author's collection, demonstrating one way to display fish. Here the fish are wired to a 4-foot-high burlap-covered pegboard. The muskie carving on the top is not a decoy but was once a decoration on the wall of a Minnesota sporting-goods shop.

part with these prizes is, of course, the dream of any collector, and one of the factors that makes collecting so rewarding. However, the rest of us who live in other parts of the country must rely on friends, antique dealers, or other fish-decoy collectors. Quite often, duck-decoy collectors also collect fish decoys or at least have a couple in their collection. For this reason, more and more fish decoys are becoming available for sale or trade at decoy shows around the country, as well as at antique shows and flea markets, where knowledgeable dealers are beginning to recognize the market for this relatively little-known form of folk art.

Once you have located one or more fish decoys, the question arises as to their worth. To date, since there is such a limited national market for this commodity, it is suggested that each decoy be judged on its own merits and valued accordingly. Needless to say, there are innumerable attributes to be considered. If, however, there was such a thing as an "average" fish decoy, it would probably be painted red and white, be about six inches long with metal fins, and command a price of anywhere from $25 to $100. Any extra work or show of ingenuity by the carver, such as carved gills, leather fins, glass eyes, or a carved wooden tail would be rewarded with an increase of value. Once a collector has seen many fish decoys, it becomes easier to compare the relative merits of each piece, but until then he must rely on the integrity of the person with whom he is dealing. Certain unusual items, such as a well-carved 40-inch sturgeon decoy, could command a price in the hundreds of dollars for its folk-art qualities alone. But pieces of this quality are extremely scarce. Sturgeon decoys were used, and are found almost exclusively, in Wisconsin, and it is interesting to note that they were often carved to the exact length of the then-current legal minimum-size sturgeon. Then, as the sturgeon swam over the decoy, it was easy to see if the fish was a "keeper" or not. In the early days, the limit was 24 inches, but this later was increased to 40 inches.

Identifiable by their shape as sunfish, these examples from 3 to 4½ inches in length are representative of decoys currently available in the $20–100 range.

A 10-inch blue-black carp decoy from Michigan with glass eyes, carved scales, and a curved carved tail. This fine example of American folk art, made about 1930, is valued at $125.

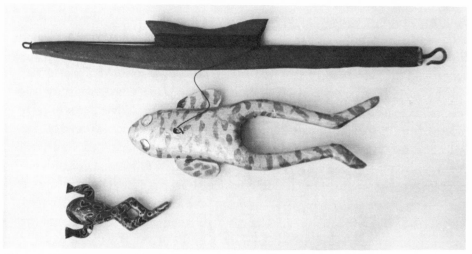

Two extremely scarce frog decoys, 2 inches and 6 inches long and valued at $40 and $75 respectively. Attached to the larger frog is an old jigging stick used to lower the decoy into the water.

Two manufactured fish decoys, each 6 inches long. On the left is a nearly perfect replica, made of molded plastic, of a pickerel. The other, made of wood with metal fins, is more stylized in shape and paint pattern.

The men who carved fish decoys had two main considerations that influenced their work. The first was to produce a functional piece that would attract fish. The second factor that guided their hands was the desire to express themselves as artists and craftsmen, for these men were proud of their efforts. Realizing that everyone who carved had varying degrees of talent in this direction, we can understand the individualism found in fish decoys and why there are so many different variations. Although it appears that the majority of fish decoys were carved by spearfishermen for their own use, there were also several professional carvers in the early 1900s, especially in Minnesota and Michigan. These artisans spent the spring and summer months carving a large inventory of decoys, and then as the winter freeze approached, they would travel around the countryside to such places as barbershops, bars, service stations, and sporting-goods stores, selling their wares for as little as 50 cents each. The work by these makers tends to be quite stylized and streamlined, varying only in size and paint pattern, but it is nevertheless avidly sought after by discerning collectors.

It should also be recorded that several attempts were made by manufacturing companies to make fish decoys. These companies, although often small, produced some very interesting and collectible items. Patents were obtained, and some ingenious creations, such as a fish with a light inside of it, were made. For the most part, manufactured fish tended to be made of some type of plastic material or composition, were boldly colored, and were extremely lifelike in appearance. They hold a definite spot in the history of fish decoys. Indeed, a collection of all the types of manufactured fish would be a formidable and extremely varied one.

It is recommended that anyone who decides to collect fish decoys should

These three 5-inch fish, which are valued at between $40 and $75, illustrate the varied styles and decorating techniques of different carvers.

weigh the attributes of a generalized, versus a specialized, approach. On the one hand, a collector could try to accumulate a well-rounded representation of all the styles and grades of fish available. This approach is advised for the collector without easy access to a source of fish decoys or for one who wants a very large collection. There are several possibilities when one considers specializing: only fish carved in New England; the work of a particular carver; or perhaps a collection of sunfish decoys only. One of the most difficult specialized collections would be one of frog decoys. Authentic old frog decoys, which were used in the same manner as fish, are extremely difficult to locate and are a prized addition to any collection.

As is the case with other types of collections, there are related items that, when displayed with the fish, enhance the understanding of how the fish were used. For example, a collection might contain at least one handmade spear. These spears, which are themselves very collectible items and are becoming quite scarce, usually were forged of wrought iron and have anywhere from three to six tines. Other related items, such as the Currier and Ives ice-fishing print or old fish boxes that were made to carry fish decoys, are also a welcome addition. The scope and range of a good collection is limited only by the imagination and the ingenuity of the collector.

An extremely realistic 7-inch bluegill from Buffalo, Minn., made about 1970. Although not very old, this piece was actually used and exhibits superb craftsmanship. It is valued at $100.

I believe that there is no better time than now for someone to acquire a fine collection of fish decoys at a reasonable price, and that the value of fish decoys will grow rapidly.

SELECTED BIBLIOGRAPHY

Bishop, Robert. *American Folk Sculpture*. New York: E. P. Dutton & Co., 1974.
Colio, Quintina. *American Decoys*. Ephrata, PA: Science Press, 1972.
Pennington, Wil. "Fish Story." *North American Decoys*. Fall 1973.

Chapter 27 ❧ Derrydale Books and Prints

F. PHILLIPS WILLIAMSON

The generally poor quality of American sporting books in comparison with English sporting books stimulated Eugene Connett, aided and abetted by Ernest R. Gee, to establish Derrydale Press in the 1920s. It soon became the finest publishing house of sporting books and prints that ever appeared on the face of the earth.

In *The Colophon 1938, The Annual of Bookmaking*, Connett wrote about the beginning of Derrydale and his objectives as a publisher:

> This press specializes in issuing limited editions of sporting books — chiefly American sporting books. If one examines a collection of the sporting books published in this country, he will be struck with the very low average of quality exhibited, and when the American books are compared to those published in England there is little cause for wonder as to why so many of the old English sporting books are avidly collected, and fairly plentiful, while the American books are sought after by only a few, and are relatively scarce.
>
> It was to remedy this situation that I established The Derrydale Press in 1927. I believed that if someone would publish a group of American sporting books in sufficiently attractive formats, these books would not be carelessly thrown away during spring house cleaning fifty years from now, but would survive in reasonable numbers through the years, just as the finer British ones have. And if these books were preserved, there would be a record of the greatest period of sport the world has yet seen — even greater than in England after the Napoleonic wars.
>
> It may be of some interest to note what we consider proper subjects for sporting books. With very few exceptions the so-called 'field sports,' such as foxhunting, fishing, riding, horse racing, yachting and breeding horses and dogs, constitute the subjects of our sporting books. Games and pastimes, such as football, boxing, tennis, swimming, and so on, rarely are included. There are exceptions, of course, such as our new book on skiing.
>
> The problem was not to design books in the modern manner, nor to seek formats which through their striking originality would call attention to themselves; but to find sound and worthwhile texts and to issue them in easy-to-read and dignified volumes which would appeal to conservative people. For sportsmen are very conservative, as a rule.
>
> They have worn pink in the hunting field for a good many generations — excellent proof that it is the best thing to wear when foxhunting; they carry on wing

shooting just as they did in 1727 when the first book on the subject in English was published, except for the minor changes made necessary by the invention of the breech-loading shotgun; and, with the exception of similar improvements in fishing tackle, angling is done exactly as it was in 1654 when the first edition of Izaak Walton's *Compleat Angler* appeared. They have kept the pedigrees of their race horses since before 1700 when the Darley Arabian and the Byerly Turk were imported into England, to found the present breed of thoroughbreds. Yes, sportsmen are conservative, and their books should be so designed.

An extended consideration of the matter convinces me that Caslon type in sizes twelve and fourteen, on pages measuring overall 6¼ × 9½, 7½ × 10 and 9½ × 12¼, provided, with generous margins, the most comfortable and easily read books. Almost all of our book pages conform to these specifications. Not very exciting, but after ten years of experience I have had no cause to change my mind as to the soundness of my choice.

As my books were made for people who would really read them, I felt that any decoration which attracted attention away from the text itself was unsound. So there is a total lack of exotic running heads and misplaced (I almost said misbegotten) folios in our books. Once in a while we have permitted ourselves the luxury of doing a book that has been pronounced fairly good looking by those whose business it is to know such things — just to keep our hand in. But as a rule we are content to stick to our very simple and easy-to-read pages. . . . if you were to ask me to state my bookmaking creed briefly, I would answer thus: first make a book that is easy to read; second make a book that is dignified and somewhat conservative in style; third make a book in tune with the finest tradition in that class of book; fourth — and this almost sums up the others — make an honest book; fifth — and most important of all — make a book for the great-grandchildren of your present customers.

The first publication Connett produced did not bear the imprint of The Derrydale Press. It came out in 1926 (*American Trout Streams* by Henry A. Ingraham, in two editions). The first publication ever to appear under the name of The Derrydale Press was a small book, cheaply bound (and said to be set on a hand press by the author), entitled *Magic Hours* by Eugene Connett. This appeared in 1927 and was the beginning of a 14-year span in which a series of sporting books and prints encompassed the hunting, shooting, fishing, yachting, skiing and coaching fields, as well as works on dogs, odd subjects, and horses. A smattering of privately printed works complemented this labor of love. A total of 222 volumes were produced by Eugene Connett.

Compared with the sporting authors that Connett had in his stable, nearly all of the so-called sporting authors of today fall short. The various works by Sheldon, Buckingham, Clard, Newman, Pickering, and Edmund Ware Smith have no equal in today's sporting publications. The books all had limited runs (total runs were set down in each work), and the deluxe bindings of a few were works of art.

In the depression of the 1930s, many of the deluxe editions were "sold out" prior to publication. In the early 1940s, ads appeared offering $100 for a copy of

A typical first-class binding and cover design by Derrydale. It is Preston Jennings' A Book of Trout Flies, *with hand-colored plates of flies. (Photo courtesy Matthew Vinciguerra)*

Nash Buckingham's most famous work, *De Shootinest Gent'man*. This was for a regular edition that was published at $7.50; a deluxe edition did not exist.

Connett's selection of both subject and author show the fine hand of a publishing genius. The paper, the bindings (with the exception of a few early works), the type, and the illustrations are praiseworthy.

Prior to establishing The Derrydale Press, Connett edited or "laid out" or designed two other publications: Mark Twain's *1601*, a 1926 limited edition of 100 copies, marked for H.D.W., with E.V.C. on the back of the title page; and *Living Contributions* for Workers Education Bureau Press in 1926.

Most prints published today can not compare in quality with Derrydale Prints. Connett brought to America, in the print line, a process that had been seldom used in the United States: aquatint, or prints watercolored by hand. The artist would do an oil painting or a watercolor, the press would print, on good-quality paper, the outline and lettering, and then the artist would watercolor what is called an artist's proof. These proofs were given to commercial artists, who would watercolor the prints by hand and return them to the publisher. The publisher or the artist would approve the coloring, then the print would be signed and/or numbered. It is evident that in several instances where the artist was deceased, Connett mostly likely gave the final approval.

The set of four polo prints by Paul Brown, the set of three fox-hunting prints by Voss (the fourth print of the set, "Tally-Ho," was published by Frank Lowe after the Derrydale Press ceased to exist), the set of four A. B. Frost prints, Schaldack's "Woodcock," Clark's "The Alarm" and "Mallard's Rising," Boyer's two fishing prints, and Megargee's "Staunch" and "Steady" are truly the pick of the crop. The color of the leaves in the A. B. Frost's "October Woodcock Shooting" is one of the best examples of a perfect aquatint print.

The prints never exceeded 250 in total run, and since they were often colored by contract tied with sales, many were never colored and finished. A few of these have come on the auction market in recent years as warehouses and storerooms have closed out.

A large number of the prints retailed at $25. Some of these prints, today, will bring $750 to $2,500. With the print-collecting craze sweeping the United States today, lithographed signed prints bring $45 and up with runs from 450 to 2,000. Derrydale prints are the real sleepers in today's art world, and the fickle public will awake one day to realize that the present craze (and prices) for lithographed long-run prints will pass. All collectors, of anything, would do well to find the time to read a book by Mackay, written in 1841 and revised in 1852, titled *The Extraordinary Popular Delusions of the Madness of Crowds*.

Some of the uncolored Derrydale Press prints that have surfaced have landed in the hands of some sharp, but uninformed, operators. The worst examples are some of Megargee's "American Shooting Scenes" in which all the woods are colored deep green (browns were the base of the originals) and the bird shooters' jackets are red. No bird shooter worth his salt ever wore anything, prior to 1941, but dark-brown duck (or some of the softer fabrics — but all *brown*). In fact, red bird-shooting coats were not even made then. (Woolrich did make a red-and-black-plaid heavy wool deer hunter's jacket!) A few other prints have been painted with colors whose bases were not made until after 1955.

If you are a serious print collector, try to buy from a reliable dealer (or owner) who will certify the past ten-year history of the print. One artist's proof that was unlettered is known to have had reproduction letters printed since 1945. One thing is fairly certain, however: the prints will never be totally reproduced again as they first were.

Any print or book collector should be aware of two major hazards — light and dampness. A good library should be in a room where the humidity is controlled and all lighting indirect. This is even more important for prints. Dampness will cause foxing, and light (sunlight and fluorescent, which is just as deadly as sunlight) will cause fading and color change. Prints should be framed in full size, uncut, and never matted. Unframed prints are best stored flat in a Hamilton-type wooden plat or drawing file with tissue paper between.

There are a limited number of dealers who specialize in sporting books, and far fewer who specialize in sporting prints. A quick review of *Bookman's Weekly* will bring forth a list of dealers specializing in sporting books, but it's every dog for himself to find the prints. There are a few print dealers — The Old Print Collector in New York, Sessler's in Philadelphia, and Purnell's Art Gallery in Baltimore, for instance.

Pick the subject you are interested in and start looking for the Derrydale Press books and/or prints. There are still bargains to be found!

PRICES OF DERRYDALE BOOKS

Note: Prices are for copies in excellent condition. Deduct up to 40 percent for copies not in top condition. All 222 volumes are listed.

A	Price
Alvard, Thomas G., Jr. *Paul Bunyon and Resinous Rhymes of the North Woods*, 166 numbered copies (blue binding), 1934	$150
332 numbered copies, signed on title page (green binding)	350
The American Shooter's Manual (printed for Ernest Gee), 375 numbered copies, 1928	100

The Anglers Club List of Members, 1929	50
The Anglers Club List of Members, 1930	50
The Anglers Club List of Members, four known copies remain, others said to be destroyed, 1931	—
Annabel, Russell. *Tales of a Big Game Guide*, 950 numbered copies, 1938	150
Ash, Edward C. *The Practical Dog Book*, 500 copies, 1931	250

B

"M.B." *The Thunderer*, 950 copies, 1933	$70
Babcock, Philip H. *Falling Leaves*, 950 numbered copies, 1937	125
Baker, Charles H., Jr. *The Gentlemen's Companion*, 2 vols., 1,250 numbered copies, 1939	120
Bandini, Ralph. *Veiled Horizons*, 950 numbered copies, 1939	100
Barber, Joel. *Long Shore*, 750 numbered copies, 1939	200
——. *Wild Fowl Decoys*, 55 numbered and signed copies with miniature decoy, 1934	4,200
Bayliss, Marguerite F. *Bolinvar*, 2 vols., 950 numbered copies, 1937	75
Baylor, Aimstead Keith. *Abdul, An Allegory*, 500 copies, 1930	75
Bigelow, Ashley. *A Bigelow Background*, 25 numbered copies, 1933	1,000
Bigelow, Horatio. *Gunnerman*, 950 numbered copies, 1939	85
Boone & Crockett Club. *Hunting Trails on Three Continents*, 250 copies, 1933	100
Bosworth, Clarence E. *Breeding Your Own*, 120 numbered copies, 1939	90
Brach, Wm. N. *In the Shadow of Mount McKinley*, 750 copies 1931	150
Briggs, L. Cabot. *Bull Terriers, the Biography of a Breed*, 500 numbered copies, 1940	150
Brown, Kenneth. *The Medchester Club*, 950 numbered copies, 1938	40
Brown, Paul. *Aintree — Grand National Past and Present*, 850 copies, 1930	200
Deluxe Edition, 50 copies	1,200
——. *Hits and Misses — A Polo Sketch Book*, 950 numbered and signed copies, 1935	190
Brown, Wm. Robinson. *The Horse of the Desert*, 750 copies	90
Deluxe Edition, 75 numbered copies, 1929	1,800
Buckingham, Nash. *Bloodlines*, 1,250 numbered copies, 1938	250
——. *De Shootinest Gent'man*, 950 numbered copies, 1934	350
——. *Mark Right*, 1,250 numbered copies, 1936	200

H

Haig-Brown, Roderick. *The Western Angler*, 2 vols., 950 numbered
    copies, 1939 $450

Harkness, William Hale. *Ho hum, the Fisherman*, 100 numbered
    copies, 1939   550

——. *Temples and Topees*, 200 numbered copies, 1936   300

Harris, Charles Townsend. *Memories of Manhattan*, 1,000
    copies, 1928   60

Hart, Scott. *The Moon Is Waning*, 950 numbered copies, 1939   45

Hell for Leather, 375 numbered copies, 1928   200

Henry, Samuel J. *Foxhunting is Different*, 950 numbered copies
    1938   35

Hervey, John. *Lady Suffolk*, 500 numbered copies, 1936   175

——. *Messenger*, 500 numbered copies, 1935   150

Heywood, G. G. P. *Charles Cotton and His River*, 50 copies, 1929   1,400

Hills, John Wallace. *Summer on the Test*, 300 copies, 1941   300

History of the Southern Grasslands International Steeplechase, 1928   150

Hood, Thomas. *The Epping Hunt*, 490 numbered copies, 1930   80

Hunt, Lynn Bogue. *An Artist's Game Bag*, 1,250 copies   350
    Deluxe Edition, 25 copies, 1936   4,000

Hunter, Anole. *Let's Ride to Hounds*, 850 copies, 1929   70
    Deluxe Edition, 50 numbered copies   400

I

Ingraham, Henry A. *American Trout Streams*, 350 numbered
    copies, 1926 $125
    Deluxe Edition, 150 numbered copies   750

J

Jennings, Preston. *A Book of Trout Flies*, 850 numbered copies,
    1935 $600
    Vol. I & Vol. II (Vol. II—*Flies*) Deluxe Edition, 25 numbered
    and signed copies   10,000

K

Keene and Hatch. *Full Tilt*, 950 numbered copies, 1938 $60

Kelland, Clarence Buddington. *Not Their Breed & The Forgotten
    Man*, 1938   70

Kendall, Lt. Paul G. *Polo Ponies, Their Training and Schooling*,
    850 copies, 1933   45

Ketchum, Arthur. *Roads and Harbours*, 150 numbered copies, 1927   200

Kirmse, Marguerite. *Dogs in the Field*, 685 numbered copies, 1935   450

——. *Marguerite Kirmse's Dogs*, 750 copies, 1930   250

L

Lanier, Henry W. *A. B. Frost*, 950 copies, 1933	$280
Lee, Amy Freeman. *Hobby Horses*, 200 numbered and signed copies, 1940	70
Lenroot, Clara C. *Will You Walk Into My Garden*, 200 copies, 1936	300
Lewis, Benjamin. *Riding*, 1,250 copies, 1936	60
Littauer, Capt. V. S. *Jumping the Horse*, 950 copies, 1931	60
Littauer, Capt. V. S. and Thayer, Bert Clarke. *Be a Better Horseman*, 1,500 copies, 1941	50
Lloyd, Anne. *Antiques and Amber*, 250 copies, 1928	100
150 numbered and signed copies	300
Loomis and Stone. *Millions for Defense*, 950 numbered copies, 1934	150
Luard, Lowes D. *The Horse—Its Action and Anatomy*, 150 numbered copies, 1936	200
Lytle, J. Horace. *Point*, 950 numbered copies, 1941	70

M

MacAskill, Wallace R. *Out of Halifax*, 950 boxed and numbered copies, 1937	$80
450 copies for Canada	160
Manchester, Hubert. *Four Centuries of Sport in America*, 850 copies, 1931	150
Markland. *Pteryplegia, on the Art of Shooting Flying*, 300 numbered copies, 1931	100
Deluxe Edition, 200 numbered, signed and colored copies	300
McCormick, Henry B. *In Memoriam, Mary Boyd McCormick*, 1930	350
Memories of the Gloucester Fox Hunting Club, 375 numbered copies, 1927	30
Montgomery, Rutherford. *High Country*, 950 numbered copies, 1938	60

N

Newman, Neil. *Famous Horses of the American Turf*, Vol. I, 750 copies, 1931	$75
——. *Famous Horses of the American Turf*, Vol. II, 750 copies, 1932	75
——. *Famous Horses of the American Turf*, Vol. III, 750 copies, 1933	75

O

O'Connor, Jack. *Game in the Desert*, 950 boxed and numbered copies, 1939	$300

P

Page, H. S. *Between the Flags*, 850 copies, 1929 $40

Page, Rodman, Jr. *War Without Fighting*, 100 numbered copies   225

Palmedo, Roland. *Skiing—The International Sport*, 950 copies, 1937   100

    Deluxe Edition, 60 copies   1,200

Phair, Charles. *Atlantic Salmon Fishing*, 950 copies, 1937   200

    Deluxe Edition, 2 vols. (one w/flies), 40 copies   8,000

Pickering, H. G. *Angling of the Test*, 297 numbered copies, 1936   200

——. *Dog Days on Trout Waters*, 199 copies, 1933   600

——. *Merry Xmas Mr. Williams 20 Pine St., N.Y.*, 267 numbered

    copies, 1940   300

    Paperback edition, 267 numbered copies   70

——. *Neighbors Have My Ducks*, 227 numbered copies, 1937   350

——. *Trout Fishing in Secret*, 99 signed copies, 1931   1,000

Pollard, Barclay, Smith and Connett. *British and American Game

    Birds*, 125 numbered, signed, and remarqued copies, 1939   800

    Special Edition, 10 copies   12,000

Poor, Charles Lane. *Men Against the Rule*, 950 numbered copies,

    1937   75

R

Records of the Town of Brookhaven, Book A, 200 copies, 1930 $400

Records of the Town of Brookhaven, Book B, 200 copies, 1932   500

Records of the Town of Brookhaven, Book C, 200 copies, 1931   400

Reeve, J. Stanley. *Foxhunting Formalities*, 990 copies, 1930   30

    Deluxe Edition, 99 numbered and signed copies   700

——. *Red Coats in Chester County*, 560 numbered copies, 1940   85

Reynal, Eugene S. *Thoughts Upon Hunting Kit*, 500 copies, 1934   200

    Deluxe Edition (quantity unknown)   300

Rives, Reginald W. *The Coaching Club*, 300 numbered copies, 1935   450

    Deluxe Edition, 30 copies   1,000

Rolston, Louis B. *Selected Poems of Louis B. Rolston*, 1931   100

S

Santini, Capt. Piero. *Riding Reflections*, 850 copies, 1932 $45

Sheldon, Col. H. P. *A Private Affair*, (for Colonel Woods King), 1940   450

——. *Tranquillity*, 950 numbered copies, 1936   125

——. *Tranquillity Revisited*, 485 numbered copies, 1940   200

Sheppard, Ted. *Pack and Paddock*, boxed, 950 numbered copies,

    1938   60

Shortt, Angela. *The Hunting If*, 100 copies, 1932   250

Simmons, Albert Dixon. *Wing Shots*, 950 numbered copies, 1936   70

Smith, Edmund Ware. *The One-Eyed Poacher of Privilege*, 750
     numbered copies, 1941   130
——. *Tall Tales and Short*, 950 numbered copies, 1938   85
——. *A Tomato Can Chronicle*, 950 numbered copies, 1937   130
Smith, Harry Worcester. *Life and Sport in Aiken*, 950 copies, 1935   50
Smith, Jerome V. C. *Trout and Angling*, 325 copies   100
     Deluxe Edition, 50 copies, 1929   600
Smith, Mary Riley. *Poems*, 200 copies, 1929   120
Some Early American Hunters, 375 numbered copies, 1928   100
Spiller, Burton L. *Firelight*, 950 numbered copies, 1937   150
——. *Grouse Feathers*, 950 numbered copies, 1935   120
——. *More Grouse Feathers*, 950 numbered copies, 1938   125
——. *Thoroughbred*, 950 numbered copies, 1936   150
The Sporting Works of Somerville and Ross (7 vols.), 500 numbered
     and signed sets including *Some Experiences of an Irish RM*,
     Further Experiences of an Irish RM, *In Mr. Knox's Country*,
     Dan Russell the Fox, *All on the Irish Shore*, *Wheel Tracks*, and
     Irish Memories, 1927   400
The Sportsman's Companion (printed for Ernest R. Gee), 200
     copies, 1930   110
The Sportsman's Portfolio of American Field Sports (for Ernest R.
     Gee), 400 copies, 1929   175
Stone, Harvey. *Yacht Racing Log*, 1933   150
Strett, William B. *Gentlemen Up*, 850 copies, 1930   85
     Deluxe Edition, 75 numbered and signed copies   1,200
Sturgis, Wm. Bayard. *New Lines for Flyfishers*, 950 copies, 1936   55

T
Taverner, John. *Certaine Experiments Concerning Fish and Fruit*,
     100 copies, 1929 $700
Thomas, Joseph B. *Hounds and Hunting Through the Ages*, 1st edi-
     tion, 750 copies, 1928   400
     Deluxe Edition, 50 copies   1,400
——. *Hounds and Hunting Through the Ages*, 2nd edition, 250
     copies, 1929   350

V
van Dyke, Henry. *The Travel Diary of an Angler*, 750 copies, 1929 $90
Van Urk, J. Blan. *The Story of American Foxhunting*, Vol. I,
     1650–1861, 950 copies, 1940   100
——. *The Story of American Foxhunting*, Vol. II, 1865–1906,
     950 copies, 1941   100

Vosburgh, W. S. *Cherished Portraits of Thoroughbred Horses*, 279
    copies, 1929 — 1,500
    Deluxe Edition with colored plates, 21 copies — 1,800

W

Walden, Howard T., II. *Big Stoney*, 550 numbered copies, 1940 — $70
——. *Upstream and Down*, 950 numbered copies, 1938 — 80
Wallner, Mary Cole. *Pydie's Poems*, 100 copies, 1928 — 200
Waterstone, Stella Sharpe. *A Collection of Verse*, 500 copies, 1938 — 100
Watson, Frederick. *Hunting Pie*, 750 copies, 1931 — 30
The Westminster Kennel Club, 100 copies, 1929 — 600
White, Frederick. *The Spicklefisherman and Others*, 740 copies,
    1928 — 150
    Deluxe Edition, 35 signed copies — 800
Whitman, Malcom D. *Tennis Origins and Mysteries*, 450 copies,
    1932 — 90
Williams, Ben Ames. *The Happy End*, 1,250 copies numbered, 1939 — 50
——. *The Happy End*, printed for the Clove Valley Rod & Gun
    Club, November 19, 1942, 1,250 numbered copies, 1942 — 85
Willock, Franklin J. *The Dalmation*, 200 numbered copies, 1927 — 220
Wise, Col. Hugh D. *Tigers of the Sea*, 950 numbered copies, 1937 — 80
Woodward, William. *Gallant Fox*, full leather, 1931 — 10,000
——. *A Memoir of Andrew Jackson Africanus*, 150 boxed and
    numbered copies, 1938 — 500

PRICES OF DERRYDALE PRINTS

B

Boyer, Ralph L. "After a Big One," 200 numbered and signed, 1936 — $400
——. "An Anxious Moment," 250 numbered and signed, 1937 — 500
——. "At the Riffle," (dry point), 60 numbered and signed proofs,
    1929 — 500
——. Fathers of American Sport (set of 6: "William Henry
    Herbert," "Thaddeus Norris," "George Washington," "Com-
    modore John Cox Stevens," "Samuel Morris," "Col. William
    Ransom Johnson"), 250 numbered and signed, 1931 — 350
——. "The Lips of the Pool," (dry point), 60 numbered and signed
    proofs, 1929 — 500

Brown, Paul. American Polo Scenes (set of 4: "Down the Field,"
    "On the Boards," "The Save," "The Goal"), 175 numbered and
    signed, 1930   3,500
——. American Steeplechasing Scenes: "The Meadowbrook
    Cup," 250 numbered and signed, 1931   2,000
——. "Hoick, Hoick, Hoick," 250 numbered and signed, 1937   600
——. "Kennel Bound," 250 numbered and signed, 1941   500
——. "Music Ahead," 250 numbered and signed, 1939   500
——. "Pressing Him," 250 numbered and signed, 1937   600
Burke, Edgar. "Canada Geese," 250 numbered and signed, 1941   400

C

Clark, Roland. "The Alarm," 250 numbered and signed, 1937 $1,200
——. "Calm Weather (Redhead)," 250 numbered and signed, 1940   750
——. "Dawn (Widgeon)," 250 numbered and signed, 1939   350
——. "Down Wind (Pintail)," 250 numbered and signed, 1937   450
——. "Dropping In (Canada Geese)," 250 numbered and signed,
    1941   800
——. "Mallards Rising," 250 numbered and signed, 1942   2,000
——. "Sanctuary (Green Wing Teal)," 250 numbered and signed,
    1938   450
——. "The Scout (Mallard Drake)," 250 numbered and signed,
    1938   450
——. "A Straggler (Broadbill)," 250 numbered and signed, 1940   600
——. "Taking Off (Blue Wing Teal)," 250 numbered and signed,
    1941   750
——. "Winter Marsh (Can)," 250 numbered and signed, 1939   750

E

Earl, Maud. "Great Dane Head" $200
Earl, T. P. "Boswell" (for William Woodward), date unknown   —

F

"Flares" (for William Woodward), date unknown   —
Frost, A. B. "A Chance Shot," 200 numbered, 1933 $1,500
——. "Coming Ashore," 200 numbered, 1934   1,500
——. "Grouse Shooting in the Rhododendrons," 200 numbered,
    1934   1,500
——. "October Woodcock Shooting," 200 numbered, 1933   2,500
Frost, John. "Maryland Marsh," 150 numbered and signed, 1936   400

G

Grant, Gordon. "Off Soundings," 250 numbered and signed, 1941 — $400
——. "The Weather Mark," 250 numbered and signed, 1941 — 400

H

Howitt, Samuel. "A Tight Line" (for Ernest R. Gee) — $100

J

"Johnstown" (for William Woodward), date unknown — —

K

Copperplate for Lester Karow — $100
King, Edward. "The Aiken Drag," 80 numbered and signed, 1929 — 200
——. American Horse Show Scenes:
   "Rochester," 250 signed, 1932 — 100
   "A Glorious Burst," 1932 — 250
——. American Shooting Scenes: "Quail Shooting," 1929 — 300
——. Belmont Terminal Lithographs (set of 2: "The Paddock," "The Finish"), 1929 — 100
——. Diana Goes Hunting (set of 4: "Her First Meet," "Alone with the Hounds," "In and Out," "Her First Brush"), 250 numbered and signed, 1930 — 300
——. Hunt Race Lithographs, American Hunting Scenes:
   I, "The First Flight," 250 signed, 1929 — 250
   II, "Well Away," 250 signed, 1929 — 250
   III, "The Check," 250 signed, 1929 — 250
   IV, "Full Cry," 250 signed, 1929 — 250
——. Hunting Lithographs (set of 2: "The Chicken Coop," "Blood Will Tell"), 250 numbered and signed, 1929 — 450
——. Quail Shooting: "The Briar Patch," 350 numbered and signed, 1930 — 100
——. Saratoga Racing Aquatints (set of 4: "Morning Exercise," "In The Paddock," "At The Barrier," "Over The Liverpool"), 80 numbered and signed, 1928 — 800
——. Woodcock Shooting: "In the Birches," 350 numbered and signed, 1930 — 100
Kirmse, Marguerite. "The Fox," 250 numbered and signed, 1931 — 800
——. "The Hounds," 250 numbered and signed, 1933 — 600

L

Lloyd, T. Ivester. "Gallant Fox" (for William Woodward), 1937 — $100

M

Megargee, Edwin. American Cock Fighting Scenes (set of 4: "Challenge," "Striking," "Struck," "Victory"), 250 signed, 1931 $1,600

———. "Closing In," 250 numbered and signed, 1939   125

———. "Grouse Shooting," 250 numbered and signed, 1931   300

———. "Pheasant Shooting," signed only, 1930   300

———. "Staunch," 250 numbered and signed, 1938   250

———. "Steady," 250 numbered and signed, 1938   250

———. "Woodcock Shooting," 250 signed only, 1931   300

S

Schaldach, William J. "Woodcock," 250 numbered and signed, 1931 $800

Sims, Joseph P. "The Rose Tree Fox Hunting Club," 150 numbered and signed, 1939   2,000

Somerville, E. E. Somerville & Ross Prints (I, "A Conspiracy of Silence." II, "Occasional Licenses." III, "Put Down One and Carry Two." IV, The Compte De Pralines.") 50 numbered and signed sets, 1929   1,500

Stainforth, Martin. "Faireno" (for William Woodward)   100

———. "Granville" (for William Woodward)   —

———. "Omaha" (for William Woodward)   100

V

Voss, F. B. Foxhunting in America:

"Over the Open," 250 numbered and signed, 1939 $750

"On a Fresh Line," 250 numbered and signed, 1939   750

"Working It Out," 250 numbered and signed, 1941   750

W

Walden and Weiler, large plate w/watermark for "Upstream and Down," 60 numbered and signed copies, 1938 $200

Bookplate for Viola T. Winmill   100

PRICES OF RELATED PUBLICATIONS

A Decade of American Sporting Books and Prints — Paper Wrappers (catalog) $25

Derrydale Sporting Books #6 1931–32 (catalog)   100

Derrydale Press & Windward House Sporting Books #7 1935 (catalog)   100

Derrydale Sporting Prints #7 1931–32 (catalog)   120
Mrs. Randolph Catlin, *The Derrydale Press*, 1957.   20
A Portfolio of Circulars Describing Sporting Books & Prints (pub-
    lished by Derrydale)   500
W. C. Thompson, *Publications of The Derrydale Press 1927–1941*,
    1953.   20

Chapter 28 ⠦ Angling Books

ARNOLD GINGRICH and ERNEST S. HICKOK

If one considers the number of books that have been written by fishermen, the inevitable conclusion is that here is a breed of man that is always questing, always optimistic, extremely inventive, and completely uninhibited concerning his own opinions. This combination of traits has resulted in some outstanding angling works, as well as a steady market for them.

Advice about book collecting in general is given in the chapter on hunting books, and there is no point in repeating it here. The purpose of this chapter is to draw attention to a representative list that, for one reason or another, has attracted the interest of anglers, and to indicate a price range where a collector can have a reasonable expectation of acquiring them, to satisfy his thirst for knowledge and/or his pride of acquisition. Within the price range, the buyer will have to decide for himself the relative importance of condition, rarity, subject matter, provenance, and the intensity of his personal desire to own.

Obviously, no such list can have any pretensions to completeness, as there are more than 5,000 angling books in English alone, and since English angling literature had a headstart of some 300 years over American, the majority of the titles of interest to collectors have always been those of English origin. In this century, however, the balance has begun to be redressed; in this selected list, intended to reflect the most active interest of present-day collectors, American books outnumber the English by around four to one — reversing the actual numerical ratio of the two literatures.

The price groupings are broad, and in general the older the book, the nearer it will approach the top end of the indicated price range. The exceptions to this usually reflect the scarcity value imparted to a volume by an extremely limited edition.

Bargains are increasingly difficult to come by, as the last decade's explosion of interest in fly-fishing has driven prices up enormously, and the listings in rare bookdealers' catalogs average three times higher now than they did in the early-to-middle 1960s. But diligent search through the secondhand book bins, particularly away from metropolitan centers, may still turn up a collector's item at a junkyard pricetag, although the reward, per manhour of time invested in such quests, is apt to work out to somewhat less than coolie wages.

Walton is a special case, since there are well over 300 editions of his unique,

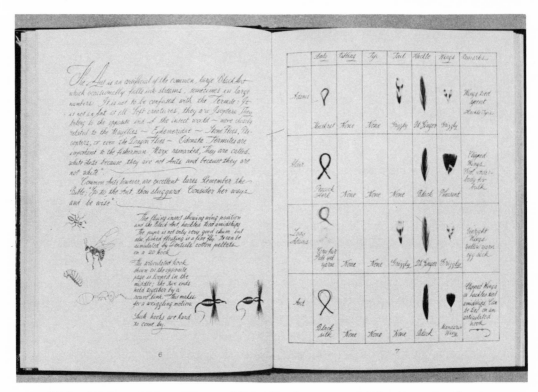

Richard Salmon's Trout Flies, *published by Sportsman's Edge Press, is a fine investment for either the advanced or the beginning collector. It was published in an autographed and numbered edition of 589 copies at $95; each copy contained, tipped in, the actual materials for almost 50 flies. (Photo courtesy Matthew Vinciguerra)*

all-time angling classic. Your chances of stumbling on one of the first five, from the seventeenth century, are less than nil of course, but copies of the last century's editions are likely to turn up almost anywhere, as the *Compleat Angler* has always enjoyed wider literary currency than any other fishing book.

The beginning collector, like the beginning fisherman, is usually interested only in quantity, as he indulges his desire to read about his favorite sport. Then, as with anglers, an inclination to specialize soon manifests itself: what was begun as a mere grab bag of wanted reading matter begins to refine itself into a collection, as the fisher-reader becomes aware of differences in editions and questions of condition. He soon feels the need for some books about fishing books, such as Hills, Robb, Wetzel, or Goodspeed (or if he has become hooked on Walton, books by Oliver, Horne, Marston, or Wood), and he finds that these books about rare books are rare books themselves. He learns, if he acquires some of them, that first editions are not always the most desired editions (it's the *third* 1851 edition of Pulman, for instance, that contains the first mention of the dry fly as such) and that a badly battered or incomplete copy of even a prized angling book is valueless as a collector's item. By this time he has either given up collecting and gone back to fishing or, if he hasn't, has acquired sufficient expertise to start to specialize — collecting Derrydale Press items, for instance, where the minimum per title is from $40 to $50 and on up to $1,000 — and has no further need of such general guidance as could be offered here.

By the same token, we have limited the scope of our listing to items under $300. Above that there are "rarities of a rarity," to echo Walton's "recreation of a recreation," such as the original 1888 Douglas edition of Dean Sage, which today commands some seven or eight times our top figure (and the only reprint itself costs $500). Prices go on up, even from there, to the rarefied fiscal stratosphere where the original editions of Walton fetch, or at least demand, a king's ransom. However, if your interest reaches this point, a reputable book dealer could be helpful. In a book of general circulation, it seems pointless to probe arcane areas of a hobby that, unless pursued to a degree of mania, should remain an innocent pastime.

Of course, unless the prices of all fishing books soon stop mounting as they have in recent years, angling may become an endangered sport, too expensive even to read about.

And the following list, if inflation continues its inexorable and unabated spiral, may become almost quaintly antiquated before it even achieves print.

$5–$25

Bergman, R. *Just Fishing*. New York: Knopf, 1943.

Brooks, Joe. *The Complete Book of Fly Fishing*. New York: A. S. Barnes, 1958.

——. *Trout Fishing*. New York: Outdoor Life, 1972.

Carroll, Dixie (Cook, C. B.). *Fishing Tackle and Kits*. Cincinnati: Stewart and Kidd, 1919.

Cross, Reuben. *The Complete Fly-Tyer*. New York: Dodd, Mead & Co., 1950.

Crowe, John. *The Book of Trout Lore*. New York: A. S. Barnes, 1947.

Farrington, S. Kip, Jr. *A Book of Fishes*. New York: Garden City Publishing, 1946.

Farson, Negley. *Going Fishing*. London: Country Life, 1944.

Flick, Art, ed. *Art Flick's Master Fly-Tying Guide*.

Foote, John T. *Anglers All*. New York: Appleton-Century, 1947.

——. *Broadway Angler*. New York: Appleton-Century, 1937.

Gabrielson and Lamonte. *The Fisherman's Encyclopedia* New York: Stackpole & Heck, 1950.

Grey, Sir Edward. *Fly Fishing*. Boston: Houghton Mifflin, 1899.

——. *The Fallodon Papers*. Boston: Houghton Mifflin, 1926.

Haig-Brown, R. L. *Pool and Rapid*. London: A & C Black, 1932.

Hallock, Charles. *The Fishing Tourist*. 1873.

Hampton, John F. *Modern Angling Bibliography*. London: Jenkins, 1947.

Henkin, Harmon. *Fly Tackle*. Philadelphia: Lippincott, 1976.

Henshall, J. A. *Bass, Pike, Perch and Other Game Fish of America*. New York: MacMillan, 1903.

Holder, C. F. *Big Game Fishes of the U. S.* New York: MacMillan, 1903.

Humphrey, Wm. *The Spawning Run*. New York: Delacorte, 1970.

Kreider, Claude M. *Steelhead*. New York: Putnam, 1948.

La Branche, George M. L. *The Dry Fly and Fast Water*. New York: Scribner's, 1951.

——. *The Salmon and the Dry Fly*. New York: Scribner's, 1951.

Lampman, Ben Hur. *A Leaf from French Eddy*. Portland: Touchstone Press, 1965.

Leisenring, James. *The Art of Tying the Wet Fly*. New York: Dodd, Mead & Co., 1941.

Lucas, Jason. *Lucas on Bass Fishing*. New York: R. M. McBride, 1947.

Marston, R. B. *Walton and Some Earlier Writers on Fish and Fishing*. London: E. Stock, 1894.

National Geographic Society. *The Book of Fishes*. Washington, D.C.: 1924.

Ritz, Charles. *A Fly Fisher's Life*. New York: Holt, 1960.

Schwiebert, Ernest. *Matching the Hatch*. New York: MacMillan, 1955.

Shaw, Helen. *Fly Tying*. New York: Ronald Press, 1963.

Sosin, Mark, and Clark, John. *Through the Fish's Eye*. New York: Harper & Row, 1973.

Swisher, D., and Richards, C. *Selective Trout*. New York: Crown, 1971.

Taverner, Eric. *Trout Fishing From All Angles*. London: Seeley, Service & Co., 1932.

Traver, Robert. *Trout Madness*. Santa Barbara: Peregrine Smith, 1979.

Van Dyke, Henry. *Fisherman's Luck*. New York: Scribner's, 1899.

Wells, Henry P. *Fly-Rods and Fly Tackle*. London: Sampson Low, 1885.

$25–$100

Allerton, R. G. *Brook Trout Fishing*. New York: Oquossoc Angling Association, 1869.

Bates, Jos. D., Jr. *Streamer Fly Fishing*. New York: Van Nostrand, 1950.

——. *Trout Waters and How to Fish Them*. Boston: Little, Brown & Co., 1949.

Babcock, Havilah. *My Health is Better in November*. New York: Holt, Rinehart and Winston, 1947.

Beebe, C. Wm. *The Arcturus Adventure*. New York: Putnam, 1926.

Beecher, Henry Ward. *Star Papers*. New York: J. C. Derby, 1855.

Bergman, Ray. *Fresh Water Bass*. New York: Knopf, 1942.

——. *Trout*. Philadelphia: Penn Publishing, 1938.

Berners, Dame Juliana. *A Treatise on Fishing With a Hook*. New York: Van Rees Press, 1933.

Best, Thomas. *A Concise Treaty on the Art of Angling*. 1787.

Blake, W. H. *Brown Waters*. Toronto: MacMillan, 1915.

Blakey, Robert. *Historical Sketches of the Angling Literature of All Nations*. London: J. R. Smith, 1856.

Bowlker, Richard and Charles. *The Art of Angling*. England: 1792–1839.

Bradford, Chas. B. *The Brook Trout and the Determined Angler*. New York: E. P. Grow, 1900.

Brooks, Joe. *Salt Water Fly Fishing*. New York: Putnam, 1950.

Chambers, E. T. D. *The Ouananiche and its Canadian Environment*. New York: Harper & Brothers, 1896.

Cleveland, Grover. *Fishing and Shooting Sketches*. New York: Outing, 1906.

Cross, Reuben R. *Tying American Trout Lures*. New York: Dodd, Mead & Co., 1938.

Curtis, Brian, *The Life Story of the Fish*. New York: Harcourt Brace, 1949.

Davy, Sir Humphry. *Salmonia or Days of Fly Fishing*. Philadelphia: Carey and Lea, 1832.

Dawson, George. *The Pleasures of Angling*. 1876.

Dunne, J. W. *Sunshine and The Dry Fly*. 1924.

Everett, Fred. *Fun With Trout*. Harrisburg: Stackpole, 1952.

Farrar, C. A. J. *Farrar's Illustrated Guide Book to the Androscoggin Lakes*. Boston: Lee and Shepard, 1884.

Farrington, S. Kip, Jr. *Atlantic Game Fishing*. New York: Garden City Publishing, 1937.

——. *Pacific Game Fishing*. New York: Garden City Publishing, 1942.

Flick, Art. *Streamside Guide*. New York: Putnam, 1947.

Forester, Frank. *Frank Forester's Fish & Fishing of the United States & British Provinces*. 1849.

Francis, Francis. *A Book of Angling*. 1867.

Gill, Emlyn M. *Practical Dry Fly Fishing*. New York: Scribner's, 1912.

Gordon, Sid. *How to Fish from Top to Bottom*. Harrisburg: Stackpole, 1955.

Grey, Zane. *Tales of Fishes*. New York: Harper & Brothers, 1919.

Grimble, A. *The Salmon Rivers of Scotland*. 1902.

Griswold, F. G. *Observations on a Salmon River.* Norwood, MA: Plimpton Press, 1921.

Grove, Alvin R., Jr. *The Lure and Lore of Trout Fishing.* Harrisburg: Stackpole, 1951.

Halford, F. M. *Dry-fly Fishing in Theory and Practice,* (Reprint edition of 100 copies). Reading, England: Barry Shurlock, 1973.

——. *Modern Development of the Dry Fly.* New York: Dutton, 1930.

Hammond, S. H. *Hills, Lakes and Forest Streams.* New York: J. C. Derby, 1854.

Harding, E. W. *The Flyfisher and The Trout's Point of View.* Philadelphia: Lippincott, 1931.

Henshall, J. A. *Book of the Black Bass.* Cincinnati: R. Clarke, 1881.

Hewitt, E. R. *A Trout and Salmon Fisherman for Seventy-Five Years.* New York: Scribner's, 1948.

——. *Secrets of the Salmon,* (Edition of 780 copies). New York: Scribner's, 1922.

Hills, John W. *A History of Fly-Fishing for Trout.* New York: F. A. Stokes, 1921.

Holland, Bob, Dan, and Ray. *Good Shot,* (Edition of 850 signed copies). New York: Knopf, 1946.

Hoover, Herbert C. *A Remedy for Disappearing Game Fishes,* (Edition of 990 copies). New York: Huntington Press, 1930.

Horne, Bernard S. *Compleat Angler—1653–1967—A New Bibliography.* Pittsburgh: University of Pittsburgh Press, 1970.

Jordan, D. S., and Evermann, B. W. *American Food and Game Fishes.* London: Hutchinson, 1902.

Knight, John Alden. *Black Bass.* New York: Putnam, 1949.

Knight, Larry R. *Taking Larger Trout.* 1950.

La Branche, George M. L. *The Dry Fly and Fast Water.* New York: Scribner's, 1914.

Marinaro, Vincent C. *A Modern Dry Fly Code.* 1950.

McClane, A. J. *McClane's Standard Fishing Encyclopedia.*

McDonald, John. *The Complete Fly Fisherman,* (Edition of 950 copies). 1907.

Mottram, J. C. *Fly Fishing—Some New Arts and Mysteries.* London: Field and Queen, 1915.

Needham, Paul R. *Trout Streams.* Ithaca: Comstock, 1938.

Norris, Thad. *The American Angler's Book.* 1864.

Oliver, Peter. *A New Chronicle of the Compleat Angler—1653–1936.* New York: Paisley Press, 1936.

Orvis, C. F., and Cheney, A. N. *Fishing With the Fly*. Manchester, VT: C. F. Orvis, 1883.

Prime, W. C. *I Go A-Fishing*. New York: Harper, 1873.

Prouty, Lorenzo. *Fish — Their Habits and Haunts*. Boston: Cupples, Upham, 1883.

Radcliffe, Wm. *Fishing from the Earliest Times*, (Second edition). New York: Dutton, 1926.

Rhead, Louis. *American Trout Stream Insects*. New York: R. H. Russell, 1961.

——. *The Speckled Trout*. New York: R. H. Russell, 1902.

Robb, James. *Notable Angling Literature*. London: H. Jenkins, 1946.

Roosevelt, Robt. B. *Superior Fishing*. New York: Carleton, 1865.

Westwood and Satchell. *Bibliotheca Piscatoria*. London: Dawsons of Pall Mall, 1966.

$100–$300

Comeau, N. A. *Life and Sport on the North Shore of the Lower St. Lawrence & Gulf*. Quebec: Telegraph, 1923.

Connett, Eugene. *See* Chapter 27, "Derrydale Books and Prints."

Coxe, Nicholas. *The Gentleman's Recreation*.

Crawhall, Joseph. *The Compleatest Angling Book That Ever Was*, (Reprint edition of 100 copies). Rockville Centre, NY: Freshet Press, 1970.

Fox, Charles K. *Rising Trout*, (Signed, limited edition). Carlisle, PA: Foxcrest, 1967.

——. *The Wonderful World of Trout*, (Signed, limited edition). Carlisle, PA: Foxcrest, 1963.

Goodspeed, Chas. E. *Angling in America*, (Edition of 795 signed copies). Boston: Houghton, 1939.

Grey, Sir Edward. *Fly Fishing*, (Edition of 150 copies, vellum). New York: Dutton, 1930.

Hackle, Sparse Grey (A. Miller). *Fishless Days*, (Edition of 591 copies). New York: Anglers Club.

Hunt, Richard C. *Salmon in Low Water*, (Edition of 500 copies). New York: Anglers Club, 1950.

Ingraham, Henry A. *American Trout Streams*, (Edition of 350 copies). New York: Anglers Club, 1926.

Jennings, Preston J. *A Book of Trout Flies*. New York: Derrydale, 1935.

Johnson, F. M. *Forest, Lake and River*, (Edition of 350 copies). 2 vols. Boston: University Press, 1902.

Lamb, Dana S. *Bright Salmon and Brown Trout,* (Edition of 350 copies). Barre, MA: Barre Publishers, 1964.

McClane, A. J. *The Practical Fly Fisherman.* 1953.

Marbury, Mary Orvis. *Favorite Flies and Their Histories.* Boston: Houghton Mifflin, 1896.

Schaldach, Wm. *Fish,* (Edition of 1,560 copies). Philadelphia: Lippincott, 1937.

Schwiebert, Ernest G., Jr. *Salmon of the World,* (Edition of 750 copies). New York: Winchester, 1970.

Scrope, Wm. *Days and Nights of Salmon Fishing in the Tweed.* 1843.

Wetzel, Chas. M. *American Fishing Books.* Newark, DE: Private printing, 1950.

Wood, Arnold. *A Bibliography of "The Compleat Angler,"* (Edition of 102 copies). 1900.

Wulff, Lee. *The Atlantic Salmon,* (Edition of 200 copies). New York: A. S. Barnes, 1958.

Chapter 29 ❧ Hunting Books

ANGUS CAMERON
Revised by Tony Lyons

M any of the items discussed in this book are of relatively recent interest to collectors. The sportsman who elects to assemble a collection of, say, all the nineteenth-century wooden fishing lures he can find is something of a collecting pioneer, and only time will tell whether he is merely enjoying a pleasant hobby or enriching his heirs.

Book collecting, however, is one of the most venerable of civilized activities. Like coin collecting and stamp collecting, it attracts tens of thousands of investors and hobbyists, supports hundreds of dealers, and has developed its own rules and media. Anyone who wants to take up book collecting seriously—hunting books or any other kind of book—would be well advised to learn the rules of the game. Although later in this chapter I will try to explain a few of the rules, and will list some current values of individual titles, be warned that the true rare-book market is not for the incautious or the ingenuous, and this brief chapter can do no more than sketch the bare outlines.

However, book collecting does not have to be approached as a way of making money, like playing the stock market. I, frankly, collect books on hunting and shooting primarily because I am a hunter and shooter and I want to read the books, and most likely reread them. And good books, whether they be "how-to" books like Jack O'Connor's *The Shotgun Book* or hunting-adventure books like Hornaday's *Campfires in the Rockies*, do increase in value. Few of the books in the field of hunting are enormously valuable (of course, a first edition of the Emperor Frederick's book on falconry would be in the big leagues), but many have prices now in the hundreds—books that could have been bought by the carton for a few dollars at country auctions of bygone decades.

Sometimes such great appreciations in value are the result simply of rarity. Sometimes there are unique or freakish considerations—an upside-down title page, an inscription of significance on the flyleaf, marginal annotations by someone famous. But it is my contention that, especially for the beginning collector, the best values are the best books. If you collect the good books, in many instances time will turn them into collector's items, and you can relax in the knowledge that the books you have enjoyed reading are never going to be worth less than when you bought them, and they may be worth a good deal more.

WHAT TO COLLECT

The essence of a good book collection, as distinguished from a mere accumulation, is not a sprinkling of titles that are expensive individually, but an overall organization or focus of some kind that gives the collection shape. In a well-rounded collection, each item's value is enhanced by its companions.

My collection, though a modest one, does include all the books written by the inimitable Frederick Selous. Selous, who was killed in his sixties in the World War I skirmishes in his beloved Africa, was one of the most notable European hunters. He flourished in those fabulous decades when a man could live the hunting life as his forebears lived during the last Ice Age, in a world of game unmatched in variety and numbers. He was a fine naturalist and a fine writer. I enjoyed reading him, bought his books whenever I could find them, and ended up with all of them — the most obvious, and certainly one of the most satisfying, ways of collecting: by author. If you enjoy reading Jack O'Connor, you might try to find all his books — from his earliest, which were novels, to his most recent, on sheep hunting. Some are in print and some are not, but there is no doubt that an O'Connor collection, not too difficult to assemble now, will increase in value. Another hunting writer well worth collecting is Elmer Keith, the doughty old mountain man and ballistics expert, whose autobiography recently appeared.

Many authors are not thought of primarily as hunters or hunting writers, yet a collection of their books would grace any hunting collection. For example, books on exploration, particularly Artic exploration, are often filled with hunting lore. Jackson's *A Thousand Days in the Arctic* included all sorts of polar-bear lore and even ballistics information. Nansen's *In the Arctic* and *Farthest North* also include much hunting material. Teddy Roosevelt is an overwhelming example (and his fine books are surprisingly inexpensive, because they were printed in very large quantities to start with). Fiction writers who deal with hunting are another category. The star is certainly Hemingway, but there are many others you can discover for yourself and whose works you can track down. Books written by or about pioneers of one type or another are bound to be of interest to the hunter — for example, Alaskan hunter-bushpilot-guide Harmon Helmericks has never written a book specifically on hunting, but all his books are rich sources of hunting lore.

Another obvious and satisfying tack to take is to collect by topic. Whatever your favorite hunting quarry — big game, upland birds, waterfowl, small game

—you can build a collection around it. If deer are your main interest, you may start with a few current and recent books, probably mostly "how-to" books. Then you may try an older book you hear of, such as Larry Koller's *Shots at Whitetails*, or a still older classic such as Theodore S. Van Dyke's *The Still-Hunter*, first published in 1886. And then you may discover that there is scarcely an account of deer hunting in English more thrilling than Charles St. John's *The Muckle Hart of Ben More*, about a seven-day hunt for a huge stag in the wild reaches of Scotland's Highlands. And this kind of bookish exploration may widen your horizons further; after all, St. John wrote other books too, and before you know it, you may find yourself with a library not just of deer books but of eighteenth- and nineteenth-century books on all kinds of hunting in Scotland. Starting with an interest in a topic, you will have acquired an interest in an author who wrote on it, an interest in a special and colorful hunting locale, and an interest in a historical period; the books you have acquired chart the course of your literary voyage, and so they form a true collection with a coherence and significance unique to you as a sportsman-collector.

Another approach, and quite a popular one, is to collect books illustrated by certain artists. I buy every book I can find that was illustrated by Carl Rungius. There are many contemporary sporting and wildlife artists — Bob Kuhn is a favorite of mine — whose illustrations will certainly enhance the future value of the books they illustrate regardless of their authors, and of course in many cases the authors are collectible in themselves.

Some specialists collect not just books but sporting catalogs. Really old ones are valuable; if you run across the first Winchester catalog to list the Model 94, you've got something. Don't throw your catalogs away as the years pass; today's catalog is tomorrow's collectible item, and even if you aren't interested in collecting them yourself, if you give them storage space you'll eventually end up with a series that can be traded or sold to other collectors.

There are numerous other ways to focus a collection, of course. Perhaps what I would emphasize most, at least for collectors like myself who are motivated more by the pleasures of reading than by the excitement of speculation in rare books, is to follow your interests wherever they take you and thus allow the focus to be your own personality.

BUYING NEW BOOKS

It is easy enough to keep abreast of current publishing. Although not too many hunting books are reviewed in the general media, many newspapers, large and small, publish outdoorsman's columns and articles that frequently contain reviews. As a hunter, you probably subscribe to specialized hunting publications that review books regularly. If you are a member of one of the outdoor book clubs, you'll be offered not only the current selection each month, but also a number of alternates.

I should say a word about the current state of hunting-book publishing. Few hunting books are printed in large numbers. First printings are apt to be around 5,000 or even less, and generally there is no subsequent printing; American hunters have never been avid book buyers. The major selections of the outdoor book clubs are an exception: they can be printed in quantities of 10,000 up to 100,000. But by and large, hunting books are printed in small quantities, and pass out of print within a few years because their long-term sale, though it may be steady, is too small to encourage publishers to reprint.

This situation is a perennial grief to me, because I am a book editor and would dearly love to publish many more hunting books than my company could sell, and if I could, I would keep the best ones in print forever. But it works to the collector's advantage in several ways.

In the first place, it means that a book you buy simply for its merit when you hear about it or see it advertised as a new book will fairly soon become a truly collectible item—an out-of-print book, available only through the rare- and used-book markets, that may increase in value.

In the second place, it means that publishers frequently "remainder" relatively new hunting books. That is, they sell their entire stock to remainder houses at a very low price, at or even below the cost of manufacture. The remainder houses, such as Marboro Books, pass these low prices on to their customers; you can get last year's $20 book for a few dollars. Thus if you take the trouble to get on a few remainder-house mailing lists and study their periodic listings closely, you can build a library of brand-new and barely out-of-print books at a quarter of the cost. In fact, this is really the only way to acquire modern hunting books at modest cost, because very few such books ever appear in paperback editions.

Limited editions of new books are in a special category. As with numbered prints and etchings, a limited edition of a book is intended to be an instant collector's item. Once the publisher's stock is sold out at his list price, no more can be printed regardless of demand, and the price on the rare-book market is free to rise. Sometimes limited editions are published simultaneously with an ordinary trade edition, and the only difference is a somewhat more expensive binding, a slipcase, and usually the author's signature. The sportsman who buys books only to read will see little point in paying several times more for the limited edition. However, there are some—serious collectors, those with a special feeling for the author, or those simply with a craving for fine bindings and other details—who appreciate them; a market for them does exist, and they can be a sound investment.

BUYING OUT-OF-PRINT BOOKS

Why do books go out of print? Because there is insufficient demand for them. Why do some out-of-print books increase in value, sometimes to hundreds of times their original cost? Because there is great demand for them. Those two statements may seem contradictory. Many an author whose book has gone out of print has upbraided his publisher when he discovered that the book is fetching $25 on the rare-book market. But there is no contradiction, just cause and effect. There are a few dozen people in the world who want the book badly enough to pay $25. Most of those few dozen would be delighted if the publisher reprinted the book and made it available again at its original price—say, $10. A couple of them would still want the original printing anyway; they specialize in first printings. Meanwhile, the publisher has had to print a minimum of several hundred—actually, usually 1,000 copies is the least it is possible to reprint at a reasonable manufacturing cost—and must try to sell them. If he doesn't think he has a good chance, he is certainly not going to reprint the book, and it almost certainly is going to cost the few who really want it more and more in the rare-book market. Thus the *absence* of sufficient demand in the new-book market *creates* a demand in the used-book market.

The price of an out-of-print book fluctuates according to supply and demand. The supply of a just-remaindered book far exceeds the demand, and the price is very low. A long-out-of-print book may be unknown to sportsmen and collectors (deservedly or not) and hence not in demand, and again the price is very low—regardless of the supply, in this case. Or a long-out-of-print book such as Roosevelt's *African Game Trails* may be in considerable demand, but also widely available because of large past printings, and hence only moderately priced.

Rare-book prices are also affected by the edition number, the condition of the binding, and other details, and thus two copies of the same book can vary considerably in price.

Since this is a supply-demand, buyer-seller situation, obviously the only way to know what the "fair" price of a book should be is to keep in touch with the action. The easiest way to do this is to get on the dealers' mailing lists and to subscribe to the rare-book periodicals (some of these are listed at the end of this chapter). If you are buying or selling, you can advertise in these periodicals yourself—though you cannot expect many big bargains this way; most of the collectors you'll be dealing with are apt to know a good deal more than you do.

The simple way to get a book you want is to go to a dealer. Say you're looking for a copy of Charles Sheldon's *Wilderness of the Denali* to complete your collection of the works of the famous hunter-naturalist-writer. You can wait till you see it listed in the dealers' catalogs at a price you're willing to pay, or you can let a dealer or two know you're looking for it. Having the dealer act as your agent in this way will drive the price up a little, perhaps, but that is fair enough, and it may be well worth it to you to complete your collection.

One of the great pleasures of any kind of collecting, of course, is satisfying the larcenous urge most of us try to repress in other areas of life. "I got it for a song" — the collector's cry of triumph, even though he may be a millionaire able to afford the going price many times over. Go ahead — look for bargains, not just on the tables of secondhand-book stores, but in dark corners in the sheds and barns of antique dealers while your wife looks for pressed glass or footed salt cellars. The prices are usually so low that you can buy anything that appeals to you; even if it turns out to be worth nothing on the rare-book market, you'll have a few hours of reading and another item for your library.

REPRESENTATIVE BOOK PRICES

There are thousands of titles that could be of interest to a collector of sporting books. The brief listing here is given as an introductory glimpse of the market.

$25–$50

Annabel, Russell. *Alaskan Tales*, (First edition). New York: A. S. Barnes, 1953.

Babcock, Havilah. *My Health is Better in November*, (Second printing). New York: Rinehart and Winston, 1948.

———. *Tales of Quails 'N Such*, (First edition). New York: Rinehart and Winston, 1951.

Barker, F. C. *Hunting and Trapping*. Boston: D. Lothrop, 1882.

Buckingham, Nash. *De Shootinest Gent'man*. New York: T. Nelson, 1961.

Burrard, Sir Gerald, et al. *Big Game Hunting in the Himalayas and Tibet*. London: H. Jenkins, 1925.

Camp, Raymond, ed. *The Hunter's Encyclopedia*, (First edition). Harrisburg: Stackpole & Heck, 1948.

Clark, Roland. *Pot Luck*, (Trade edition). New York: A. S. Barnes, 1945.

Connett, Eugene V. *Duck Shooting Along the Atlantic Tidewater*, (First edition). New York: W. Morrow, 1947.

Evans, George B., ed. *The Woodcock Book*, (Edition of 1,000 copies). Clinton, NJ: Amwell Press, 1977.

Everett, Fred. *Fun With Game Birds*. Harrisburg: Stackpole, 1954.

Farrington, S. Kip. *The Ducks Came Back*. New York: Coward, McCann, 1945.

Faulkner, William. *Big Woods*, (First edition). New York: Random House, 1955.

Foote, John Tainter. *Dum-Bell of Brookfield*, (First edition). New York: Appleton, 1917.

Forester, Frank (H. W. Herbert). *American Game in Its Season*, (First edition). New York: Scribner's, 1853.

Grand, Gordon. *The Millbeck Hounds*. New York: Scribner's, 1947.

Grinnell, George B. *American Game-Bird Shooting*. New York: Forest & Stream, 1910.

——. *Hunting Trails on Three Continents*. For Boone & Crockett Club. New York: Derrydale, 1933.

Haig-Brown, R. L. *Panther*, (First edition). 1946.

Heilner, Van Campen. *A Book on Duck Shooting*. New York: Knopf, 1947.

Hornaday, Wm. T. *Campfires on the Canadian Rockies*, (First edition). New York: Scribner's, 1906.

Janes, E. D. *Ducks and Geese*, (First edition). 1954.

Knight, John Alden. *Ruffed Grouse*, (First edition). New York: Putnam, 1947.

——. *Woodcock*, (First edition). New York: Putnam, 1944.

Koller, Larry. *Shots at Whitetails*, (First edition). Boston: Little, Brown, 1948.

Lytle, Horace. *Gun Dogs Afield*. New York: Putnam, 1942.

Murray, Wm. H. H. *Adventures in the Wilderness*, (First edition). Boston: Lee & Shepard, 1869.

National Geographic Society. *The Wild Animals of North America*. 1963.

O'Connor, Jack. *The Art of Hunting Big Game in North America*, (First edition). New York: Knopf, 1967.

——. *The Shotgun Book*, (First edition). New York: Knopf, 1965.

Ormand, Clyde. *Hunting in the Northwest*, (First edition). 1948.

Parker, Eric, et al. *Shooting by Moor, Field and Shore*, (First edition). Philadelphia: Lippincott, 1929.

Roosevelt, Theodore. *The Wilderness Hunter*. New York: Putnam, 1893.

——. *African Game Trails*. New York: Syndicate, 1910.

Ruark, Robert. *The Old Man and the Boy*, (First edition). New York: Holt, 1957.

Rutledge, Archibald. *Hunter's Choice*, (First trade edition). New York: A. S. Barnes, 1946.

Schaldach, William. *Upland Gunning*, (Second printing). New York: A. S. Barnes, 1946.

Scharff, Robert. *Complete Duck Shooter's Handbook*, (First edition). New York: Putnam, 1957.

Shields, G. O. *Hunting in the Great West*. 1884.

Smith, Edmund Ware. *A Treasury of the Maine Woods*, (First edition). New York: F. Fell, 1958.

Spiller, Burton. *Grouse Feathers*, (First trade edition). New York: Macmillan, 1947.

Whelen, Townsend. *American Big Game Shooting*, (First edition). 1932.

$50–$150

Annabel, Russell. *Tales of a Big Game Guide*, (Edition of 950 copies). New York: Derrydale, 1938.

Babcock, Havilah. *I Don't Want to Shoot an Elephant*, (First edition). New York: Holt, Rinehart and Winston, 1958.

——. *My Health is Better in November*, (First edition). New York: Holt, Rinehart and Winston, 1947.

Babcock, Philip. *Falling Leaves*, (Edition of 950 copies). New York: Derrydale, 1937.

Barber, Joel. *Wild Fowl Decoys*, (First trade edition). New York: Derrydale, 1937.

Bigelow. Horatio. *Gunnerman*, (Edition of 950 copies). New York: Derrydale, 1939.

Boone & Crockett Club. *American Big Game Hunting*. 1893.

Buckingham, Nash. *De Shootinest Gent'man*, (First trade edition). New York: Scribner's, 1941.

Camp, Raymond. *Duck Boats: Blinds: Decoys*, (First edition). New York: Knopf, 1952.

Clark, Roland. *Pot Luck*, (Edition of 460 copies). New York: A. S. Barnes, 1945.

Connett, Eugene V. *Wildfowling in the Mississippi Flyway*, (First edition). New York: Van Nostrand, 1949.

Derrydale Press. *A Decade of American Sporting Books and Prints*, (Edition of 950 copies). 1937.

Doughty, J. and T. *Some Early American Hunters*, (Edition of 375 copies). 1928.

Edward, Duke of York. *The Master of Game*. New York: Duffield, 1909.

Foote, John T. *Jing*, (Edition of 950 copies). New York: Derrydale, 1936.

Forester, Frank. *The Warwick Woodlands*, (First illustrated edition). 1851.

A Gentleman of Philadelphia County. *The American Shooter's Manual*, (Edition of 375 copies). 1928.

Grand, Gordon. *Old Man and Other Col. Weatherford Stories*, (Edition of 1,150 copies). 1939.

Hawker, Peter. *Instructions to Young Sportsmen in All That Relates to Guns and Shooting*. London: Longman, Rees, Orme, Brown, and Green, 1830.

Hazleton, William C., ed. *Tales of Duck and Grouse Shooting*, (First edition). 1916.

Heilner, Van Campen. *Our American Game Birds*, (First edition). Garden City, NY: Doubleday, Doran, 1941.

Hunter, A. *Let's Ride to Hounds*, (Edition of 850 copies). 1929.

Knight, J. A. *Ol' Bill*, (Edition of 1,929 copies). New York: Scribner's, 1942.

Leffingwell, Wm. B. *The Art of Wing Shooting*. Chicago: Rand, McNally, 1894.

Milnor, W., Jr. *Memoirs of the Gloucester Fox Hunting Club Near Philadelphia*, (Edition of 375 copies). New York: Ernest Gee (Derrydale), 1927.

Nansen, Fridtjof. *Farthest North*. New York: Harper & Brothers, 1897.

O'Connor, Jack. *Game in the Desert*, (Edition of 950 copies). New York: Derrydale, 1939.

Phillips, John C. *Shooting-Stands of Eastern Massachusetts*, (First edition). Cambridge: Riverside Press, 1929.

Phillips, John C., and Hill, Lewis Webb. *Classics of the American Shooting Field*, (Edition of 150 copies). Boston: Houghton Mifflin, 1936.

Pollard, Hugh B. C., and Barclay-Smith, P. *British and American Game Birds*, (First trade edition). London: Eyre & Spottiswoode, 1945.

Prichard, H. H. *Hunting Camps in Woods and Wilderness*, (First edition). New York: Sturgis and Walton, 1910.

Roosevelt, Theodore. *Ranch Life and the Hunting Trail*, (Edition of 1,250 copies). New York: Scribner's, 1906.

Rosene, Walter. *The Bobwhite Quail*, (Edition of 250 copies). New Brunswick, NJ: Rutgers University Press, 1969.

Rutledge, Archibald. *Hunter's Choice*, (Edition of 475 copies). New York: A. S. Barnes, 1946.

Schaldach, Wm. *Upland Gunning*, (First printing). New York: A. S. Barnes, 1946.

Sheldon, Charles. *The Wilderness of Denali*, (First edition). New York: Scribner's, 1930.

Sheldon, H. P. *Tranquillity*, (Edition of 950 copies). New York: Derrydale, 1936.

Smith, Edmund Ware. *Tall Tales and Short*, (Edition of 950 copies). New York: Derrydale, 1938.

Spiller, Burton. *Grouse Feathers*, (Edition of 950 copies). New York: Macmillan, 1938.

Ward, Rowland. *Records of Big Game*. London: R. Ward, 1962 and later.

$150–$500

Beebe, Wm. *Pheasants — Their Lives and Homes*, (Edition of 201 copies). Garden City, NY: Doubleday, Page, 1926.

Betten, H. L. *Upland Game Shooting*, (Edition of 124 copies). New York: Knopf, 1940.

Bishop, Richard E. *Bishop's Wildfowl*, (First edition). St. Paul, MN: Brown & Bigelow, 1948.

Brown, Paul. *Ups and Down*, (Edition of 750 copies). New York: Scribner's, 1936.

Buckingham, Nash. *De Shootinest Gent'man*, (Edition of 950 copies). New York: Derrydale, 1934.

Clark, Roland. *Pot Luck*, (Edition of 450 copies). West Hartford, CT: Countryman Press, 1945.

Connett, Eugene V. *Upland Game Bird Shooting in America*, (Edition of 850 copies). New York: Derrydale, 1930.

Forester, Frank. *Frank Forester's Fugitive Sporting Sketches*, (First edition). 1879.

——. *The Warwick Woodlands*, (Edition of 250 copies). New York: Derrydale, 1934.

Grand, Gordon. *The Silver Horn & Other Sporting Tales of John Weatherford*, (Edition of 950 copies). New York: Derrydale, 1932.

Grinnell, Geo. B. *American Duck Shooting*, (Deluxe edition). New York: Forest & Stream, 1901.

Hawker, P. *The Diary of Colonel Peter Hawker*, (First edition). New York: Longmans, Green, 1893.

Hazelton, Wm. *Duck Shooting and Hunting Sketches*, (First edition). Chicago: 1943.

Holland, Ray R. *Shotgunning in the Lowlands*, (First edition). West Hartford, CT: Countryman Press, 1945.

Knight, J. A. *Ruffed Grouse*, (Edition of 210 copies). New York: Knopf, 1947.

——. *Woodcock*, (Edition of 275 copies). New York: Knopf, 1944.

Millais, J. G. *Game Birds and Shooting Sketches*, (First edition). London: Southeran, 1892.

Phillips, John C. *George Washington — Sportsman: From His Own Journals*, (Edition of 100 copies). Cambridge, MA: Cosmos Press, 1928.

——. *Bibliography of The Natural History of Ducks*, (Edition of 75 copies). 1926.

Queeny, Edgar M. *Prairie Wings*. Philadelphia: Lippincott, 1947.

Roosevelt, Theodore. *Big Game Hunting in the Rockies and Great Plains*, (Edition of 1,000 copies). New York: Putnam, 1899.

Schaldach, Wm. *Upland Gunning*, (Edition of 160 copies). New York: A. S. Barnes, 1946.

Scott, Peter. *Morning Flight*, (Edition of 750 copies). New York: Scribner's, 1935.

Sheldon, H. P. *Tranquillity Revisited*, (Edition of 485 copies). New York: Derrydale, 1940.

$500-and up

Anonymous. *The Sportsman's Portfolio of American Field Sports*, (First edition). 1855.

Barber, Joel. *Wild Fowl Decoys*, (Deluxe edition of 55 copies). New York: Derrydale, 1937.

Davis, Edmund, Jr. *Woodcock Shooting*, (Edition of 100 copies). 1908.

Doughty, J. and T. *The Cabinet of Natural History and American Rural Sports*. 3 vols. Philadelphia: J. & T. Doughty, 1830.

Ellison, Frank. *A Journal of a Trip Down East—Aug. 1858*, (Three known copies). 1858.

A Gentleman of Philadelphia County. *The American Shooter's Manual*, (First edition). 1827.

Hagerbaumer, David, and Lehman, S. *Selected American Game Birds*, (Edition of 190 copies). Caldwell, ID: Caxton Printers, 1972.

Harris, Cornwallis W. *Portraits of the Game and Wild Animals of Southern Africa*, (Edition of 550 copies). Mazoe, Rhodesia: Read Press, 1976.

Huntington, D. W. *In Brush, Sedge and Stubble*, (First edition). 1898.

McAleenan, Joseph. *Hunting with Rifle and Camera in the Canadian Rockies*, (Edition of 25 copies). N.D. (1915).

Morris, Beverley R. *British Gamebirds and Wildfowl*, (First edition). London: Groombridge, 1855.

Phillips, John C. *A Natural History of Ducks*. New York: Houghton Mifflin, 1922.

Queeny, Edgar M. *Prairie Wings*, (Edition of 225 copies). Philadelphia: Lippincott, 1946.

Schaldach, Wm. J. *Carl Rungius—Big Game Painter*, (Edition of 160 copies). West Hartford, CT: Countryman Press, 1945.

Schwerdt, C. F. G. R. *Hunting, Hawking, Shooting*, (Edition of 300 copies). 4 vols. London: Waterlow, 1928.

Stoddard, Herbert L. *The Bobwhite Quail*, (Edition of 260 copies). New York: Scribner's, 1931.

Tome, Philip. *Pioneer Life; or, Thirty Years A Hunter*, (First edition). Buffalo: 1854.

DEALERS IN HUNTING BOOKS

Any good book dealer — and there are many hundreds — will know something about sporting books. Those listed here make a specialty of them.

Angler's and Shooter's Bookshelf
Goshen, CT 06756

The Charles Daly Collection
36 Golf Lane
Ridgefield, CT 06877

Morris Heller
Swan Lake, NY 12783

Ernest Hickok
382 Springfield Avenue
Summit, NJ 07901

The Sporting Collector
Box 1042
Laurence Harbor, NJ 08879

Chapter 30 ❧ Catalogs and Periodicals

F. PHILLIPS WILLIAMSON and ALLAN J. LIU

Austin Hogan, curator of the American Museum of Fly Fishing, once stated: "Catalogs and periodicals are where you separate the men from the boys. Anyone with the money can get the books. It takes hard work to get the catalogs and periodicals." Austin is not far from wrong, but it's still fun to find a $100 book for a $1 at a garage sale.

Catalogs have been long overlooked, but they recently have started catching collector's interest. How can one collect guns, rods, reels, decoys, shells, or waterfowl calls without eventually desiring to document them with catalogs? Designs change over the years, and a catalog is the best evidence for dating an item, *if* you can acquire a run of catalogs so the date can be established when the "collectible" was first introduced and when it last appeared.

While catalogs and periodicals are great reading, you get something more important: a feel and mood of the time. You sense the pride of workmanship and the feeling of quality—and sometimes the despair when the market failed to appreciate the product. Like the story of the man who reportedly made a fantastic goose call—it is said to have really worked, but it failed to sell because the call could not be heard by the human ear; only a goose could hear it.

Today, if Madison Avenue does not tell you something is good, you just know it isn't! In the old days, the best ad was a satisfied customer. Testimonials were an important section of any catalog (Weatherby still carries them from the world's best hunters). If a buyer was satisfied, he would tell his friend. The friend would seek out a catalog to find out what models were available and the price range.

Currently there are few real markets (or dealers) specializing in catalogs or periodicals. Occasionally a book dealer will list one or two. The only way to really find them is to work. Look. Tell your friends, the rubbish man, the bulk-paper collector. Send out want lists. And above all, keep at it. Our want lists have had some items on them for 30 years (some of them have been bought and sold in that time, but either the word came too late or a dollar problem prevailed). Get there first, as most folks clean out Grandpa's house after it's sold, and catalogs and periodicals are the first thing in the trash.

It is really hard to hang a dollar sign on a catalog or periodical now, but things are looking up. A 1951 Payne Rod Company catalog has sold for $150. The World's

The 1939 World's Fair issue of Stoeger's catalog has sold for more than $200. (Photo courtesy Matthew Vinciguerra)

The 1951 Payne Rod Co. catalog. (Photo courtesy Matthew Vinciguerra)

Fair edition of Stoeger's Gun Catalog has sold for $300. Recently, at auction, a group of Derrydale flyers and catalogs brought $600. Prewar Abercrombie & Fitch catalogs are a treasure. In fact, all of the original Abercrombie & Fitch catalogs are in demand. For war buffs, try some of the early Bannerman catalogs.

About 1914, the famous story "De Shootinest Gent'man" by Nash Buckingham appeared in a periodical entitled *Recreation Magazine*. A Nash Buckingham collector might just have to have a copy.

Some authors never wrote books. Theodore Gordon, considered to be the founding father of fly-fishing in America, was a prolific periodical contributor. His notes were never found, and Gordon never wrote a book. Magazines with his work are certainly collectible. As a sidelight, Gordon also wrote articles on upland gunning—rare items if you can find one.

If you are a gun buff, look for issues of *The Rifleman* published when Thomas G. Samworth was editor. Samworth was the greatest gun book/magazine editor.

Other periodicals to look for include *Forest and Stream* (weekly), *Recreation*, *Anglers Club Bulletins*, and many more.

There is no hard and fast rule in collecting periodicals. Look! You have to find something that will interest you. Get the periodical intact—especially with front and rear covers.

It is somewhat easier to suggest what catalogs to collect. Any with a legendary name is worthwhile. Parker, Winchester, Stoeger, L. C. Smith, and Stevens had fine gun catalogs.

Fishing catalogs have gained attention with the publication of *Great American Fishing Catalogs*, by Samuel Melner and Hermann Kessler. Use this as a starter, but look for catalogs of rodmakers (instead of dealers); they will have the greatest future demand.

Keep your eye peeled for anything by Derrydale, Frank Lowe, Abercrombie & Fitch, Herter's, L. L. Bean, or David Abercrombie, prior to 1945. It may be only a paper flier, but it may be collectible to someone.

When you have what is a real treasure and of great interest to you, protect your investment. Either bind it or have a slipcase made. The reason some of the publications are so scarce and sought after (like *Forest and Stream*'s little paper book "Shore Birds" that came out at 15 cents) is that they failed to survive the years.

Chapter 31 ❧ Decorating

JAYNE W. TEAGLE

In decorating, both for myself and for others, I have learned that one of the most important, and often the most difficult, effects to achieve is the integration of the owner's personality into the home. No matter how beautiful a room is, it is a failure if, upon entering it, there is no feeling for the type of person who lives there. One of the things that most beautifully expresses this individuality is a collection. Whether it is a collection of guns, duck decoys, paintings, or antique salmon reels, it pronounces something about the owner; something that differentiates him and his home from anyone else's. Whether the collector is a beginner, or one who has been collecting for so long that his collection exceeds the limitations of displaying it, he should give considerable thought to the placement of the pieces so that he and others may derive the greatest amount of enjoyment from them. To my mind, there are two methods of decorating with attention to a sporting collection, and the choice should be determined by the answer to the question, "Which is of greater importance—the collection or the decoration?" Most collectors whom I have met would answer that the collection takes precedence, and if they live alone, or have a sufficiently large home or office, this is fine. However, many collectors must accommodate their collection either to limited space, to other people, or to both. Under either circumstance, these are some guidelines and suggestions that I would offer.

DECORATING, WITH FOCUS ON THE COLLECTION

If an entire room can be decorated with a specific collection, it should become a showcase for that collection, with each of the elements of decoration—architecture, wall, treated fabrics, and lighting—working toward the glorification of that collection.

Architecturally, much can be done to enhance a collection. For instance, if an area is being designed or restructured to accommodate a collection, consideration should be given to recessed cabinets, both for beauty and protection. Adequate shelving and cabinetry cannot be stressed too much for the collector

A wall over a fireplace makes a wonderful focal point for the exhibition of decoy carvings and antique pistols.

of three-dimensional items, who does not want to end up with most of his collection in the attic or cellar. Not all shelves, however, need to be built into the room. Besides cabinets and étagères, one of the nicest ways to display collections such as duck decoys and fishing paraphernalia is in a pine hutch, similar to those used in country kitchens in earlier times. Other architectural features that can enhance a collection room are chair-rail picture moldings and wooden beams. A collection of fox-hunting prints and original paintings achieves the feeling of an English manor house when it is hung over an applied chair rail. The look is completed by adding moldings where the walls meet the ceiling. These picture moldings have the dual benefit of being functional as well as elegant because they enable the collector to move the paintings around without having to put lots of holes in the walls. In fact, some English decorators hang paintings exclusively from the moldings, using ribbon or silk cord to cover the wires. Wooden beams can also be used to create a framework within a room. One room I worked on had cathedral ceilings. The beams served as dividers, creating partitions in which trophy animal heads could be hung, leaving space on the walls below for a collection of African art.

It is not always possible to suit the architecture to the collection. However, it is often possible to turn an architectural liability into an asset where a collection is concerned. In rooms in which vertical support columns are visible and immovable, shelving can often be attached to the column to display artifacts, either by hanging glass shelves between two such columns or between a column and the wall, or by attaching bracket shelves at different heights along the columns to hold individual objects. A cannister light attached to the top of the column, downlighting the shelves, would complete the transformation of the unsightly columns into a sculpture center.

Another element of decoration that can enhance a collection is the correct choice of wall-treatment and selection of fabrics. The criteria on which these things should be judged is their similarity in feeling to the collection. In a room designed for the display of fishing rods or duck decoys, I might suggest a wall covering of grass cloth, pigskin, or suede. For the exhibition of English hunting prints and original paintings, a nice background would be wood panelling or simply a top-quality paint job, perhaps in a stippled or stained effect. These are not definite rules at all, but are simply meant to help you coordinate the feeling of the room with that of the collection. Similarly, when choosing fabrics, let the formality or informality of the collection be your guide. In a room I decorated for a couple who are avid sportsmen, the fabric was of primary importance. They had a very large game room. It had to double as a family room and as a showcase for their various collections of animal trophies, duck and goose decoys, art, and artifacts collected on hunting and fishing trips all over the world. Three of

An avid decoy collector has turned his office into a splendid showcase for his collection.

These wood-panelled walls make an elegant backdrop for a collection of Winchester rifles, paintings, and Indian artifacts.

the four walls were glass so that when the curtains were drawn they surrounded the room. The difficulty was in choosing a fabric that wouldn't overshadow the room, nor challenge the focus by drawing continual attention to itself. In this case, we chose a fabric with a pattern of a rain forest, which contributed to the feeling already created by the collections.

Another point that this particular room raises is that the mixture of collections in a room is to be encouraged. The greater variety of things to look at, the more interesting the room. Some collections lend themselves to being intermixed with others, such as fishing rods hung on walls alongside guns and paintings, while others are better displayed on their own. A collection of small knives, or Indian arrowheads, would have greater impact in its own cabinet or on a table around a lamp, than if it was scattered around.

While it is often difficult for a collector to have an entire room for a collection, it is sometimes easier, and often more desirable, to use a hallway as the display area. One of the most interesting halls I have decorated was that of a couple who are devoted fishermen. We used one wall to display their stuffed and mounted fish, while we covered the other wall with their framed fishing photographs.

One collection that has the greatest need for its own room is that of animal trophy heads and full mounts. All trophies should be displayed together. I would suggest that the collection not be displayed in the main entertaining room because it is rare for anything to be discussed in a trophy room except hunting. Of course, if all of your friends are hunters, this will probably be the desired effect rather than a problem. However, I would still urge hunters to display all their animals in one room. I vividly remember one weekend spent at a

Curtains with a rain forest motif are appropriate for a game room displaying African trophies, decoys, and duck stamp and hunting prints.

Hand-tied trout and salmon flies are beautifully displayed in a shadowbox case.

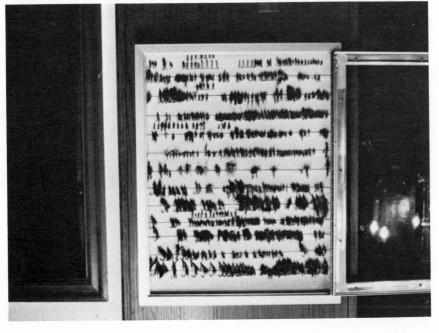

A front hall is used to display a fine collection of Winchester rifles and a shell board.

A well-lit cabinet becomes a treasure trove in a hallway.

private hunting lodge where I shared the guestroom with half of a mountain goat that was hung over the dresser. I draped my bathrobe over it for the duration. I was not, however, so adroit at covering the buffalo who glowered down at me from eight feet above my head.

INTEGRATING A COLLECTION INTO THE DECOR

Those who cannot spare an entire room for their collections can still easily, and somewhat more pleasurably, incorporate them into their existing environment. For those with paintings and prints, the solutions are numerous since wall space is usually more plentiful than anything else. If possible, however, I would still urge that the paintings and prints be hung in settings compatible with their mood. For instance, realistic hunting paintings generally dominate a room. Whether they exude excitement and adventure, or serenity and reminiscence, they generally ask to be hung near fireplaces and good books. I know of one house in which Pleissners hang on hand-painted Chinese wallpaper, thereby diminishing both the beauty of the paintings and the beauty of the wallpaper.

Three-dimensional collections can be displayed in several ways. They can be contained within cabinets, étagères, and collection tables, which gives them the previously mentioned impact of a grouping while also protecting them from damage. Single duck decoys or bronze sculptures will look lovely on a bookshelf among the volumes. Likewise, a fishing reel becomes a beautiful treasure placed among shells and fossil rocks on a mantlepiece or coffee table. This is a more sentimental means of display because it enables the collector to continually rediscover his finds and spark the memories associated with them.

This brings up the point of protection of collections. If a collection is fragile, valuable, or both, pay specific attention to its placement. In the case of break-

A guest room doubles as a display room for a fine set of A. B. Frost prints.

Lucite sconces and a bookshelf turn an office wall into a display case for treasured decoys.

A collection table with treasures in each of its 12 drawers, which are interchangeable.

ables, the safest places are behind glass doors or inside collection tables and shadowboxes. I have put Boehm bird collections on shelves in bay windows where they are some distance from the seating arrangements in the room, and further protected them by putting *display* tables in front of them as decorative roadblocks. Similarly, when handling rare books, I suggest putting the more valuable ones on the higher shelves so that people will not be tempted to reach for them. This extra effort will have the dual effect of protecting your collection and making your guests feel more comfortable, because they don't have to worry about touching anything they shouldn't. If three-dimensional objects are not fragile and each can stand alone without losing importance, it is nice to display them randomly. For instance, pianos and windowsills serve as excellent shelves, or an unused corner can be mirrored on both sides with triangular glass shelves suspended from its walls, thereby creating a sculpture nook.

SUGGESTIONS

There are very few absolute rules in decorating. However, I would like to make a few suggestions that might guide and inspire ideas of your own.

For one thing, when buying or building cabinetry for your collectibles, try to make the shelves movable. This is easiest when the shelves are on tracks, and gives you the advantage of being able to rearrange and replace collections so that they don't stagnate. I find this important with paintings as well. When first acquired, a painting is treasured, hung, and looked at often. As time passes, however, the collector often becomes so accustomed to seeing it that it tends to fade into the background. In one house, all of the paintings were taken down so that a room could be repainted. By the time the paint had dried, the painters had forgotten where each painting belonged and rehung them at random. Although they did not all fit where they were hung, their owners left them for several months because the rearrangement caused them to rediscover the art they had taken for granted.

Another component of design that should not be neglected is lighting. In addition to ceiling lights, which are costly as well as sometimes structurally prohibited, there are excellent picture lights that not only can be attached to paintings, but also can be secured into wooden shelves to cast light on articles within. Most cabinets tend to become dark and gloomy after dusk. They should be wired by an electrician, if possible. In the case of antique cabinets, however, a specialist should be consulted first, to avoid diminishing the value of the piece by drilling holes in it. In a room with beautiful paintings and objects, it is a good idea to subordinate all lighting to them; that is, you should let the picture lights be the stronger in the room, making any lamps dimmer. With the costs of acquiring and caring for a collection today, it is surprising how many people refuse to go to the small additional expense of correctly lighting it, thereby sacrificing much of their enjoyment.

One plea made by artists themselves to collectors concerns the choice of framing: a frame should suit the painting, not the room. This does not mean that a sporting painting hung in a French room must have a cypress frame, but it should have a simple frame that doesn't contrast with either the painting or the room. The frame is meant to enhance the painting, and the painting is meant to enhance the room. There are many creative ways to frame paintings, prints, and photographs. For instance, one fishing collector has put his fishing flies on the matting around his fishing paintings. The matting on a shooting print could display duck stamps or feathers. If the prints are part of a series, they should be matted and framed identically, so that the viewer's eye goes from one to the next with ease. This is particularly effective in a large living room in which all the prints in a series can be hung at the same level around the entire room.

Framing need not be reserved exclusively for paintings, prints, and photographs. One of my favorite uses of frames is as a display board for collages made up of ephemera. Few people are admitted collectors of ephemera, and yet most of us are in one way or another. *Ephemera* is a term that refers to odds and ends that memories are made of, and if you have drawers full of old letters, lodge bills,

Windowsills make a casual perch for carved decoys.

and hunting licenses, you are a collector of ephemera. Why not get them out of the drawers and up on a worthy wall? One such ephemera-frame might focus on a fishing trip to Canada. The collage would include photographs, the fly that caught the largest fish, and perhaps a few other flies that did their utmost. Added to these might be your fishing license, a map of the river, a railroad ticket, or wildflowers from the lodge. In the case of more unwieldy ephemera, such as flies or knives, shadowboxes could replace the framing format. These can be placed on tables or mantlepieces, as well as hung on walls.

As I mentioned before, there are very few rules in decorating; however, there are as many ideas as there are objects to use in decorating. The primary thing to remember is that the function of decorating is to give pleasure. Therefore, what you are trying to create when you set about decorating around your sporting collection is an environment in which you will derive the most enjoyment from your possessions. The ways in which this is achieved will vary from collector to collector, and it is that difference that gives each the distinct character that is the essence of good design.

About the Contributors

ALLAN J. LIU

One of the most enjoyable tasks in compiling this book was contacting and working with the various contributors. Each of them is an expert in the particular field I asked him or her to discuss — which means that each of them has an intense interest in some facet of collecting. A true collector is never bored and, at least to another collector, never boring; the enthusiasm is infectious and carries over to many areas of life. *The American Sporting Collector's Handbook* crew are a fascinating bunch, and I want to say a few words about each of them.

Patricia Janis Broder *(Rodeo Bronzes)* writes expertly on the West and bronzes. Her book, *Bronzes of the American West*, is a "must" for Western collectors.

Angus Cameron *(Hunting Books)* has been collecting books on hunting, fishing, and other outdoor subjects for a great many years, and he has also been making them: since 1935 he has been in publishing, first at Little, Brown and Company and since 1959 at Alfred A. Knopf. His own book on owls, *The Nightwatchers*, illustrated by Peter Parnell, is a classic, and, of course, he has assisted at the birth of many of the distinguished sporting books that have come from Knopf.

Henry Christmann *(Modern Sporting Firearms Valuation, English Game Guns)* is a connoisseur, noted *bon vivant*, sportsman, collector, dealer, and restorer of fine guns. He lives in Valley Stream, New York.

Len Codella *(Split-Cane Rods)* is the proprietor of the Angler's Den, a tackle shop specializing in fly-fishing. In the fall of 1975, he associated with the Thomas & Thomas Rod Company, and he now operates out of Turners Falls, Massachusetts. He is a member of the Henryville Conservation Club and is active in Trout Unlimited.

Margot F. Conte *(Photographs)* is a full-time nature photographer who has had one-person exhibits at Abercrombie & Fitch and other fine galleries. Her photographs have appeared in *Time-Life, Smithsonian, Geo Magazine, National*

Geographic, and *National Wildlife*. Winner of the 1979 Eastern Waterfowl Festival photography contest, she teaches photography in the adult education program in White Plains, New York, where she lives.

Jack Dugrew *(Hardy Reels)* has been an eager collector of fishing tackle for many years. He is an avid fly-fisherman, fly-tier, and photographer who has served as a fly-fishing instructor for the H. L. Leonard Rod Company. He has traveled throughout this country and Canada in pursuit of his interests. He is a member of the Federation of Fly Fishermen and Trout Unlimited.

Russell A. Fink *(Wildlife Stamp Prints, State Duck Stamps)* received his degree in Fine Arts from Ohio University in 1959. He also holds a degree in architecture, but after 10 years in that field, decided to return to fine arts and is one of the most respected dealers in wildlife and sporting art. He is the author of *Wild Turkey Stamp Prints* and co-author of *Duck Stamp Prints*, books that are considered to be the most definitive works on their respective subjects.

Norm Flayderman *(Sporting Firearms)* is one of the best-known authorities and dealers in collector's arms; his regularly issued catalogs are the most often cited in the business. He is Staff Arms Consultant to the U.S. Springfield Armory Museum, Arms Consultant to the U.S. Marine Corps Museum, Arms Consultant to the State of Connecticut for its Colt collection, and an appraiser for both the Winchester Gun Museum and the Gettysburg National Museum. He has written many articles on gun collecting and is currently compiling a book that will undoubtedly become the American gun collector's bible. Flayderman is also well known in the fields of American art and whaling history, and is the author of a classic work on the folk art of scrimshaw.

Edward C. German *(Contemporary Carvings)* is a practicing lawyer, lecturer, author, and partner of the law firm German, Gallagher & Murtagh in Philadelphia. When not involved in business, he may be found collecting contemporary carvings, shooting quail in Georgia, salmon fishing in Iceland, or trout fishing in Henryville.

Arnold Gingrich *(Angling Books)* has written several classic books on fishing — *The Joys of Trout, The Well-Tempered Angler, The Fishing in Print* (the last an excursion through five centuries of angling literature) — and is best known to general readers for his monthly page in *Esquire*, the magazine he founded over 40 years ago. He has many other interests, from music to motor cars, but perhaps none so keen as fishing and books on fishing.

Alan G. Haid *(Wildfowl Decoys)* spends all his free time searching for decoys, which isn't easy when you're from Hamilton, Ohio. All that time and travel is well spent, and Alan is a true expert.

Ernest S. Hickok *(Angling Books)* is a leading collector and dealer in books, prints, and paintings and a well-known expert in the field of hunting and fishing artifacts. A member of the New Jersey State Council of the Arts and the Advisory Council of the New Jersey State Museum, he is one of the directors of the Summit Art Center.

Drew Holl *(Original Art)* left the advertising business when the opportunity arose to purchase The Crossroads of Sport, Inc. His lifelong interest in field sports and the collecting of its art now became his vocation. Besides being an active partner in Crossroads, Drew belongs to the African Safari Club of New York, Ducks Unlimited, and Anglers Club of New York.

Mary Kefover Kelly *(Antique Reels)* lives in Tryon, North Carolina. Her lifelong interest in fishing has turned her into a true expert on fishing reels. Mary is one of few people I know who has studied the patents on these reels.

William C. Ketchum, Jr. *(Western Memorabilia)* was born in Missouri at the eastern end of one of the many western wagon trails. He is an avid student of the Old West and the author of 14 books on American and European antiques, including Western memorabilia. He lives in New York City, teaches at New York University and the New School for Social Research, and lectures throughout the United States. He is a museum and auction house consultant and an associate editor of *Antique Monthly*.

Alfred F. King, III *(State Duck Stamp Prints)* sold his seat on the New York Stock Exchange in 1973 and decided to make his longtime hobby of collecting into a career. He is the owner of Sportsman's Edge, Ltd., which has become one of the finest sporting and wildlife galleries in the country.

Sid Latham *(Modern Handmade Knives)* has worn a knife from the Arctic to the Amazon and from North Africa to New Guinea. He is a New York–based photographer, specializing in outdoor subjects. A few years ago he was commissioned to photograph some knives for a magazine—and was bitten by the knife bug. Characteristically, he went after the craftsmen to find out all he could, and in 1973 published *Knives & Knifemakers*, now an essential guide and reference for knife collectors.

Tony Lyons *(Hunting Books)* is a full-time college student and an avid collector of sporting books. He is the director of Sportsmen's Encore, New York, a dealer in sporting books.

Theodore A. Niemeyer *(Fishing Flies)* is one of the few experts who can identify almost any fly tied by past and present masters. He is a master tier himself, his nymph patterns are considered among the finest. He is a member of the Federation of Fly Fishermen and United Fly Tyers, Inc. With William Cushner and Charles DeFeo, he has assembled a collection of flies unmatched anywhere.

Harold L. Peterson *(Antique Knives)* is chief curator of the National Park Service and has been in the museum field for more than 30 years. He is the author of 24 books and hundreds of articles on arms and antiques in general. He has served as honorary curator of edged weapons at the West Point Museum, consultant to Colonial Williamsburg, Plymouth Plantation, and the Henry Ford Museum, and associate curator of the Field Artillery Museum at Fort Sill. He is also founder and past president of the Company of Military Historians, a member of the Executive Council of the International Association of Museums of Arms and Military History, and a member of the Board of Advisors of the National Historical Society.

Seth R. Rosenbaum *(Fishing Lures)* has a collection of more than 3,000 plugs. A computer consultant by trade, he tries not to let business interfere with fishing. His New York apartment features mounts of both a record Icelandic salmon and a 12-foot broadbill swordfish, as well as a number of sergeant majors, which he captured himself in the Dry Tortugas.

Leo Scarlet *(Federal Duck Stamps and Postage Stamps)* has been in the stamp business since 1929 and is known as an authority on the stamps of the United States and Canada. He is a member of all major stamp societies. He was president of the American Stamp Dealers' Association for four years.

Ernest Schwiebert *(Split-Cane Rods)* published his first book, *Matching the Hatch*, in 1955, and since then his name has become a byword among fly-fishermen. His other books include *Remembrances of Rivers Past*, *Nymphs* and the massive *Trout* — perhaps the first book to come along worthy of borrowing Bergman's title. Schwiebert is an architect and urban planner.

Robin Starr *(Fish Decoys)* got the collecting bug from his father, George Ross Starr, Jr., MD. He has been collecting fish decoys since 1972; his other fields of interest include duck decoys and Derrydale and other sporting books.

Charles R. Suydam *(Cartridges, Shotshells, and Accessories)* is the author of *The American Cartridge* (1960) and *American Pistol and Revolver Cartridges 1790–1975*, as well as numerous articles in magazines. He is currently on the editorial staffs of *The Gun Report*, *The American Rifleman*, *Arms Gazette*, and *The International Cartridge Collector*.

Jayne W. Teagle *(Decorating)* is an interior decorator, as well as a sportswoman who has hunted and fished all over the world. Her office and home are in New York City.

Charles Ward *(Shorebird Decoys)* is an "ex" bayman from Oceanside, New York, who collects shorebird decoys and now works full time at buying and selling them.

William B. Webster *(Federal Duck Stamp Prints)* is owner of Wild Wings, Lake City, Minnesota. He has had a lifelong interest in duck stamps.

F. Phillips Williamson *(Derrydale Books and Prints, Catalogs and Periodicals)* began his sporting library in the late 1930s; it now covers the entire range of hunting throughout the world and includes books in many languages. He has a nearly complete collection of both the Derrydale books and the Derrydale prints; the list of Derrydale publications he supplied for his chapter had never been compiled before. He has hunted throughout the world—but says his best trophy is the memory of a thousand campfires.

Thomas A. Winstel *(Wildfowl Decoys)* is a heating and air-conditioning executive from Cincinnati, Ohio. As with Alan Haid, all his spare time is spent buying, selling, trading, appraising, and searching for fine wildfowl decoys.

Robert F. Wohlers *(Sporting Calendars and Posters)* is a certified public accountant who lives and works in Lincoln, Nebraska. Though an avid collector of many things, his true love is sporting calendars and posters.

Index

Boldface page numbers indicate photographs.